Smithsonian

AMERICAN TABLE

Smithsonian

AMERICAN TABLE

THE FOODS, PEOPLE, AND INNOVATIONS THAT FEED US

LISA KINGSLEY
in collaboration with Smithsonian Institution

HARVEST
An Imprint of WILLIAM MORROW

SMITHSONIAN® and the Smithsonian® logo are registered trademarks of the Smithsonian Institution. Used under license.

Back cover photographs: Ken Carlson/Waterbury Publications, Inc. (Siu Mai, Korean Beef [Bulgogi] Tacos, and Matzoh Ball Soup); Brent Hofacker/Shutterstock (crawfish boil); B&W from top to bottom: Hulton Deutsch/Getty Images; Bettmann/Getty Images; Courtesy Of Newcomb Archives And Vorhoff Library Special Collections, Tulane University (Lena Richard)

Page 296 constitutes an extension of the copyright page.

HarperCollins books may be purchased for educational, business, or sales promotional use. For informaiton, please email the Special Markets Department at SPsales@harpercollins.com.

FIRST EDITION

Design by Waterbury Publications, Inc.

Library of Congress Cataloging-in-Publication Data has been applied for.

ISBN 978-0-358-00866-8

23 24 25 26 27 TC 10 9 8 7 6 5 4 3 2 1

CONTENTS

A TASTE OF PLACE 12

Where we live shapes what we eat. The environment, available foodstuffs, and migration have determined the diets of Indigenous peoples, colonizers, immigrants—and their descendants.

THE MARK OF HISTORY 84

Across time and cultures, foodways are not static. They are moved and changed by social, political, and environmental forces. Enslavement, immigration, legislation, war, social movements, and economic realities have all had profound effects on the American table.

FOOD FADS & TRENDS 148

While food is basic to survival, it is also subject to the vagaries of fashion. Some culinary practices have been born of necessity only to return as trends many decades later, while others emerge in response to a single moment in history.

INNOVATORS & CREATORS 194

There have always been those who push forward with new ways of doing and thinking about things, and who, whether intentionally or not, have changed what we eat and how we go about feeding ourselves.

TASTE MAKERS 240

What we're eating at any given time depends on the foods that are available to us, our own personal backgrounds and histories, personal preferences, and our exposure to those who seek to share their food knowledge and culture with the wider world.

HISTORY BY THE FORKFUL

"Tell me what you eat, and I will tell you who you are," the French gastronome Jean Anthelme Brillat-Savarin famously wrote. How and what we feed ourselves is ever evolving due to migration; climate change; political, economic, and environmental movements and events; new technologies; and human creativity and innovation. Food offers a powerful lens through which we can increase understanding of science, art, history, and culture.

A search across the Smithsonian Institution's collections for the word "food" yields tens of thousands of results. That number includes exhibitions, stories, historical narratives and interviews, events, film and video, and objects ranging from cooking utensils to serving vessels to packaging to cookbooks to restaurant menus and other ephemera—and much, much more.

Across the wide breadth of its museums, research centers, cultural centers, and programming, the Smithsonian tells the ongoing stories of the American table—and those of the American people. The American Food History Project at the National Museum of American History has taken a leading role in this work. For more than 25 years, the project has used the power of food and drink to engage audiences in conversations about culture, technology, labor, memory, and more—the ingredients of our daily sustenance. With a deeper understanding of the history of food in the United States, we can come to the table to create a more just, sustainable present and future.

American Table is a multifaceted look at how place, historical events, and diverse people have influenced how and what we eat in the United States. It's not just the story of those who have pushed the culinary arts forward, but also of activists, scholars, inventors, and everyday people who are opening our eyes to history and trying to make change in the present to better their communities. Learn how Native Americans have been working to reclaim their traditional foodways and achieve food sovereignty to improve the health of their communities, how a Black female chef gained renowned and culinary influence by showcasing her skills on her own television show in Jim Crow–era New Orleans, and how everything from fondue to Jell-O salads to pumpkin spice (even in hummus) became national obsessions.

While this book highlights in snapshots many stories around food, it is not even a fraction of the whole narrative.

We hope reading it spurs more exploration of the rich tapestry of the American story—the foods, people, and innovations that have fed us through history to the present, and those who will feed us in the future.

THE NATION'S MUSEUM

For more than 175 years, the Smithsonian Institution has sought to preserve, study, and increase understanding of science, history, art, and culture. Across its museums, more than 156 million objects help visitors—in person, in publications, through programming, and online—explore who we are, where we've been, and where we're headed.

An Evolving Endeavor

History is what happened in the past, but it informs and shapes the present. In that spirit, the Smithsonian constantly seeks to increase understanding of science, history, art, and culture among all Americans and the ability of all to have their story told.

It is an ongoing process. In 2004, the National Museum of the American Indian opened its doors to the public, and in 2016, the National Museum of African American History & Culture did the same. In 2020, Congress appropriated funds to create two new museums—the National Museum of the American Latino and the American Women's History Museum.

It is something of a quirk of history that the Smithsonian was established not by an American, but by a British scientist named James Smithson (1765–1829). Smithson left his estate to the United States to found "at Washington, under the name of the Smithsonian Institution, an establishment for the increase and diffusion of knowledge."

Congress authorized acceptance of the Smithson bequest on July 1, 1836. After a decade of debating, on August 10, 1846, the U.S. Senate passed the act organizing the Smithsonian Institution, which was signed into law by President James K. Polk.

Once established, the Smithsonian became part of the process of developing an American national identity—an identity rooted in exploration, innovation, and a unique American style. That process continues today as the Smithsonian looks toward the future.

A Lasting Legacy

Smithson was the child of a wealthy Englishman. He traveled much during his life but never set foot on American soil. Why, then, would he decide to give the entirety of his sizable estate—which totaled half a million dollars, or 1.5 percent of the United States' entire federal budget at the time—to a country that was foreign to him?

Some speculate that he was inspired by the United States' experiment with democracy. Others attribute his philanthropy to ideals inspired by such organizations as the Royal Institution, which was dedicated to using scientific knowledge to improve human conditions. Smithson never wrote about or discussed his bequest with friends or colleagues, but his gift has had a profound impact on the arts, humanities, and sciences in the United States.

Since its founding more than 175 years ago, the Smithsonian has become the world's largest museum, education, and research complex, with 19 museums that contain more than 156 million objects, the National Zoo, and nine research facilities.

▶ The Smithsonian Institution Building, popularly known as the Castle, is an iconic symbol of the museum. It served as the home and office of the first Secretary of the Smithsonian, Joseph Henry.

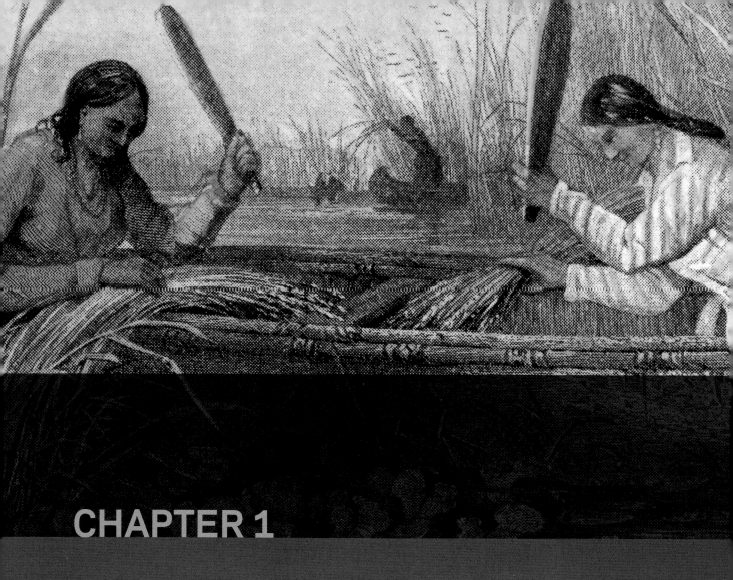

CHAPTER 1

A TASTE OF PLACE

Where we live shapes what we eat. The environment, available foodstuffs, and migration have determined the diets of Indigenous peoples, colonizers, immigrants—and their descendants. From the wild rice harvest by the Ojibwe of Minnesota since precolonial times to the lemongrass- and fish sauce–infused crawfish boil that bubbled up with the arrival of refugees from Southeast Asia to Houston, there is both continuity and creativity in the story of American food.

FIRST PEOPLE, FIRST FOODS

For thousands of years before Europeans arrived, Native people had healthful diets based on foods they hunted, gathered, fished, and grew. Colonization disrupted that, but a movement—that of food sovereignty—seeks to reclaim and return to those holistic and culturally significant foodways. "Food sovereignty," writes activist and author Winona LaDuke in the foreword to *Indigenous Food Sovereignty in the United States*, published in 2019, "is an affirmation of who we are as Indigenous peoples, and a way, one of the most sure-footed ways, to restore our relationship with the world around us."

NATIVE AMERICAN CULTURAL REGIONS

Millennia before the arrival of Europeans to North America, Native people fostered communities and cultures, and devised ways to survive and thrive.

ARCTIC

NORTHWEST COASTAL

SUBARCTIC

PLATEAU

GREAT BASIN

PLAINS

NORTHEAST

CALIFORNIA

SOUTHEAST

SOUTHWEST

NORTHWEST COASTAL Tribes living in this area were less agriculturally oriented than those in other areas, relying on the lush land and ocean.

PLATEAU The network of rivers and streams here provided salmon, a primary food source.

CALIFORNIA More than 1,000 miles of coastline and a highly diverse geography provided a wealth of resources to the people of this area.

GREAT BASIN The extremes of hot and cold, along with limited rainfall, meant the diets of the Native people of this region relied heavily on small game, nuts, and seeds.

SOUTHWEST Although the diets of the people of this region included wild plants and game, corn was the defining food source.

ARCTIC Modern-day Alaska is divided into two cultural regions—Arctic and Subarctic. Winters in the Arctic are very cold and the topography is flat. Native people lived almost exclusively on sea mammals and fish.

SUBARCTIC The people of this region also relied heavily on marine mammals, but areas of lush rain forest also provided berries, roots, and greens.

PLAINS The people of the Great Plains practiced agriculture and fished, but the hunt for buffalo came to dominate the culture.

NORTHEAST Hunting, gathering, fishing, and agriculture all played a role in the foodways of the Indigenous people of this region, but its vast forests also provided a wealth of nuts and maple syrup.

SOUTHEAST Abundant rich soil and a long growing season made agriculture central to the diets of the people here, allowing the establishment of permanent settlements.

ALASKA

From the arrival of the first Alaskans from Asia at least 13,000 years ago to the beginning of Russian colonization in the 18th century, the Native diet was almost exclusively one of subsistence.

The first inhabitants of Alaska arrived there from elsewhere in two major movements in history.

The people of the Arctic Culture Area—which ranges from the Aleutian Islands across the northernmost and down along the easternmost parts of the state—came later than those of the Subarctic Culture Area, defined as most of the vast interior. Arctic peoples sailed from Siberia in boats beginning about 2,500 BCE, while the very first arrivals likely came from Asia across the Bering Strait land bridge 13,000 or more years ago.

Most Native Alaskans identify with one of 231 federally recognized tribes—all of whom have their own cultures and customs and some 20 distinct languages among them—but it is helpful in understanding the Native foodways that developed in Alaska by exploring each of them in a broad sense.

The Iñupiat and St. Lawrence Island Yup'ik established themselves in Alaska's northern and northwestern region. Winters are very cold and the topography is generally flat. Because it is so far north, the diurnal cycle has a dramatic effect on the amounts of sunlight it receives throughout the year. During deepest winter, the sun barely peeks above the horizon for just an hour or so each day, while in the summer the reverse is true. While most of the year the people of this region subsisted on whales, seals, walrus, birds, and—when the weather permitted—fish and berries, the long hours of sunlight in the summer created a burst of vegetation growth that attracted caribou and other large animals.

The Athabascans settled in the vast interior of the state and to this day have the largest land base of any other Native group. The Athabascans were migratory. In the summer, they set up fishing camps along major river systems—such as the Yukon, Tanana, Innoko, Chandalar, Koyuk, and Tolovana rivers—and in the winter they hunted game such as moose and caribou.

The relative proximity of Alaska's southeastern panhandle—the Inside Passage region—to the northwest coast of the mainland United States means the Tlingit, Haida, Eyak, and Tsimshian who put down roots there share many cultural similarities with the Native people of Washington and Oregon. The maritime environment provided salmon, halibut, shellfish, and sea plants, while the cool and temperate rain forest—with an annual rainfall of up to 200 inches—was rife with berries, roots, and greens. The people of this region also hunted deer, moose, and mountain goats.

Southwestern Alaska became home to the Yup'ik and Cup'ik. They had a seminomadic lifestyle, and their diets depended on exactly where they lived in the region. Those who lived along the coast relied most heavily on sea mammals such as seal, walrus, and whale and the plethora of Pacific fish—salmon, herring, trout, halibut, flounder, burbot—as well as shellfish and sea plants. Inland, freshwater fish, moose, caribou, migratory birds

▼ A hunter in Point Hope, Alaska, sits on the carcass of a whale that has been hauled onto the ice to be butchered, circa 1955.

and eggs, berries, greens, and roots provided sustenance.

It is no surprise that water determined the way of life of the Unangax and Sugpiaq (also called Alutiiq) people of southwest Alaska and the Aleutian Islands, a 1,200-mile-long chain of virtually treeless volcanic islands surrounded by the Pacific. The staples of their diet came from the

> After the arrival of Russian fur traders, an estimated 80 percent of the Indigenous Aleut population died from diseases to which they had no immunity.

ocean—seals, whales, sea lions, otters, fish, and mollusks—although in some areas they hunted bears and caribou, and gathered wild plants such as Arctic cloudberries, wild greens, and roots that came from bog orchids.

Fur Trade Drives Destruction

The way of life of these island people remained harmonious and symbiotic until the arrival of Russian fur traders—who gave them the name Aleut—in the 18th century. It changed everything for them, and eventually for all of Alaska's Native people.

In 1743, Russian traders began hunting in the Aleutian Islands. By the 1770s, Russia had laid claim to Alaska, primarily occupying the coastal areas because of the large populations of sea otters, whose pelts were highly prized. Skilled Native Aleut hunters were enslaved by the Russians. An estimated 80 percent of the Indigenous Aleut population died from introduced diseases to which

▼ An 1818 watercolor by Russian painter Mikhail Tikhanov depicts an Aleut man in festival dress. Tikhanov was the expeditionary painter of Captain Vasily Golovin's circumnavigation aboard the frigate *Kamchatka*.

they had no immunity. In 1784, trader Gregorii Shelikhov landed on Kodiak Island with a crew. They killed hundreds of the island's Natives and established the first permanent Russian colony in Alaska.

Over the next near-century, as Native Alaskans spent more time hunting for the Russian occupiers, they spent less time hunting for themselves and began trading some of their catch for Russian foodstuffs such as flour and barley. Russia continued to extract resources from the land and people of Alaska until the territory was sold to the United States in 1867.

Although the dietary changes brought on by colonization had a highly detrimental effect on the health of Native Alaskans, traditional foodways remain strong in many areas, particularly in the southwest part of the state.

As in many Native communities across the United States, there are Indigenous Alaskans working to create programs and initiatives that provide healthful, sustainable food sources to their people. In the coastal Native village of Tyonek, residents are working with the Tyonek Tribal Conservation District to plant, maintain, and harvest organic vegetables from a community garden. The Kodiak Archipelago Leadership Institute and Alaska Village Initiatives provide funding and grants to build economic stability and food security in Native commmunities across the state.

Each year, the Inuit Circumpolar Council (ICC) holds a summit, which draws Native delegates from all over Alaska. "Going back to managing our own resources, as hunters and the ladies on the land, we know what is most important," said JakyLou Olemaun, a North Slope Youth Delegate from Utqiagvik at the 2019 gathering. "I think that many people try to have a say on how to manage our food, and they don't know what is going on. We do."

GREAT BASIN

In a region whose climate is by turns very hot and very cold, the Indigenous people of this land of mountains and deserts cultivated expertise in hunting small game and waterfowl—where there was water—as well as gathering nuts and seeds.

Geographically speaking, a basin is an area with a lower elevation than the land that surrounds it. Basins are generally deserts because the mountains around them force rain clouds to shed their water before they reach the lower elevation.

The Great Basin is an area of about 200,000 square miles that covers almost all of Utah and Nevada, large areas of Oregon, Idaho, Wyoming, and Colorado, and slivers of Arizona, Montana, and California. The terrain includes many small basins, mountains, and plateaus, but most of it is desert, which means much of it gets very little rain.

Summers can be very hot and dry, and winters can be very cold. The region includes Death Valley, the lowest point in all of the Americas, where temperatures frequently top 120°F in the summer and the annual rainfall is 2.36 inches. Large stretches of alkaline flats—soil that contains mineral salts

So much of the Great Basin is desert, many anthropologists refer to its Indigenous people collectively as "The Desert Culture."

from lakes that have since evaporated—were inhospitable to agriculture.

Generally, the tribes of the north and east—most notably the Shoshone, who acquired horses from the Spanish in the late 17th century—used horses, and those in the south and west did not until the mid-19th century.

Whether they traveled on foot or by horseback, the challenges of the environment required them to make annual rounds to various ecological zones in search of seasonally available plants, animals, and fish. Depending on where they lived, the people of the Great Basin hunted

antelope, mountain goats, and jackrabbits. Where there was water, there were waterfowl. A 1924 excavation of Lovelock Cave in western Nevada yielded a cache of 2,000-year-old duck decoys made from tule reeds and feathers that were once used to lure waterfowl to hunters in the marshlands of the ancient Lake Lahontan.

The dominant plants were sagebrush and grasses. Seeds were a staple food, in particular pine nuts from the piñon (pinyon-juniper) tree. Grasses were woven into intricate baskets so tight they could carry water. Baskets were also used to cook food, winnow grass seeds, and store pine nuts.

Pine nuts are still an important and symbolic food source for Indigenous people of the Great Basin. Darlene Dewey, a member of the Yomba Shoshone Tribe in central Nevada, heads out with her grandson in late summer and early fall to gather them.

Dewey, who was born in the 1940s in Yomba, told *Bitterroot* magazine she remembers as a child bringing home 100 pounds or more of pine nuts each fall to help sustain her family through the harsh winters when they could not leave their home.

"We didn't have any TV as kids," she said. "We used to eat pine nuts and do our homework."

▲ A Paiute woman makes a basket in the Yosemite Valley, circa 1900. Pine nuts were one of the primary food sources for the people of the Great Basin.

GREAT PLAINS

Although the people of the vast grasslands practiced all forms of food acquisition—agriculture, gathering, hunting, and fishing—the hunt for buffalo came to dominate the culture.

Historically, the Native people that once comprised the more than 30 tribes of the Great Plains—a huge region ranging from east of the Rocky Mountains in the west to the Mississippi River in the east, as far north as North Dakota and as far south as central Texas—belonged to two broad groups depending on whether they were primarily nomadic and mostly engaged in hunting or primarily sedentary and mostly engaged in agriculture.

The agriculturally oriented tribes generally settled in fertile river valleys, where they cultivated crops such as sunflowers, corn, squash, and beans, supplementing with some hunting. For the hunting tribes, the buffalo was by far the most important food source and, in fact, central to their way of life.

The trajectory of the Plains tribes differs somewhat from those of other culture areas because their dominant means of providing food for their communities evolved after the arrival of Europeans due to a single factor: the horse.

The Spanish brought horses to North America in the early 16th century. Animals that escaped migrated north from Mexico and began expanding their numbers in the Southwest, eventually reaching the Great Plains, where they were adopted by the people living there.

▼ An 1845 painting by American painter John Mix Stanley depicts the buffalo hunt. Stanley's primary subject were Native people and the landscape in which they lived.

The Horse Changes Everything

Prior to acquiring horses, Plains people hunted bison primarily by two techniques—the buffalo jump and the buffalo impound. In a buffalo jump, a herd was driven down a steep slope or over a cliff. If there was no access to a cliff or steep hill, hunters would lure a herd into a timber corral or impound—about 10 to 15 feet high, with a 100-yard chute—where the animals would be killed with bows and arrows.

Hunting on horseback was much easier, less dangerous, and more efficient than hunting on foot. It also provided the opportunity to follow the food source as it ranged over the vast territories of the Plains. Tepees that could easily be put up and taken down became the primary source of shelter for these increasingly nomadic tribes.

The importance of the buffalo to Native people was not lost on the white settlers of the Plains. Some of the last of the "Indian wars" were between the U.S. government and citizens of Plains tribes, who fought for their way of life until the late 19th century, when they were forcibly removed to reservations after white settlers intentionally destroyed herds of bison. The population of buffalo roaming North America fell from an estimated 60 million prior to contact to just a few hundred. By 1900, the era of the nomadic, buffalo-hunting Plains people was over, but the importance of the buffalo was not forgotten by the people themselves.

In 1992, the InterTribal Buffalo Council was established with a mission "To restore bison on Tribal lands for cultural and spiritual enhancement and preservation." Today, membership in the ITBC—based in South Dakota—comprises 58 tribes in 19 states and a collective herd of more than 15,000 buffalo.

NORTHEAST WOODLANDS

The first people of this region—diverse in both its climate and geography—utilized the trees of the wide-ranging, dense, and giving forests for shelter, tools, transportation, and food.

The Northeast Woodlands Culture Area spans east to west from the Atlantic Ocean to the Mississippi River and north to south from Nova Scotia through southern Quebec and Ontario to the Ohio River Valley.

It is geographically diverse, with coastal areas, waterways, the Great Lakes, and the Appalachian and Adirondack ranges. Much of it is near-boreal forest, a biome of coniferous trees such as pine, spruce, and fir as well as broadleaf species such as poplar, birch, oak, maple, hickory, and chestnut.

The Native people of the region practiced a combination of hunting and gathering and agriculture. Bountiful waters provided fish, shellfish, and waterfowl. Forests yielded seeds, roots, berries, nuts, and game animals, most prominently deer.

Where there was a short growing season and more extreme cold, people depended more on

The journals of Europeans in the area describe the maple sugar-making process of Native people as early as 1609.

fishing and hunting. The more temperate climate in the central and southern areas was more conducive to growing crops—primarily corn, beans, and squash.

The Bounty of Trees

The plentiful trees provided two food sources in particular that—although not unique to this region—played a more significant role in the diets of the people of the Northeast Woodlands than in other areas: maple sugar and tree nuts.

Families set up camps near stands of sugar maples each year as winter waned. A V-shape slash was cut into the trunk and sap was collected. The sap—which is 98 percent water—was then boiled in vessels made of hollowed-out logs, clay, or birch bark into which hot stones were dropped. Because there was no good way to store syrup long-term, it was boiled down into one of three types of sugar. "Grain sugar" was similar to modern brown sugar. "Cake sugar" was poured into wooden molds when the syrup was hot to form hard cakes. And "wax sugar" was made by boiling the syrup until very thick, then pouring it over snow to create a taffy-like consistency.

Other types of trees provided a valuable source of protein and fat. Acorns, beechnuts, black walnuts, butternuts, chestnuts, and hickory nuts were all used in a variety of ways. *Kanuchi*, a traditional Cherokee hickory-nut soup, was made by pounding shelled and dried nuts to a consistency that could be formed into balls. The balls were then simmered in boiling water until the soup was the desired consistency.

When the United States government forcibly removed the Cherokee from their Appalachian homeland as part of the Trail of Tears, they brought the tradition of *kanuchi* with them to Indian Territory (present-day Oklahoma), where it is still made today.

▲ The Indigenous people of this region had been turning the sap of the maple tree into syrup and several types of sugar long before the arrival of Europeans. Here, a woman boils sap, circa 1964.

SOUTHEAST WOODLANDS

While the people of this region engaged in hunting and gathering, abundant rich soil and a long growing season were conducive to farming—and the establishment of permanent settlements.

Like all Indigenous peoples of North America, the peoples of the Southeast Woodlands—bordered on the east by the Atlantic Ocean, west roughly to the Mississippi River (although it includes all of Louisiana and some of southeastern Texas) and north to south approximately from the Tennessee and Potomac rivers to the Gulf of Mexico—hunted, gathered, and fished.

The region is heavily forested but also includes saltwater marshes, stands of cypress trees, savanna grasslands, the floodplain of the Mississippi, the jungle and swamplands of the Everglades, and the imposing mountain ranges of southern Appalachia.

Wild game and fowl—deer, elk, black bears, beavers, squirrels, rabbits, otters, wild turkeys, partridges, pigeons, quail, ducks, and geese—were plentiful. Wild spinach was picked in the woods. Fresh and salt waters teemed with fish. People who lived along the coast gathered oysters, crabs, clams, and mussels. In present-day Florida, turtles and alligators were a crucial food source.

In addition to the rich plant and animal supply, one of the most significant natural resources of the region was its large swaths of dark, fertile soil—including a crescent-shape stretch of land about 25 miles wide and about 300 miles long mainly in central Alabama and northeast Mississippi that was once referred to as the Black Belt. (The term is now primarily used in a geopolitical sense to describe the areas of the South where large numbers of Black people were enslaved on plantations prior to the Civil War.)

The productivity of the land, coupled with a long growing season that allowed the planting of many fields twice in a year, meant that many of the region's Native people fed themselves primarily through farming. The most important crop was corn, but they also grew beans, squash, melons, sweet potatoes, and sunflowers. Wild fruits such as grapes, plums, and berries—and perhaps walnut and pecan trees—were incipiently domesticated, meaning that some propagation techniques were applied, but they were not fully domesticated.

An Ancient City Along the Mississippi

The ability to produce enough food to support a sizable population had a profound effect on the development of the region's cultures. While many Indigenous peoples of North America were nomadic or seminomadic—following fish or game migrations—the peoples of the Southeast generally stayed in one place, establishing permanent settlements, often in river valleys.

The most sophisticated of these was Cahokia, a pre-Columbian city located across the Mississippi River from present-day St. Louis, Missouri. At its zenith, about 1100 CE, it's estimated to have been the home to between 8,000 and 20,000 people of the Mississippian culture, a population larger than London in 1250. The remains of the city—including the largest man-made earthen mound on the North American continent—can be seen today at the Cahokia Mounds State Historic Site near Collinsville, Illinois.

▼ This engraving of a strainer used by Florida Seminoles to prepare coontie arrowroot flour, also called Florida arrowroot, appeared in an 1887 report by Clay MacCauley called "The Seminole Indians of Florida." MacCauley studied the Seminoles for what was then the Smithsonian Bureau of American Ethnology.

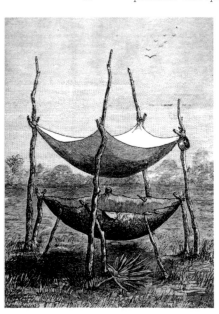

PLATEAU

Salmon was a primary food source for the Native people of this region, which is networked with rivers and streams filled with water that flows into it from the Rocky and Cascade mountain ranges that border it.

There have been people living in the Plateau—a region of highlands cut through by the Columbia River—continuously for at least 10,000 years. Bordered in the north by the Fraser River in British Columbia, it stretches south to present-day central Idaho. Most significantly, it's flanked on the west by the Cascades and on the east by the Rocky Mountains, a location that has a tremendous impact on its geography and climate.

Because the Cascades block the rain clouds that blow in from the ocean, the region doesn't get much rain. Although there are some forested areas at the edges near the mountains, the vegetation of the Plateau was largely sagebrush and grasses. There was some large game in those forested areas—such as deer, elk, and caribou—but the people of the Plateau primarily hunted smaller game such as antelope and jackrabbits, as well as foraging for wild carrots, onions, camas bulbs, parsnips, and berries.

Honoring the first salmon of summer ensures there will be plenty to harvest in the future.

Their most important food source, though, came from the water. The elevation of the Columbia Plateau ranges from 200 feet to about 5,000 feet above sea level. Mt. Rainier in the Cascades is more than 14,000 feet, and Mt. Robson in the Canadian Rockies in British Columbia is nearly 13,000 feet. Water runs downhill from the mountains, creating numerous networks of rivers and streams that teemed with salmon, which was eaten fresh roasted over a fire, steamed in ovens dug into the ground, or dried by smoke or sun.

Salmon was by far their primary food source until the Shoshone, who lived in the Great Basin, acquired horses in the late 17th century and began supplying their Plateau neighbors to the north with them. Increasingly, the peoples of the Plateau came to rely on buffalo, traveling on horseback to the Great Plains to hunt.

Following the Food

Traditionally, the people of the Plateau lived a seminomadic lifestyle, staying in permanent villages in the winter and then moving to semipermanent camps, following the migration of game and fish and the seasonal availability of wild plants.

An important ritual was—and still is—the first foods ceremony celebrating the arrival of salmon from the ocean to spawn in the region's rivers. A fish is caught, cooked, cut into small pieces, and shared among all participants. The carcass is then returned to the water.

"What the ancestors have taught us is that when we get the first fish and bring it in, we need to treat it properly and with all due respect," the late Chinook Tribal Chairman Ray Gardner told the *Chinook Observer* in 2008. "And then when that fish is released back to the river, it has the ability to go back out in the ocean and tell the other fish that we have treated it the way we were supposed to, and then the others will come in for us to harvest."

▲ A Wishram man fishes for salmon with a net, circa 1909. The Wishram lived along the north bank of the Columbia River. Salmon rest in the quiet pools along the rocky shore after their journey upstream.

NORTHWEST COAST

The tribes living in the pre-Columbian coastal Northwest were less agriculturally oriented than some of the nations living in different areas of the continent. The ocean and lush land yielded plenty.

One of the most important food sources for the Native people of the Pacific Northwest was salmon. They cooked salmon over an open fire or smoked and dried as a means of preservation. Salmon was—and continues to be—a source of sustenance and also of spiritual and ceremonial significance.

Other protein sources included trout; halibut; herring; shellfish such as oysters, mussels, prawn, and crab; whales; otters; seals; bears; beavers; lynx; deer; elk; and small game such as rabbits and hares.

And while the people of the coastal Northwest didn't engage in agriculture in a formal sense, they used controlled burning to clear land and improve growing conditions for a variety of foraged plants. "In almost all cases, the immediate reason for environmental fire use in the Northwest related to the food quest," writes anthropologist Robert Boyd in the introduction to *Indians, Fire and the Land in the Pacific Northwest* (1999, Oregon State University Press). "Northwest Native Americans used fire in fire drives of deer and elk and in gathering species such as grasshoppers and tarweed. But more than this, they used it to create environments suitable for some of their most-favored food plants, such as camas and other root crops and many species of wild berries. Firing in the camas beds, huckleberry fields, oak groves, and tule flats, as well as other environments, took place after harvest, as a kind of post-use cleanup process, with ecological consequences in following seasons."

The production of wild foods was enhanced with these controlled burning techniques. Oregon grapes, chokecherries, wild currants, and a variety of berries that included huckleberries, serviceberries, raspberries, bunchberries, and blackberries were all gathered and eaten fresh or dried for the winter. The mountain patches in which they grew were burned after the harvest to improve the soil and increase yields the following year. Burns were also used to clear areas for gathering sunflower seeds.

A Generous Land

One of the most important land-based food sources was camas, a type of edible lily in the asparagus family. The people dug bulbs from the ground around rivers with a hardwood stick, then boiled or roasted them in a pit. A cooked camas bulb resembles and tastes a bit like a baked sweet potato, but is sweeter and more fibrous. Dried and pounded, it was turned into a flour.

The land also yielded wild onions, carrots, grasses, herbs, and nuts, including beaked hazelnuts, which are smaller than the variety grown for commercial purposes. The nuts were eaten fresh and also buried for future use. The stems of the shrub—which grows from 3 to 15 feet tall—were used to weave baskets and fish traps.

Through a combination of good fortune at the riches the water and land provided—and a cultivated knowledge in sustainably managing it—the people of the Northwest coast prospered.

▼ A Salish man smokes salmon on the Tulalip Indian Reservation in 1906.

CALIFORNIA

With a coastline of more than 1,000 miles and incredible diversity of geography, California was home to Native people who skillfully harvested and manipulated its vast resources to feed themselves.

More than 300,000 Indigenous people lived in present-day California, estimated to be about 13 percent of all Native people in North America, when Spanish colonizers arrived in 1769. Though there was certainly dietary overlap among the Native Californians who spoke as many as 135 different dialects, there was one aspect of Indigenous culture that was the same everywhere.

"One activity shared by all [N]ative Californians was interaction with and manipulation of the environment," writes historian Joshua Paddison in a 2005 essay titled "Before 1768: Pre-Columbian California," for the University of California's California Cultures project. "Many groups dried, shelled ground, washed, and cooked acorns into soup and bread, flavored with berries, seeds, and nuts. Some caught trout, salmon, and shellfish with harpoons and nets. Others hunted elk, deer, rabbits, and fowl with bows and obsidian-tipped arrows. Whether they lived in mountains, valleys,

There were as many as 135 dialects spoken by Native Californians. A common thread is that all groups had deep knowledge of their environment and developed the skills to survive and thrive.

deserts, forests, or beaches, [N]ative peoples continually tended and cultivated the land through controlled burnings, weeding, pruning, tilling, irrigation, and selective replanting."

The Importance of the Acorn

Acorns were one of the foods shared by most of the Indigenous people of California. They were abundant and high in fat, carbohydrate, protein, and vitamins. Each fall, they were harvested and dried. After drying, they were cracked and winnowed to remove the hulls, then ground into flour with a stone mortar and pestle. Because acorns contain tannic acid, a poisonous and bitter acid, the flour was leached to remove it. The flour was spread out into a shallow sand basin in the ground and covered with branches. Water was poured through the branches to soak the acorn meal. When the meal was no longer bitter, it was drained and scooped out of the hole, ready to be made into soup, mush, or bread.

The use of acorns through adaptation is just one example of the ingenuity and resourcefulness employed by the Indigenous peoples of California to make use of everything the land and water offered.

"When I was a small girl, I went on root-digging trips with my mother and helped her to collect plenty of roots to dry for winter use," Marie Potts, a Maidu woman, recalls in *The Way We Lived*, a compilation of reminicenses of Native Californians of various tribes. "These would be gathered in baskets. Some were cooked whole, or sometimes we pounded them and cooked them like mush . . . I also remember as a child living in the cedar bark house with my grandparents. How wonderful it was lying awake at night sometimes, to hear the coyotes bark, and the hoot owls uttering their calls among the trees."

▲ A woman pours water on acorn meal to leech out tannic acid, which makes it bitter, on the Hoopa Valley Reservation in 1902 in Humboldt County in northwest California.

SOUTHWEST

The first people who lived here knew how and where to look for foraged foods and developed methods of cultivation to grow essential crops. Corn, or maize, became the most culturally and culinarily significant of these.

The geography of New Mexico, southern Colorado, Arizona, and northern Mexico includes mesas, mountains, and desert. Even so, the people who lived here prior to contact with Europeans—the Apache, Hopi, Navajo, Pueblo, and Zuni—figured out how to coax sustenance from the land.

Wild plants, including the fruit of the giant saguaro cactus, as well as piñon nuts and seeds, were gathered. Game such as bison, deer, elk, and bighorn sheep were a valuable protein source, as were fish where there was water.

And while each group had a unique diet depending on the environment in which they lived, there is a thread that connects them all: corn.

▼ An Apache bride holds a basket of maize, circa 1900.

"The story of America is essentially the story of corn, and the Native cultures from all over the Americas that developed it," writes Lois Ellen Frank in her 1991 book, *Foods of the Southwest Indian Nations*. "Corn made cultural development possible by supporting dense concentrations of populations."

Cultivating Life

Many Indigenous peoples cultivated corn, or maize, but it was perhaps most significant culinarily and culturally to the nations of the Southwest.

While scientists still do not completely agree on how the plant—originally a wild grass called *teosinte*—became domesticated, there is evidence from a cave in southern Puebla in Mexico that suggests it might have first been cultivated between 5,000 and 7,000 years ago. Domesticated corn arrived in the Southwest about 4,000 years ago, and as early as 500 BCE, it became the primary calorie source for the Puebloan people.

Selective breeding of plants that could adapt to different environments was crucial. Corn developed by the Hopi was specifically adapted for a dry environment. While most maize cannot surface from more than 4 inches belowground, Hopi corn can emerge from more than 18 inches—where the dry desert soil retains more moisture. While many of these varieties of maize could thrive without supplemental water, there were tribes that also developed technologies of irrigation.

The Hohokam people, who lived in what is now Arizona from 300 to 1500 CE, built hundreds of miles of canals to carry water from the Rio Verde, Salt, and other rivers to water fields of corn, beans, squash, and cotton. The network of canals in what is now the Phoenix metropolitan area was the most sophisticated in North America at the time. While they were once nomadic hunters and gathers, agriculture allowed them to stay in one place and build stable, permanent communities.

For the Indigenous people of the Southwest, corn was not just food, but also a metaphor for life.

"We see corn as our children," Hopi farmer Donald Dawahongnewa told *The Cortez Journal* in an August 2013 article. "When we go to the field we sing a song and the corn grows, just like you do to your children."

THE UNITED EATS OF AMERICA

Today the United States of America is tremendously diverse. It can be a challenge to achieve consensus on much of anything—except this: there is a special place in our hearts for the iconic foods of the places we live. Every bite of a rich and buttery Maine lobster roll, spicy Ethiopian doro wat in a D.C. neighborhood, or crisp masa pocket stuffed with creamy beans and melty cheese at an L.A. pupuseria is a coming together of food, people, and place.

NEW ENGLAND AND THE MID-ATLANTIC

The proximity to the Atlantic Ocean and its rocky coastline has had no small measure of influence on the foods of the Northeast—consider the iconic lobster roll of Maine and the crab cakes of Maryland. But of course so does the continuing impact of the Indigenous peoples, as well as those who arrived in waves of immigration from Europe and elsewhere. The traditional New England clambake has its roots in the Wampanoag method of cooking clams and other shellfish in holes in the ground covered with hot rocks. As with any area of the country, innovation, thrift, and a longing for home have found their way into the food culture of the region.

Connecticut: Steamed cheeseburger
For many residents of Connecticut—particularly the central part of the state—the charred crust and smoky flavor of a grilled or pan-seared burger has nothing on the allure of a grayish but exceedingly juicy steamed beef patty topped with a 2-ounce block of cheese, also steamed, to create a gooey avalanche of goodness over the top of the meat. The beautiful mess is served on a Vienna roll that soaks up the juices with every bite, along with the conventional toppings—lettuce, tomato, onion, condiments—of choice. The steamed cheeseburger (also called a steamer or cheeseburg) started out in the early 20th century as steamed cheese on a roll sold from a horse-drawn cart. The beef patty is believed to have been added at a restaurant called Jack's Lunch in Middletown, Connecticut, sometime in the 1920s or '30s. During this era, steaming was being promoted as a healthful alternative to frying. According to *Images of America: Middletown* from the Middlesex County Historical Society, the steamed cheeseburgers at Jack's Lunch

were "cooked in a tall copper box filled with simmering water for 18 tin trays of square ground-beef patties." Cheddar cheese could be added for 5 cents. Today, the epicenter of cheeseburg mania is in Meriden, at a family-owned lunch counter called Ted's, which has been turning out the succulent sandwiches since 1959.

Delaware: Scrapple
A colonial-era proverb—"waste not, want not"—is exemplified in one of the most enduring and iconic foods in the whole mid-Atlantic region: scrapple. Devised by 17th- and 18th-century German immigrants who settled in Pennsylvania to make use of every last bit of the pigs they slaughtered during the fall and winter—heads, brains, hearts, livers, and skin—scrapple consisted of those pork scraps simmered with stock and cornmeal or buckwheat (or a blend) to make a porridge flavored with onion, spices, and herbs. The mixture was poured into a loaf pan to solidify, then sliced and pan-fried. Now, as then, it is an

offal-based dish—one made of various animal parts. Although scrapple—also known as *pon haus* (pan hare or rabbit) in Pennsylvania Dutch—wasn't born in Delaware, the scrapple-loving citizens of that state have raised its profile and popularity through the centuries. The Apple-Scrapple Festival is held each fall in Bridgeville, home of the country's largest scrapple producer, and one of the state's craft breweries even created a beer brewed with scrapple.

▼ Scrapple was created by German immigrants to Pennsylvania in the 17th and 18th centuries as a way to use every possible part of the pigs they slaughtered during fall and winter.

Innovative chefs have made goat scrapple, duck scrapple, and bison scrapple. But most scrapple is made with traditional ingredients and eaten the classic way—topped with maple syrup or applesauce and served alongside fried eggs for breakfast.

Maryland: Crab cakes

The blue crab—which ranges along the Atlantic Coast from Nova Scotia to Argentina—is a prolifc reproducer. Although environmental factors have an impact on the abundance of the harvest (and, consequently, the price per pound), with careful management, the commercial harvest each year in Chesapeake Bay and its tributaries is generally between 50 and 60 million pounds of crab. No small amount of it ends up in Maryland's famous crab cakes, which fall into two general styles. Restaurant- or gourmet-style crab cakes are made from large chunks of meat. They eschew fillers such as minced red pepper, celery, scallion, and parsley, and are usually not breaded but rather broiled over an open flame or pan-seared in butter. Boardwalk-style cakes are made from smaller bits of crab—usually claw meat—and are more heavily seasoned than restaurant-style cakes. They're breaded before being fried. Either way, the appeal of a crab cake lies in how the crisp exterior gives way to a tender, almost creamy, and vaguely sweet interior. Although there's much disagreement among Marylanders about what makes the perfect crab cake, the one thing they can all agree on is that

▶ Boardwalk-style crab cakes are made from smaller bits of crab than restaurant-style cakes and are breaded before being fried.

they have to be made with the meat from blue crabs—named for the azure color of their claws before they are cooked, when they turn coral. In fact, the scientific name of blue crab is *Callinectus sapidus*, or "beautiful swimmer."

Massachusetts: The Fluffernutter

For many Bay Staters, there is one peanut butter sandwich that surpasses even PB&J: the Fluffernutter—creamy peanut butter and marshmallow crème on soft white bread. The reason likely has to do with the origin stories of the stuff. The first holds that in the early 1900s, a former soda fountain

equipment salesman named Armory Curtis created a marshmallow spread in the basement of his house in Melrose, Massachusetts. By the early 1910s, his Curtis Marshmallow Factory was making Snowflake Marshmallow Crème on a commercial scale, and by 1915, it was selling nationwide. His sister, Emma, was something of a marketing phenom and came up with all kinds of ways to use the product, which she shared in a weekly newspaper column and radio show. In 1918, when Americans were asked to go meatless one day a week to aid in rationing and help the war effort, she published a recipe for what she called

the "Liberty Sandwich"—a combination of peanut butter and marshmallow crème—and, in today's parlance, it went viral. The other begins with Somerville, Massachusetts, entrepreneur Archibald Query selling his version of marshmallow crème door-to-door in 1917. Sugar shortages during the war caused his business to begin to fail, so in 1920, he sold it to candymakers H. Allen Durkee

A 1960s commercial gave the flutternutter its name: "Oh, you need fluff, fluff, fluff to make a flutternutter. Marshmallow fluff, and lots of peanut butter!"

and Fred Mower, who created the Marshmallow Fluff empire.

New Hampshire: Grape Nuts ice cream

Health food and indulgence come together in this frozen treat that is a favorite in the Granite State—and in fact all over the Northeast. Cereal and milk are natural companions, so why not cereal and ice cream? Grape-Nuts were first introduced by Battle Creek, Michigan–based Post Cereal in 1898, one of the first packaged breakfast

cereals. Post sponsored recipe contests using the cereal, which prompted cooks to incorporate the "grain nuts" into pudding, baked goods, even meatloaf. It wasn't too many years after its debut that Grape-Nuts and ice cream came together for the first time. In a January 2014 blog post, Paul Young of Hantsport, Nova Scotia, put forth one theory about how this frozen treat came to be. His grandmother, Hannah Young, and her son, Cecil (Paul's father), ran an ice cream parlor in Wolfville, Nova Scotia, in the early 20th century. They added various ingredients to their ice cream to create different flavors—maple syrup, fresh fruit, nuts, bits of ribbon candy at Christmas. One day in 1919, Young writes, Hannah ran out of fresh fruit to add to her latest

batch of ice cream, so she added several handfuls of Grape-Nuts instead. The combination of creamy, sweet ice cream speckled with crunchy, salty, malty bits of cereal—some of which soften slightly in the frozen custard, just like the cereal does in milk—became so popular that Farmers Dairy asked for permission to produce it. That, combined with the movement of people and food between Canada and the U.S. over the northern border, spurred its spread throughout the area and eventually throughout New England.

New Jersey: Pork roll, egg, and cheese sandwich

Most beloved regional foods migrate beyond the state of their origin simply due to the movement of people and word of mouth. Not so the pork roll, egg, and cheese sandwich—a New Jersey original that has pretty much stayed within the borders of the state. The star ingredient—pork roll (also called Taylor Ham)—is a processed meat made from minced pork, sugar, spices, and salt that is formed into rolls and hickory-smoked before being packaged in Trenton, New Jersey, and just about nowhere else. New Jersey businessman and state senator John Taylor created the product in 1856 and formed Taylor Provisions Company in 1888 in Trenton. He called his product Taylor's Prepared Ham, but had to change the name when it didn't meet the new legal definition of "ham" established by the Pure Food and Drug Act of 1906. It's been made in Trenton since then. He rebranded it and sold it under the name Taylor Pork Roll and Trenton Pork Roll. Competitors saw the potential and began making "Rolled Pork" and "Trenton-Style Pork Roll." George Washington Case began selling his version of pork roll in Belle Mead, New Jersey, in 1870. Case's product was originally wrapped in corn husks. Today, that company—the Case Pork Roll Company—is also based in Trenton, making the city truly the epicenter of pork roll culture in the country.

New York: New York-style pizza

Between 1876 and 1930, approximately 5 million Italians immigrated to the United States. Fully 80 percent of them were from impoverished southern Italy, including the region of Campania, home to the city of Naples—considered the

▶ The classic New Jersey breakfast sandwich is made from thinly sliced pork roll, griddled until crispy, and served on a hard roll with melted American cheese and a fried egg.

birthplace of pizza as we know it today. One of those new arrivals was Gennaro Lombardi, who had learned the craft of pizza-making in Naples. In 1897, he settled in New York City's Little Italy neighborhood, where he opened a small grocery store. He and his employee, Antonio "Totonno" Pero, began making pizzas to sell at the store. Slices went for 5 cents. The pizza became so popular they opened up a dedicated pizzeria,

Some young Black chefs in Philadelphia are reviving pepper pot soup as a way of bringing to light the story of a Black food tradition that hasn't always been told.

Lombardi's, close by in 1905. Iconic New York–style pizza was born—inspired by Neapolitan-style pizza, but different. The crust, made with high-gluten bread flour, can be stretched and hand-tossed until very thin without tearing. The result is a crust that is crisp but foldable, meaning it can be eaten on the go. The sauce is heavily seasoned and made from cooked tomatoes instead of a simple uncooked tomato sauce flavored only with salt. Traditional slices of *mozzarella di bufala* were replaced by shredded low-moisture mozzarella. The finished pies are large—usually about 18 inches in diameter—and the slices are also large and wide. Although perhaps not unique to New York City, the by-the-slice and on-the-go phenomenon of pizza-eating is very much part of the street food culture there. "A slice of pizza is one of the greatest walking-and-eating devices ever invented," writes Robert Sietsema in "An Ode to the Pleasures of Walking and Eating" in an October 2015 post on Eater.com, "especially a bare-bones cheese slice if you employ the fabled New York fold and decant the excess oil first."

Pennsylvania: Pepper pot soup
Although the first food that might come to mind in association with Pennsylvania is the Philly cheesesteak, there is one that is equally iconic and with a much longer backstory—pepper pot soup. For centuries, it was more than just sustenance. It was a hangover cure—and the one food visitors had to have. It was sold all over town at diners, cafes, taverns, and on the street. There are many versions of it, but it is usually some combination of peppers, spices, root vegetables, beef tripe, and leafy greens, such as collards. Some versions have dumplings. The creation of free Africans and Caribbean people who came to Philadelphia after the Revolutionary War, it likely has its roots in similar dishes from West Africa, such as *soupe kandia* from Senegal. By the end of the 18th century, Pennsylvania had passed the first abolition act. From the end of the war to about 1815, free Blacks from rural areas around the city and the South migrated in significant numbers to Philadelphia. By 1790, the city was home to about 2,000 free Blacks. So it was not uncommon to hear the cries of the "pepper pot women" on the streets of Philadelphia advertising their warming concoction. It was so popular that the Campbell Soup Co. sold pepper pot soup from 1899 to 2010, when it was discontinued. But now, some young Black chefs in Philadelphia are reviving pepper pot soup as a way of bringing to light the story of a Black Philadelphia tradition that hasn't always been told.

Rhode Island: Hot wieners with coffee milk
The hot dog may be a distinctly American invention, but there are many regional variations on it, including one that you should never, ever call a "hot dog." Rhode Islanders are very protective of their highly regionalized specialty—the hot wiener. Also called a New York System Wiener, it is a 4-inch pork, beef, and veal wiener served in a steamed bun and topped with yellow mustard, chopped white onions, celery salt, and a finely minced ground beef sauce. The beverage of choice for washing it down is another distinctly Rhode Island specialty—coffee milk, which is simply cold milk flavored with coffee syrup. The creation of the hot wiener is largely credited to Greek immigrants who came through Ellis Island in the early 1900s, settled in Brooklyn, ate Coney dogs,

then moved out of the area to other places, including Providence. They brought with them the wieners they had eaten in New York but gave them their own twist. Because hot dogs were associated with New York, the phrase "New York System Wiener" was attached as a marketing term to denote authenticity. The first vendor to sell hot wieners in Providence was the aptly named Original New York System, in 1927. Olneyville N.Y. System opened in 1946. Both institutions are still in operation today—and more followed. While every hot wiener joint has its own secret sauce recipe, it is often spiced with some combination of cumin, chili powder, paprika, and allspice—a spice Greek cooks often use to season beef or lamb. As for the coffee milk, that was likely an invention of thrifty Depression-era diner owners (some also say Italian immigrants) who ran water and sugar through used coffee grounds, then boiled it into a syrup and stirred it into milk. "People assume that hot wieners and coffee milk won't go together," says Greg Stevens, owner of Olneyville N.Y. System. "But they try it and find it works somehow. It's one of those things."

Vermont: Maple creemee

Two of Vermont's most vaunted agricultural products—maple syrup and dairy—come together in a creamy, dreamy frozen treat found all over the state at summer fairs and festivals, food trucks, ice cream shops, and even at maple sugar processors and dairies themselves: the maple creemee. And yes, that's creemee—

► Maple syrup and dairy—two of Vermont's most important agricultural products—come together in the maple creemee.

no "a" or "y" necessary. Richer and thicker than soft-serve but ethereal nonetheless, the maple creemee is made with milk, cream, sugar, vanilla, some stabilizers, and of course, pure maple syrup, all whipped together and swirled on top of an ice cream cone. Its nomenclature and origin are somewhat in dispute, but Vermonters' enthusiasm for their singular treat is not. Some speculate that because Vermont sits just across the border from Quebec, it's possible that "creemee" is a derivative of the Québécois term for ice cream, crème glacée. Burr Morse, a Montpelier maple producer and operator of a sugarhouse business featuring maple creemees, told

the [Lebanon, New Hampshire] *Valley News* in 2016 that he remembers going to an ice cream stand with his parents in the 1950s at age 8 or 10 and ordering a vanilla or chocolate creemee, but there was no maple. According to an October 2018 article in the *Rutland Herald*, in 1981, C. Blake Roy, markets inspector for the Vermont Department of Agriculture, approached the Rutland County Maple Producers with an idea for a new frozen treat to be sold to the thousands of visitors to the RCMP Rutland fairgrounds sugarhouse. They thought the idea to be a winner and, hundreds of thousands of maple creemees later, it seems they were right.

LOBSTER ROLLS

Long before Europeans arrived in North America, Indigenous peoples of the Northeast—the Passamaquoddy, Eastern Abenaki, Wampanoag, and Algonquin—caught and ate lobsters, boiled or covered in seaweed and baked over hot rocks. The lobsters were so abundant—said to wash ashore in piles up to 2 feet high—they became an important protein source when other foods were scarce. Considered a luxury food today, it is hard to imagine that lobsters were so abundant they were fed to prisoners, enslaved people, and servants, some of whom allegedly specified in their contracts that they would not have to eat lobster more more than twice a week. The commercial fishery for lobster coincided in the late 19th century with increased demand for the sweet, succulent meat among wealthy diners in Boston, New York, Philadelphia, and points west. The first lobster pound—a tank or pen with recirculating water to keep the crustaceans alive until they are cooked—was established in 1876 in Vinalhaven, Maine.

By the 1950s, as postwar vacationers explored coastal communities and beaches, local entrepreneurs set up lobster shacks, where lobster rolls became a menu favorite. Today, eating a lobster roll—or many—is on the list of nearly every visitor to the state. Like many regional foods, what comprises a proper lobster roll is hotly debated. Connecticut-style lobster rolls—first served in 1929 by Perry's Restaurant in Milford, Connecticut—are simply chunks of warm butter-poached lobster tucked into a toasted center-split ("New England-style") hot dog bun. Most Mainers insist a real lobster roll is simply cold lobster dressed only in mayonnaise, to allow the delicate flavor of the lobster to shine through, served in the same top-split bun. The addition of celery for crunch and a little bit of lemon is acceptable to some, anathema to others. If you'd like the purist's version, leave those—and the chives—out.

SERVES 4

- 4   1¼-pound lobsters
- ⅓   cup good-quality mayonnaise
- Kosher salt and freshly ground black pepper
- 1   rib celery, finely chopped
- Juice of ½ lemon
- 2   tablespoons butter, divided
- 4   top-split or regular side-split hot dog buns
- Chopped chives, for garnish

1. Prepare a large ice-water bath. In a very large pot of boiling salted water, cook the lobsters until they turn bright red, about 10 minutes. Using tongs, plunge the lobsters into the ice-water bath for 2 minutes; drain.

2. Twist off the tails and claws and remove the meat. Remove and discard the intestinal vein that runs the length of each lobster tail. Cut the meat into ½-inch pieces and pat dry, then place in a strainer set over a bowl and refrigerate until very cold, at least 1 hour.

3. In a large bowl, combine the lobster meat and mayonnaise. Stir gently until combined. Season with salt and pepper to taste. Fold in the diced celery and lemon juice.

4. Heat a large skillet over medium-low heat. Melt 1 tablespoon of the butter, swirling around pan. Toast 2 of the buns on both sides of the exterior until golden-brown, turning once, about 5 minutes. Remove from the pan. Repeat with the remaining butter and buns.

5. Divide the lobster salad among the toasted buns. Garnish with chives.

DORO WAT (SPICED CHICKEN STEW)

The nation's capital is home to the largest population of Ethiopians outside of Africa, which is reflected in the number of Ethiopian restaurants in the city and the community's embrace of Ethiopian food. It began with an influx of students in the 1950s who were drawn by an opportunity to study abroad, many of them at Howard University. Then, a revolution in 1974 and the ensuing civil war caused many Ethiopians to flee their home country. In 1978, the first Ethiopian restaurant in D.C.—Mamma Desta's—opened. Doro wat—considered to be the national dish of Ethiopia—is a mainstay on the menus of D.C.'s Ethiopian restaurants. A wat is a highly spiced stew made with chicken, beef, or lamb and a variety of vegetables. This recipe was inspired by one taught to chef Marcus Samuelsson by a friend in Addis Ababa. Two crucial ingredients in all versions of doro wat are niter kibbeh, a spiced clarified butter, and berbere, a complex spice blend.

SERVES 4 TO 6

- ¼ cup Niter Kibbeh (recipe follows) or prepared niter kibbeh
- 3 tablespoons grated fresh ginger
- 3 medium red onions, very finely chopped
- 5 cloves garlic, minced
- 3 tablespoons Berbere (recipe follows) or prepared berbere
- 1 small tomato, chopped
- ½ teaspoon ground cardamom
- ½ teaspoon ground coriander
- 4 chicken drumsticks, skinned
- 4 bone-in chicken thighs, skinned
  Kosher salt and freshly ground black pepper
- 4 hard-cooked eggs
  Injera, for serving (recipe page 39)

1. In a large pot, heat the Niter Kibbeh over low heat. Add the ginger, onions, and garlic. Cook, stirring occasionally, until soft, about 30 minutes. Add the Berbere and tomato. Cook, stirring occasionally, until reduced and darkened, about 15 minutes.

2. Add 4 cups water, the cardamom, coriander, and chicken. Season to taste with salt and pepper. Bring to a boil over medium-high heat. Reduce heat to medium-low. Cook, covered, until the chicken is done, about 1 hour.

3. Transfer the chicken to a serving platter. Bring the sauce to a boil. Reduce heat and simmer until the sauce is reduced, about 15 minutes.

4. Pierce the eggs in several places with a fork. Add to the pot and simmer until heated through, about 5 to 6 minutes. Peel and coarsely chop.

5. Pour the sauce over the chicken. Sprinkle with the chopped egg. Serve with Injera.

NITER KIBBEH: In a medium pot, combine 1 pound unsalted butter; 1 yellow onion, chopped; 4 cloves garlic, minced; 1 tablespoon grated fresh ginger; 1½ teaspoons coarsely ground black pepper; 4 cardamom pods, lightly smashed; 1 teaspoon coriander seeds, coarsely crushed; 1 teaspoon fenugreek seeds; ½ teaspoon cumin seeds; ½ teaspoon ground turmeric; and ¼ teaspoon freshly grated nutmeg. Bring to a simmer over medium-low heat. Allow to simmer for 30 minutes, or until the bubbles that rise to the top are clear and the mixture is no longer milky. Line a strainer with a few layers of cheesecloth. Place over a heatproof jar with a lid and strain mixture into it. Discard solids. Store in the refrigerator for up to 2 months.

BERBERE: In a small dry skillet, toast 1 teaspoon whole black peppercorns, 6 cardamom pods, 1 teaspoon coriander seeds, and 1 teaspoon fenugreek seeds over medium heat until fragrant, about 4 minutes. Let cool completely. Grind in a spice grinder with ¼ cup dried onion flakes. Transfer to a bowl. Whisk in 3 tablespoons paprika, 1 tablespoon cayenne, 1 teaspoon garlic powder, 1 teaspoon ground ginger, ½ teaspoon ground cinnamon, ½ teaspoon freshly grated nutmeg, ¼ teaspoon ground allspice, and ¼ teaspoon ground cloves. Store in an airtight container in a cool, dark place for up to 6 months.

INJERA

Most types of Ethiopian *wat*, or stew, are served communally on a large platter on top of injera, a spongy, slightly sourdough flatbread made with teff flour, ground from the seeds of an annual grass native to the Horn of Africa. The stew is scooped up with the bread and eaten by hand. Most Ethiopian restaurants in the United States serve injera made from a blend of teff and all-purpose wheat flour—many Ethiopian cooks who came to the U.S. adapted the recipe to the grains that were available to them.

SERVES 4 TO 6

2 cups teff flour

2 cups unbleached all-purpose flour

½ teaspoon salt

5 cups lukewarm water

1. In a large mixing bowl, combine the teff flour, unbleached flour, and salt. Whisk until well-combined. Add the water, whisking until smooth. Cover the bowl with a few layers of cheesecloth and let stand at room temperature overnight.

2. Gently stir in the morning with a wooden spoon. (There should bubbles forming on the surface and fermenting water will have come to the top of the mixture.)

3. Cover again with cheesecloth. Let stand at room temperature overnight. The next morning, stir, cover, and let stand again overnight. Repeat the process for 3 to 5 days or until the batter has a pleasantly sour smell and is very bubbly.

4. To cook, heat a large nonstick pan over medium-high heat. Stir the batter and ladle about ½ cup of the batter into the pan. Swirl to coat the bottom. Cook, undisturbed, until bubbles appear on the surface, 1 to 2 minutes. Cover the pan and continue to cook until the top of the injera is dried out and slightly glossy, the edges begin to curl, and the middle is cooked through, about 2 minutes more.

5. Invert pan so the injera falls onto a platter or cutting board. Repeat with remaining batter. Serve warm or at room temperature.

THE SOUTH

The Black Belt South is a geographic band that cuts through Arkansas, Louisiana, Mississippi, Alabama, Georgia, and beyond. Originally named for its rich, dark, fertile soil, the name later took on cultural significance as the area where the greatest number of enslaved people labored on plantations. The South and the Southeast share many things, including a common history of enslavement, but topographically, they diverge. The Southeast is dominated by the Atlantic Coast, the South by the Gulf of Mexico.

Georgia: Boiled peanuts

In late summer and early fall in parts of the South, signs begin to appear along roadsides for "boil p-nuts." While the uninitiated may wonder at this, Southerners know exactly what it is: boiled peanuts. The signs are reminders that it is peanut-harvest season and that this singular snack should be enjoyed right now. Peanuts were brought to the Southern United States by enslaved people from West Africa—where they had been introduced by the Portuguese around the turn of the 16th century. They were similar to the native groundnut, which

▼ Fresh peanuts are highly perishable and need to be boiled or roasted to prevent them from spoiling in just a few days after harvest.

African cooks put to use in a variety of dishes, most notably a soup or stew, and they spread across the continent. Fresh peanuts—also called green peanuts—are highly perishable due to their high moisture content and will spoil in a matter of days after harvest if they are not air-dried or cooked. African American cooks cooked them by boiling them—in the shell—in heavily salted water. W. H. Shelton, a captured Union solider who escaped from a prison camp in Columbia, South Carolina, in 1864 and traveled east to Charleston, was given food by Black freedmen along the way, often boiled peanuts. White cooks didn't begin boiling peanuts until after the turn of the 20th century, when the nuts began being served at festivals, fairs, weddings, and parties. Peanuts are a legume. Roasting them, writes Robert Moss in "The Real Origin of the Boiled Peanut" for Serious Eats, enhances their nuttiness. Boiling them, he says, "brings forward their essential pea-ness." The result is soft (some say almost mushy), fresh-tasting, and salty. It may be an acquired taste, but it is not one many Southerners want to relinquish any time soon.

Louisiana: Crawfish étouffée

According to Cajun food expert Dickie Breaux—former owner of the now-closed Café des Amis in Breaux Bridge, Louisiana—sometime in the 1940s, a banker from nearby Lafayette got a scent of something wonderful emanating from the kitchen at the Rendezvous Restaurant and walked into it to ask the cook, Aline Champagne, what she was doing. She reportedly said, *"Mais, justement étouffe mes ecrivisses,"* or "I am simply smothering my crawfish tails." He tried the dish and returned the next week with a group of his employees—and lots of other people did too. While both Cajun and Creole traditions feature versions of crawfish étouffée—a stew featuring crawfish tails, butter, onions, and bell peppers served topped with rice—its origins lie in Cajun country, specifically in Breaux Bridge, self-declared "Crawfish Capital of the World." *Étouffée* means "stifled" or "smothered" in French. The most authentic recipe, Breaux says, is made with crawfish "fat," which is not really fat at all but rather the hepatopancreas (essentially the liver) of the crawfish. Often referred to as "crawfish butter," it

▲ Crawfish étouffée is thought to have originated in Breaux Bridge, Louisiana, deep in Cajun country.

is considered the heavenly nectar of traditional Cajun cooking. Its commercial sale was outlawed in the early 20th century, but cooks who peel their own crawfish can still taste the real thing. Others substitute dairy butter. Like gumbo, étouffée is based on a roux, but it is a blonde roux, meaning the flour and fat mixture is not cooked as long as it is for gumbo, resulting in a more delicate flavor and color than that storied stew.

Arkansas: Chocolate gravy on biscuits

Whether you call it chocolate gravy or "soppin' chocolate," it serves the same purpose—to be served in some form with the daily bread of the region, biscuits, as a special breakfast or dessert. Chocolate gravy is not made with meat drippings—although some Southern cooks do start with bacon drippings—but it is thickened with flour, as most gravies are, by starting with a roux. Its ingredients are just sugar, flour, butter, milk, and cocoa powder. There are multiple theories about how this combination came to be, some of which reach far back into the region's history. The *Oxford Encyclopedia of Food and Drink in America* suggests that chocolate gravy might have been a creation that came from a trading network between Spanish Louisiana

Man!" Legendary bluesman Robert Johnson released "They're Red Hot" in 1936. Delta-style hot tamales are similar to their Mexican counterparts but smaller in size, made with coarse cornmeal instead of masa, and, as the name implies, the filling—which can be pork, beef, or turkey—is heavily seasoned with cumin, paprika, garlic, and generous amounts of cayenne. The cornhusk- or parchment-wrapped packets are simmered in peppery water and served drizzled with some of the cooking liquid, often on saltine crackers. There are several theories about the origin of hot tamales, but the most commonly held one is that beginning around 1916, when Blacks began leaving the Jim Crow South for northern cities like Chicago—the massive movement of people known as the Great Migration— Mexican laborers moved in to take their place. They would bring tamales to the cotton fields in coffee cans that could be thrown on a fire. Their Black

and the Tennessee Valley, bringing "Mexican-style breakfast chocolate to the Appalachians." Another theory holds that it spread from Spanish colonies on the East Coast in the 16th and 17th centuries by a group of people referred to by some white Southerners as "Melungeons," who may have been of Portuguese origin or somehow connected to the Lumbee tribe of North Carolina. The name probably comes from the French word *mélange*, a slur used to refer to darker-skinned Southerners during the Jim Crow era. Southern food expert and writer Sheri Castle thinks it probably goes back to a time when people began working in coal mines and there was a company store or a local general store where they could source the ingredients. "To me, it is the epitome of resourcefulness," she told "The Spoken Dish," a video series from

the Southern Foodways Alliance. "You had this wonderful porous bread that you eat your soppin' chocolate with, and it was a humble dessert, and it is utterly and completely delicious."

It's thought that Mexican laborers brought tamales to the cotton fields. Their Black co-laborers tasted them and then made them their own.

Mississippi: Delta-style hot tamales
Mississippians are so fond of hot tamales that they've been enshrined in song. Reverend Moses Mason (recording as Red Hot Ole Mose) cut "Molly Man" in 1928. Giving voice to the Black vendors who sold hot tamales on the street, he sings, "Good times are comin,' don't you see the signs? White folks standin' 'round here spendin' a-many dimes, red hot, whoo! The 'Male

co-laborers tasted them, then took the tamale and made it their own. While Greenville is considered the epicenter of the hot tamale, this unique food is so closely associated with the whole state that the Southern Foodways Alliance has created an interactive Hot Tamale Trail Map to guide visitors to tamale hot spots as far north as Dilworth's Tamales in Corinth to Doris' Hot Tamales on the Gulf in Biloxi.

LANE CAKE

In 1898, Emma Rylander Lane of Clayton, Alabama, published a cookbook called *Some Good Things to Eat*. One of the recipes would rise up above all the others in the book to become an iconic Southern dessert—even making mention in a classic work of literature—the Lane Cake. The cake made its first public appearance at a county fair in Columbus, Georgia, when Lane entered it in a baking competition. She won first prize and initially called it Prize Cake, until a friend convinced her to name it eponymously. Lane's original recipe was difficult to come by until it was shared by her granddaughter, Emma Rylander Law, in a 1967 article run by the Associated Press. Originally a four-layer sponge cake filled with a rich custard spiked with bourbon, studded with raisins, and covered with fluffy boiled white frosting, it changed over the decades as cooks tried different ingredients to make it their own. Some featured sponge cakes with butter, some without, some with four layers, others with three. Some Lane Cakes call for pecans, candied cherries, and/or coconut in the filling. Lane's original recipe specified that the raisins be "seeded and finely clipped" and for "one wine-glass of good whiskey or brandy." The one constant of most Lane Cakes is that they're soaked in spirits. Scout Finch of Harper Lee's *To Kill a Mockingbird* acknowledges as much. Miss Maudie Atkinson, the Finches' neighbor, is famed in the fictitious town of Maycomb for her Lane Cakes. "Miss Maudie Atkinson baked a Lane cake so loaded with shinny," Scout says, "it made me tight." "Shinny" is slang for liquor and "tight" refers to being inebriated. And while that might be a bit of an exaggeration, a fairly generous amount of bourbon does tame the sweetness of the cake. This is a special-occasion cake—it does take a bit of effort. Make it at least one day ahead of when you plan to serve it.

SERVES 12 TO 16

FOR THE CAKE

3 cups cake flour

1 tablespoon baking powder

¼ teaspoon salt

1 cup unsalted butter, softened at room temperature

2 cups granulated sugar

1 teaspoon vanilla extract

1 cup milk

8 large egg whites, room temperature

FOR THE FILLING

½ cup unsalted butter

1 cup granulated sugar

8 large egg yolks

¾ cup flaked coconut

¾ cup pecans, toasted and chopped

½ cup raisins, chopped

½ cup candied cherries, quartered

½ cup bourbon

1 teaspoon vanilla

¼ teaspoon salt

FOR THE FROSTING AND DECORATING

1½ cups granulated sugar

⅓ cup water

2 large egg whites

¼ teaspoon cream of tartar

Pinch salt

¼ cup coconut flakes, toasted

Maraschino cherries with stems

1. **FOR THE CAKE:** Preheat the oven to 350°F. Grease and flour three 9-inch round cake pans. Set aside.

2. Sift the flour, baking powder, and salt into a medium bowl. In a large bowl, beat the butter and sugar with an electric mixer until light and fluffy, 3 to 5 minutes. Add the vanilla and beat until combined, about 1 minute.

3. Add one-third of the flour mixture and one-third of the milk to the butter mixture. Beat on low until combined. Continue alternating between the flour mixture and milk, beating between additions and ending with flour.

4. Thoroughly wash and dry the beaters. In another large bowl, beat the egg whites until soft peaks form, about 5 to 7 minutes. Fold one-third of the egg whites into the cake batter. Fold in remaining two thirds in two additions.

5. Divide the batter among the prepared cake pans. Lightly tap on the counter to release any large air bubbles. Bake until a toothpick inserted into the center of the cakes comes out clean, 18 to 22 minutes. Cool in pans on a wire rack for 10 minutes, then remove from the pan and cool completely.

6. **FOR THE FILLING:** In a medium saucepan, melt the butter over medium-low heat. Whisk in the sugar and egg yolks, and cook, whisking constantly, until thickened, 7 to 10 minutes. Remove from heat. Stir in the coconut, pecans, raisins, cherries, bourbon, vanilla, and salt. Let cool completely.

7. TO ASSEMBLE THE CAKE: Place one cake layer on a cake stand or serving plate. Top with half of the filling, leaving a ½-inch border around the edge. Top with a second layer, followed by the remaining filling. Top with the final cake layer. Wrap snugly in plastic wrap and refrigerate for at least 12 hours.

8. FOR THE FROSTING: Remove the cake from the refrigerator. Bring 2 inches of water to boiling in a double boiler. In the top of the boiler, combine the sugar, water, egg whites, cream of tartar, and salt. Beat with an electric mixer on low for 30 seconds, then increase speed to high and beat until light and fluffy, about 7 minutes.

9. Immediately frost the sides and top of the cake. Sprinkle the top with the toasted coconut and decorate with maraschino cherries. Serve at room temperature.

THE SOUTHEAST

Geographically, this area spans the Tidewater regions of northeastern North Carolina and southeast Virginia, the Appalachian Mountains, dense forests, and rolling hills. At its southernmost tip, it is surrounded by water—the Atlantic on one side and the Gulf of Mexico on the other. It was the original home of the Cherokee nation, who taught colonizers from northern Europe in the early 18th century how to grow corn and beans; to Lowcountry fishermen, whose signature legacy dish—shrimp and grits—can be traced to Mozambique; and, more recently, to an influx of immigrants from Latin America and Asia, who have left their mark on the cuisine of the region.

North Carolina: Vinegar-sauced BBQ pork

Although there are now four distinct styles of American barbecue—Carolina, Memphis, Texas, and Kansas City—North Carolina, in particular, lays claim to being the originator of this uniquely American cooking style. North Carolina–style barbecue is divided into two types—Eastern, which is a whole hog cooked low and slow over a wood fire and seasoned with a thin, vinegary sauce; and Western or Lexington-style, which calls for just shoulder and a similar sauce, but with the addition of ketchup. The geographic split—roughly along the Piedmonts—occurred when Heinz began bottling and selling ketchup commercially in the early 20th century. German immigrants who lived in the western part of the state began adding this new product to their sauce, as it created a flavor reminiscent of the sweet-and-sour flavors of Germany. The story of barbecue in North Carolina is much older than this regional tussle, though. Cooking meat over an open fire was a technique used by Indigenous peoples long before Europeans arrived. British colonists contributed the technique of basting meat with a vinegary sauce to keep it from drying out as it cooks, and enslaved people from the Caribbean—where meat was cooked over smoky fires fueled by green wood—brought a taste for spice and hot peppers. These enslaved cooks were often charged with preparing whole hogs for large gatherings on the plantations on which they were held. Much has changed in the ensuing centuries, but some things haven't. Purists maintain that the only ingredients in Eastern-style barbecue sauce are cider vinegar, black pepper, red pepper, and salt. The smoke—and the pit master—work the rest of the magic.

Tennessee: Meat and three

The main thing you need to know as a first-timer to a meat-and-three establishment is how to go through the cafeteria-style line. The food is unapologetically old-school, homey Southern fare—crispy fried chicken, juicy slices of roast beef, thick slabs of meatloaf, hamburger steak with gravy, chicken-fried steak, baked chicken, fried-to-order catfish, chicken and dumplings, honey-cured ham. As implied by the name, the "three" in the equation are sides. First you pick your protein, then your go-withs. The biggest share of the options are Southern-style vegetables—collards and/or turnip greens cooked in a smoky pork broth, fried okra, mashed potatoes, creamed corn, candied yams, cauliflower casserole, fresh tomato salad, fried apples,

▼ Purists insist that the only ingredients in real Eastern-style North Carolina barbecue sauce are cider vinegar, black pepper, red pepper, and salt.

and a plethora of beans (pinto, butter, or white). Although not a vegetable, mac and cheese is a must-have on the menu of any meat and three. Biscuits, cornbread, or a homemade roll are often included—and dessert too, a seasonal cobbler, pie, or pudding (banana is a favorite). The beverage of choice to wash it all down is a glass of sweet tea. Although there are meat-and-threes throughout the South, the epicenter is Nashville, and—according to John T. Edge, director of the Southern Foodways Alliance at the University of Mississippi—they likely came into being as a response to workers moving from the farm to the city in the early decades of the 20th century. "It was food for people who plowed the back 40 [side of the farm], reinterpreted for people who work in desks and factories," he told *Eater* in a December 2016 interview. "[The meat and three] offers a multitude of choices, as if your grandmother made three meats and 10 vegetables and said, 'Okay, pick what you want.' There's a bounty to the meat and three."

▶ The Cuban sandwich is an amalgam of contributions made by Cuban, Italian, Spanish, German, and Romanian Jewish immigrants to Florida.

Florida: Cuban sandwich

A person would be hard-pressed to find a Cuban sandwich in Cuba. Although it could be argued that one ingredient—the citrusy mojo-roasted pork—has its roots there, the way the sandwich came together is a distinctly American story. Between 1868 and 1898, Cuba was fighting for independence from Spain. A wave of Cubans left the island and landed in Key West, drawn both by a desire to escape the conflict and to seek work in the city's

80 or so cigar factories. They discovered the classic American ham-and-cheese sandwich and gave it a Cuban twist. The sandwich, made of crusty Cuban bread, pickles, ham, roast pork, Swiss cheese, lettuce, tomato, and mayonnaise, was called a *mixto*, meaning it was simply a mixture of different meats. In 1886, when a fire destroyed a cigar factory owned by Vicente Martinez Ybor, he moved it to Tampa, specifically to an area that came to be known as Ybor City. It was there that the Cuban immigrants

worked alongside Italian immigrants, who introduced Genoa salami to the mix. In the decade from 1880 to 1890, Tampa's population swelled from 700 to 5,000, due largely to an influx of Cubans, Spanish, Italians, Germans, and Romanian Jews, all looking for jobs in the city's cigar industry. Each group contributed something to what would come to be called the Cuban sandwich. The sandwich eventually migrated south to Miami in the mid-20th century, when a new wave of Cuban immigrants continued to make tweaks, which included dropping the salami. Although the "Historic Cuban Sandwich" was declared in 2012 by the Tampa City Council to be the city's official sandwich, it is the Miami version, the "Cubano"—Cuban bread layered with ham, roast

pork, Swiss cheese, pickles, and yellow mustard, pressed and cooked until crunchy and melty—that is found on menus throughout the world.

Virginia: Ham biscuits

While the phrase "ham biscuits" may imply an immediate understanding of this Southern specialty, it's not quite as simple as it seems. Virginians, in particular, have developed variations on the theme. Smithfield, Virginia, a town of fewer than 10,000 people in the southeast area of the state, lays claim to being "The Ham Capital

◄ Virginia's ham biscuits are likely a descendant of the biscuits filled with a slice of salt pork eaten by enslaved Black people.

of the World." Virginia ham is a regional variation on the country ham. Although there's no longer a legal stipulation to this effect, it used to refer to a ham cut from a hog that had been fed primarily a diet of peanuts and peaches. Country ham is cured with a dry rub, then hung to age in a temperature- and humidity-controlled environment. The result is a rich, dry, salty, slightly sweet, and intensely flavored product with an earthy aroma. At its most essential, a ham biscuit is a few slices of ham tucked into a flaky biscuit. Toni Tipton-Martin writes in her 2019 book *Jubilee: Recipes from Two Centuries of African American Cooking* that ham biscuits are descended from biscuits filled with a slice of salt pork eaten by enslaved Africans. After emancipation, the salt pork was replaced with thinly sliced ham—or even deviled ham. In her classic *The Taste of Country Cooking*, Edna Lewis writes that ham biscuits were fixtures at "ball games and suppers, and always at Sunday Revival." These days, ham biscuits can include a smear of hot or sweet mustard, horseradish, honey, jelly, or jam. There's a variation—also called "funeral biscuits"—that doesn't call for biscuits at all, but rather yeasted rolls layered with ham, Swiss cheese, and butter flavored with poppy seeds, mustard, onion, and Worcestershire sauce that are wrapped in foil and baked until warm—and they're still called "ham biscuits."

West Virginia: Pepperoni rolls

The signature food of West Virginia has a direct line to the state's immigration and industrial history. The pepperoni roll—a crisp-crusted, fluffy white yeasted roll into which pepperoni is baked—is a staple that can be found in nearly every West Virginia grocery store, convenience store, and gas station—and even on the menus of school cafeterias. In the early 20th century, Italian immigrants flooded into West Virginia, most looking for work as pick-and-shovel coal miners. By 1910, there were more than 17,000 Italian immigrants in West Virginia, most from southern Italy, and most of whom settled in the north-central part of the state. Miners worked long days and needed a filling, simple, portable, and nonperishable lunch to take with them into the mines. Giuseppe Argiro, an immigrant from Calabria who came to work in the mines, noticed that his compatriots would eat a stick of salami or pepperoni with one hand and a piece of bread with the other. The natural conclusion he came to was to combine the two. In 1927, he opened the Country Club Bakery in Fairmont, and began making pepperoni rolls. Miners could hold the roll in one hand and drink water with the other. Other bakeries soon followed, including Tomaro's Bakery—the oldest in the state—just a few miles away in Clarksburg. Both bakeries still make pepperoni rolls and even ship them to expatriate West Virginians longing for a bite. There are now many variations on the roll—some bakers add cheese or peppers—but the classic, a simple bread infused with spicy, flavorful pepperoni fat and basted with melted butter after baking, is still the standard bearer.

▶ West Virginia's pepperoni rolls were created by an Italian immigrant miner looking to make a filling, simple, portable, nonperishable lunch to take to the mines.

SOUP BEANS & CORNBREAD

There is a direct line between the Indigenous people of what is now Kentucky and the development of soup beans and cornbread as a staple food of the (mostly) European descendants of modern-day Appalachia. Nearly 1,000 years before the Scots-Irish, Germans, and English began arriving in the early 18th century, the Native people—primarily Cherokee—were using fire to clear areas of the forest to cultivate crops, most notably corn and beans. The Europeans adopted their agricultural practices and adapted these foodstuffs into their own dishes, often incorporating meat from hogs they let range free in the forest. "Farming in the Appalachian Mountains is hard now, and used to be nearly impossible," writes author and Southern food expert Sheri Castle in a 2016 issue of *Southern Living*. "The land is combative . . . The growing season is fickle and fleeting. The terrain is steep . . . Given those conditions and exigencies, it's easy to see why dried beans, bread made from dried corn, and home-canned chow chow—a sweet-and-sour pickle relish—made from a homegrown garden would be essential. At one time, mountain families relied on this meal as an affordable source of sustenance. Most of us modern-day mountaineers no longer eat soup beans because we have to, but because we want to."

SERVES 6

1 pound dried pinto beans

2 slices thick-cut bacon, diced

1 large sweet onion, chopped

2 bay leaves

8 ounces country ham, left whole

1 to 2 teaspoons ground black pepper

¼ teaspoon salt, plus more to taste

Prepared chow chow, for serving

Cornbread (recipe follows)

1. Pick through the beans and discard any chaff or pebbles. Rinse and drain the beans. Place in a large bowl and cover with water to a depth of 3 inches. Let stand overnight; drain.

2. In a large pot, cook the bacon over medium heat, stirring occasionally, until it renders, browns, and begins to crisp, about 10 minutes. Transfer with a slotted spoon to drain on paper towels.

3. Add the onion to the pot and cook, stirring occasionally, until tender, about 5 minutes.

4. Add the beans, 8 cups water, bay leaves, ham, pepper, and salt. Bring to a boil. Reduce heat and partially cover the pot. Cook beans at a gentle simmer until tender and creamy, about 1 hour. Begin checking for doneness after they have cooked for 45 minutes, then check every 5 minutes. Shred ham into coarse chunks. Stir cooked bacon into beans.

5. Serve topped with chow chow and a wedge of Cornbread.

CORNBREAD: Preheat the oven to 425°F. Place 2 tablespoons bacon fat or butter in a 9- or 10-inch cast-iron skillet. Place in oven until fat is melted and starts to sizzle, about 2 to 4 minutes.Meanwhile, in a large bowl, combine 2 cups stone-ground white cornmeal, 1 teaspoon salt, and 1 teaspooon baking soda. In a medium bowl, whisk together 1¾ cups buttermilk and 1 egg. Add to the cornmeal mixture and whisk until a smooth batter forms. (Batter should have a sheen—add more buttermilk if necessary.) Pour the hot fat into the batter and whisk to combine. Pour batter into hot skillet. Bake 25 to 30 minutes or until golden. Cool in the pan for 5 to 10 minutes. Carefully remove from the pan. Cut into wedges and serve warm.

SHRIMP & GRITS

This dish evolved from a simple Lowcountry fishermen's breakfast to pricey modern restaurant versions that involve Creole cream sauce and pork belly croutons or wild-caught head-on shrimp tossed with andouille sausage and crawfish, but its origins are thousands of miles from the shores of South Carolina. According to food historian Michael Twitty, author of *The Cooking Gene*, shrimp and grits has its roots in Mozambique, where dishes that combined corn and shellfish have been cooked and eaten for centuries. The combination was brought to this country in the minds of enslaved Africans, many of whom landed at the port of Charleston. A printed recipe first appeared in 1930, in *Two Hundred Years of Charleston Cooking*, a cookbook compiled by the wife of the longtime mayor of Charleston. Calling it "shrimps and hominy," she credited it to her Black butler, William Deas. He was 78 years old at the time—meaning it's likely he was born into slavery—and had been eating the dish every morning during shrimp season for as long as he could recall. In the 1980s, a profile of chef Bill Neal of Chapel Hill's Crook's Corner by *New York Times* food editor Craig Claiborne catapulted the dish into the national mainstream. Neal's version—shrimp sautéed with bacon, mushrooms, garlic, and hot sauce and served on a bed of cheesy grits—became the new standard-bearer. This is inspired by that classic recipe.

SERVES 4

FOR THE GRITS

- ¾ teaspoon salt
- 2 tablespoons unsalted butter, divided
- 1 cup coarse stone-ground white grits
- 1 cup whole milk
- ¼ teaspoon ground black pepper

FOR THE SHRIMP

- 4 slices thick-cut bacon, finely chopped
- 2 cloves garlic, minced
- 1 pound large shrimp, peeled and deveined
- ¼ cup lager beer
- 4 tablespoons butter, cubed
- 1 tablespoon fresh lemon juice
- 1 teaspoon hot sauce (optional)
- Salt and freshly ground black pepper
- Sliced scallions, for garnish
- Lemon wedges, for serving

1. **FOR THE GRITS:** In a large pot, bring 4 cups water, the salt, and 1 tablespoon of the butter to boiling. Add the grits gradually, stirring constantly with a wooden spoon. Reduce heat and cook at a bare simmer, covered, stirring frequently, until the water is absorbed and the grits are thickened, about 15 minutes.

2. Stir in ½ cup of the milk and simmer, partially covered, stirring occasionally to keep grits from sticking to bottom of pan, about 10 minutes. Stir in remaining ½ cup milk and simmer, partially covered, stirring occasionally, until the liquid is absorbed and the grits are thick and tender, about 35 minutes more. Stir in the pepper and remaining 1 tablespoon butter.

3. **FOR THE SHRIMP:** In a large skillet, cook bacon over medium-high until browned and crisp. Remove from the pan with a slotted spoon and drain on a paper towel–lined plate.

4. Add the garlic and shrimp to the pan and cook, stirring occasionally, about 3 to 4 minutes. Add the beer. Whisk in the butter, lemon juice, and hot sauce, if using. Reduce heat to low and simmer for 2 minutes or until the shrimp are cooked through. Stir in the cooked bacon and season to taste with salt and pepper.

5. Ladle the grits into shallow bowls. Top with the shrimp and scallions. Serve with lemon wedges.

THE MIDWEST

In this, the so-called "heartland," vast stretches of land devoted to agriculture are punctuated by muscular industrial cities and the largest system of lakes in the country. What was first called the "Middle West" beginning in the 1880s is culturally defined by many factors, most notably the movement of people—the migrations of the Ojibwe from lands in the northeast in the 17th century, and waves of Germans, Scandinavians, and other Europeans in the mid-1800s. In the early 20th century, people from Lebanon, Palestine, Syria, and other parts of the Middle East arrived in Michigan to work for Henry Ford, while many Black Americans moved north during the Great Migration.

Illinois: Italian beef

The city of Chicago has a trifecta of iconic foods that includes deep-dish pizza and the Chicago dog, but it could be argued that none is more beloved than the Italian beef sandwich. Its specific origins are genially disputed by several longtime purveyors of it, but all agree that it was created by immigrants in the early 1900s. Those who worked in the Union Stock

▼ Chicago's Italian beef sandwiches were created by immmigrants without much money who served thinly sliced roast beef at so-called "peanut weddings."

Yards would bring home the tougher, less desirable cuts of meat and oven-roast them slowly in highly seasoned liquid to make them tender and flavorful. These roasts were served at so-called "peanut weddings." Because the recent immigrants had very little money, they served inexpensive foods such as peanuts and thinly sliced roast beef at weddings. Enterprising Italian Americans began setting up Italian beef stands around the city, some of which are still in operation today. While the exact recipe varies from cook to cook, there are similarities. A top sirloin or top or bottom round roast is seasoned with lots of garlic, oregano, basil, black pepper, crushed red pepper, and sometimes nutmeg and cloves. As it roasts, the fat melts into liquid, creating a flavorful jus, called "gravy." The meat is cooled, then very thinly sliced and kept warm in the liquid until it's piled on a French-style roll and served. "Regular" is a ladle of gravy over the top. "Dry" means the gravy is shaken off the meat. "Dipped" means the sandwich is quickly dunked

in the gravy, and "wet" means it gets a good soaking. It's finished with strips of roasted bell peppers ("sweet") or giardiniera ("hot")—a vinegary and spicy mélange of pickled vegetables that cuts the richness of the beef.

Indiana: Sugar cream pie

Like so many beloved foods, sugar cream pie was created in response to scarce resources. The crust—made with flour, butter or lard, salt, and water—is like that of most other pies, but it's the filling that sets it apart. Made with milk and sugar and thickened with cornstarch or flour, the pie is flavored with cinnamon, nutmeg, and/or vanilla. The result is creamy, sweet, and simple, similar to crème brûlèe. Although some recipes include an egg or two, sugar cream pie purists say that makes it a custard pie. It likely originated in the early 1800s in the Shaker community in the eastern part of the state as a solution to a lack of seasonal fruit. For that reason, it is also sometimes called "desperation pie." Although the oldest recorded recipe for the pie was in 1816, its identification with resourcefulness was further bolstered by its widening popularity during the Depression, when hard times spurred creativity. Kate Scott, a reference librarian at the Indiana Historical Society, has combed through what she calls the "wealth" of historic cookbooks in the library's collection that range from early statehood (Indiana became a state in 1816) to the present, and all but two included a recipe for sugar cream pie. Also called Hoosier Pie, Amish milk pie, and finger pie, this simple pie reflects the resilience of the state's home cooks.

▶ Sugar cream pie was likely a creation of the Shaker community in eastern Indiana as a solution to a lack of seasonal fruit.

Iowa: Loose-meat sandwich

One of Iowans' most nostalgic and favored foods is a burger served with a spoon. The loose-meat sandwich, tavern sandwich, and Maid-Rite all refer to a sandwich that consists of finely ground beef seasoned with salt—maybe some pepper—and served on a bun with yellow mustard, pickles, and diced raw onion. The spoon is for scooping up the "loose" meat that invariably falls out while eating. According to Jane and Michael Stern's *Roadfood Sandwiches*, this deconstructed burger is said to have been invented in the 1920s by the proprietor of Ye Olde Tavern Inn in Sioux City, who called them tavern burgers. Then in 1926, butcher Fred Angell opened up the first Maid-Rite in Muscatine, selling loose-meat sandwiches that eventually defined the dish for many Iowans. Angell franchised the idea and sold rights to the Maid-Rite name to a proprietor in Newton in 1927 and in Marshalltown in 1928.

Although Maid-Rites dotted much of rural Iowa throughout the ensuing decades, Taylor's Maid-Rite in Marshalltown—still in operation—is one of the most well-known. Although most loose-meat shops in Iowa put ketchup out for those who want it, Taylor's did not for the first 78 years in business. The reason? Because the beef, ground fresh daily, was considered so delicious it didn't need it and to do so would insult the cooks. In 2016, the restaurant took a vote from customers on the ketchup question. There were more than 1,000 votes. While the "nos" had a slight margin, in the interest of pleasing the entire clientele, the owners offered it anyway—and no one has refused a Maid-Rite because of it.

Kansas: Chili and cinnamon rolls
Some foods go together naturally— peanut butter and jelly, cheese and crackers, and soup and bread, to name a few. A twist on that last combination has been heartily embraced by many Kansans and Midwesterners in general: chili and cinnamon rolls. Among the origin stories for this much-loved pairing, the most prevalent points to a frequent offering at public school cafeterias. Some sources say the genesis was actually in Iowa, when, in 1944, 35-year-old Marietta Abarr—a newly-single mother of seven children—took a job as a school cook for $12.50 a week in the southwest Iowa town of Clearfield, where she worked on and off for 30 years. She began serving

chili and cinnamon rolls together, and the combination became a comfort-food classic. In the 1930s, during the Great Depression, the federal government began providing schools with commodity products such as flour, dried beans, tomatoes, and ground beef—so the makings were in

▲ The combination of chili and cinnamon rolls served in school cafeterias throughout the Midwest came about during the Depression using ingredients supplied by the federal government.

ample supply. Even without glancing at the school lunch menu, the homey smell wafting through the hallways on chili–cinnamon roll day was a harbinger of good things to come. Fans differ on how to enjoy the duo. Some eat the chili first, then the cinnamon roll as dessert. Others eat them alternately, together. And some tear pieces off of the rolls and dip them in the chili. "It's just a good combination," says one fan. "The sweet spiciness of the cinnamon rolls complements the flavor of the chili. It's a match made in heaven."

Missouri: St. Paul sandwich

St. Louis has several hyper-regional food specialties, including "T-ravs," or toasted ravioli—deep-fried ravioli dusted with Parmesan and served with marinara for dipping—and Provel, a highly meltable processed cheese made with cheddar, Swiss, and provolone. But perhaps the most highly localized is the St. Paul sandwich. The St. Paul is a savory, crispy egg foo yung patty served on soft white bread slathered with mayonnaise and topped with lettuce, tomato, onion, dill pickles, and optional meat, poultry, or shrimp. It's likely a derivation of "the new and popular St. Paul sandwich" touted in a 1903 newspaper ad for Mills Sandwich Room in St. Paul, Minnesota. At some point, it evolved into the Egg Foo Yung sandwich purveyed by Minneapolis' Yuen Faung Low—commonly called John's Place—in the mid-1930s. How the Egg Foo Yung sandwich became the St. Paul sandwich and became so closely associated with St. Louis is still not

The original, early-20th-century St. Paul sandwich consisted of bread slices filled with eggs scrambled with ham, onions, and parsley.

completely known. The most commonly told story is that Steven Yuen, a native of St. Paul, put something called the St. Paul sandwich on his menu at Park Chop Suey in St. Louis in the 1970s. He may have been the first to add the lettuce, tomato, pickles, onion, and mayo, but it seems he didn't invent it entirely. Today, variations can be found throughout the city, but it's nowhere to be found in St. Paul. "St. Louis-based food writers have been chasing this recipe's origins for many years," says Deborah Reinhardt, co-author with Suzanne Corbett of *A Culinary*

History of Missouri: Foodways & Iconic Dishes of the Show-Me State. "It remains one of St. Louis' delicious mysteries, I'm afraid."

Nebraska: Bierocks (Runza)

At any given Nebraska Cornhuskers football game at Memorial Stadium in Lincoln, more than 10,000 yeasted bread pockets stuffed with meat, vegetables, and seasonings are sold. They're called runza, and they have a long history that begins more than 250 years ago and almost 6,000 miles away. In the 1760s, Russia was experiencing famine. Empress Catherine II invited Germans—primarily from Swabia in southern Germany who were known for their skills as farmers—to settle along the Volga River near Saratov. She promised 75 free acres per family, freedom of religion and language, and freedom from military service. By 1869, there were more than 250,000 *Wolgadeutsche* (Volga Germans) living there. While they didn't adopt the local language, religion, or traditions, they did create a new food based on Russian *pirozhki*, a baked or fried stuffed yeasted bun. They called them *bierock*, and they are traditionally filled with ground beef, cabbage or sauerkraut, onions, and seasonings. By 1875, the special protections had been revoked and thousands of Volga Germans began immigrating to the United States, specifically to the Midwest. By 1910, there were approximately 4,000 *Wolgadeutsche* living in Lincoln, which had a population of just under 44,000 at the time. While those who moved to Kansas continued to call the buns *bierock*, in Nebraska, they evolved to be called runza. A Nebraska woman named Sally Everett adapted her family's recipe for bierock into a stuffed

▶ The bierock, also called runza, was a creation of Germans living in Russia in the 19th century. Immigrants brought them to Nebraska.

sandwich she called a runza, from another name for the German dish—krautrunz, or the Low German, runsa. In 1949, she founded the modern Runza restaurant chain in Nebraska—a branch of which is located at Memorial Stadium and feeds all of those football fans.

Ohio: Cincinnati chili
Cincinnati's most famous food might more accurately be called Cincinnati chili sauce. While some Cincinnatians eat it straight from a bowl, it is most often ladled over spaghetti or hot dogs, then topped with shredded cheese or some combination of cheese, diced raw onion, kidney beans, and hot sauce, if desired. Serving styles aren't the only thing that distinguishes it, though. It's all in the spicing. Cincinnati chili is flavored with chili powder and cumin, yes, but also crushed red pepper or cayenne, and, most importantly, is redolent with sweet spices such as cinnamon, nutmeg, cloves, and allspice. It has been referred to as "Greek bolognese," and there's good reason for that. Two restaurateurs and brothers, Thomas and John Kiradjieff, immigrated from Macedonia (now Argos Orestiko in Greece) to Cincinnati in 1921, and began serving spiced chili at their restaurant, Empress Chili, next to the Empress Burlesque Theater, in 1922. "It was just something my dad concocted," Thomas' son, Joseph, told the *New York Times* in 1989. At first, they cooked the spaghetti with the chili—likely a spin on the classic Greek dish pastitsio, which

◀ Sometimes referred to as "Greek bolognese," Cincinnati chili is seasoned with sweet spices such as cinnamon, nutmeg, cloves, and allspice.

features Greek macaroni, cheese, béchamel sauce, and a ground beef sauce flavored with tomato, allspice,

nutmeg, and cinnamon—but customers asked for it with the chili on top. Empress Chili expanded throughout the city and was the largest chili parlor chain until 1949, when Nicholas Lambrinides, a former Empress employee, started Skyline Chili. Today, it is estimated that there are more than 250 chili parlors in Cincinnati, and it's not just for tourists. "Yes, we eat the stuff," writes Cincinnatian Keith Pandolfi on *The Takeout.com*. "We eat it all the time."

North Dakota: Knoephla
The story of North Dakota's knoephla soup has a through line that connects it to that of Nebraska's runza—the immigration of Germans to Russia in the 18th century and their subsequent immigration to the Midwest in the late 19th century. Knoephla soup, eaten all over the state and almost nowhere else, is a creamy chicken soup made with celery, carrots, potatoes, milk, and dumplings called knoephla, from the German *knöpfle*, meaning "little knobs" or "little buttons." The German element in this

Oyster crackers are sometimes sprinkled over the top of the spaghetti version of Cincinnati chili as a crunchy crowning touch.

comfort-food soup is the dumplings, which are similar to spätzle—chewy noodles made with flour, salt, water, and eggs—but the other components were likely borrowed from bits of other cultures over time. Potatoes—known as a "second bread" in Russia—were added at some point. The celery and carrots are crucial elements of the Russian *smazhennya* or *zazharka*—the French version of the cooking base called mirepoix—which also includes onion. "The Russian diet has always been one rich in soups," writes Victoria R. Rumble in *Soup Through the Ages: A Culinary History*

with Period Recipes, "many of which were created in the medieval era and vastly improved during the 18th and 19th centuries." One of these was a chicken soup made with milk that was adapted from the Tatars. The Volga Tatars, usually just referred to as the Tatars, were a Turkic people who invaded Russia in the

▲ Sometimes knoephla, a type of dumpling, are eaten simply—just buttered and seasoned—but most often they are enjoyed in soup.

13th century. Many of them eventually settled in the same region in Russia as the Germans who came at Empress Catherine II's invitation in the 1760s—and who arrived in North Dakota in the 19th century, bringing their soup with them.

Oklahoma: Fried onion burger
It is no news to burger fans that beef and onions are a congenial combination, and equally unsurprising to Oklahomans that their fried onion burger is one of the simplest and best burgers around. Once called the Depression burger, it is said

top bun, followed by the heel of the bun so that as the patty finishes cooking, the steam rising from the beef moistens and flavors the bun. The patty—smothered in cheese and imbued with caramelized onions, is placed between the bun halves. Pickles are optional. The result is enough to make some cry—not from the onions, but from joy.

South Dakota: Chislic

Cooked meat on a stick is certainly not a novel concept, but a certain type of cooked meat on a stick is unique in America to South Dakota—and, like Nebraska's runza and North Dakota's knoephla soup, has its roots in the food of German immigrants who came to the state from Russia in the late 19th century. Chislic, simply put, is cubes of meat—traditionally lamb or mutton but

to have been created in the late 1920s or early 1930s by Ross Davis, proprietor of the Hamburger Inn in El Reno along Route 66. He was looking for a way to make ground beef, which was expensive, go further. His solution: Use less meat and lots of onions. According to John T. Edge's book, *Hamburgers & Fries: An American Story*, Davis would "smash a half-onion's worth of shreds into a five-cent burger." Davis' burger proliferated throughout western

Some versions of chislic are marinated and served with dipping sauces, but purists prefer the classic: deep-fried meat cubes seasoned with garlic salt.

Oklahoma. The technique for making it is perhaps even more important than how it came to be. For the most classic version, a ball of ground beef is thrown on a hot flat-top, sprinkled with salt, and topped with a large mound of paper-thin sliced onions. A large spatula is used to smash everything together and flatten the patty until very thin, with irregular edges that get lacy and crispy. The onions that stray beyond the edges of the patty get very caramelized and browned, almost burnt. The burger is flipped, then topped with cheese and the

sometimes beef—that are deep-fried, seasoned with garlic salt, and served on skewers with saltine crackers. Chislic is likely an anglicization of the Turkic word *shaslik*, referring to something on a skewer. ("Shish," as in shish kebabs, means skewer.) According to Marnette Honer, executive director and archivist at the Heritage Hall Museum & Archives in Freeman, South Dakota, chislic was introduced to southeastern South Dakota by Johann Hoellwarth, who came to Dakota Territory from Crimea sometime in

the 1870s. With very few trees available on the plains from which to obtain wood for grilling the meat—as was the traditional way Tatar cooks in Russia prepared it—South Dakota cooks fried the cubes of meat in the tallow of the sheep they butchered. While in Russia the meat was marinated in onions and other seasonings for hours, in America garlic salt came to be used. Saltine crackers supplanted the flatbread. From Freeman, chislic spread in a circle of about 30 miles surrounding the town, often referred to as the "Chislic Circle," though today it is served at bars and restaurants throughout the state.

Wisconsin: Friday night fish fry

The roots of this entrenched Wisconsin tradition can be traced to the Vatican in Rome and the year 1249, when a canonical law was passed forbidding the eating of meat on Fridays. Specifically, its inception can be traced to Milwaukee in the late 19th century, when large numbers of German and Polish Catholics began arriving there. The city's proximity to Lake Michigan made fish a natural solution to this religious imperative. Over time, it became a social one as well. Whether dining at Earl's Sister Bay Bowl and Supper Club in Door County, the VFW Hall in Kenosha, or Toby's Supper Club in Madison, the impetus is twofold—food and friendship. The menu is pretty much the same no matter where you are: beer-battered deep-fried perch, bluegill, walleye, catfish, or cod; french fries or potato pancakes; coleslaw; beer; and rye bread. "The conviviality of a table that exists at a . . . Wisconsin fish fry is unlike any other meal," says culinary historian Kyle Cherek. "If you're sitting at the end of one of the long tables and you don't know the people across from you, you will within 7 or 8 minutes."

Wisconsin's classic Friday night fish fry tradition took hold when large numbers of German and Polish Catholic immigrants—who didn't eat meat on Fridays—began arriving in Milwaukee in the 19th century.

MICHIGAN

FALAFEL

Southeast Michigan, with Dearborn at its epicenter—is home to the largest Arab American population in the country. The first Arab immigrants arrived there in the late 19th century, but the real influx began in the early 1900s, when—according to local legend—there was a chance encounter between Henry Ford and a Yemeni sailor working on the Great Lakes. The story goes that Ford told the sailor that his automobile factory was paying $5 a day. The sailor took word back to Yemen, where it spread throughout the region. In the ensuing decades, as people fled conflicts in the Middle East, many sought economic opportunities in and around Dearborn. Hundreds of thousands left Lebanon, Iraq, Palestine, Yemen, and North Africa, bringing their food traditions with them. None is more prevalent than the crisp, tender, spiced chickpea patties made by home cooks or in falafel shops across the region. This recipe comes from Patty Darwish of Dearborn, whose great-grandfather immigrated from Lebanon in the late 1800s.

SERVES 4

FOR THE FALAFEL

2   cups dried chickpeas

1   cup coarsely chopped fresh parsley

1   cup coarsely chopped fresh cilantro

1   small onion, coarsely chopped

¼   of a green bell pepper

1   serrano chile, seeded and coarsely chopped (optional)

1   tablespoon ground cumin

½   teaspoon garam masala

½   teaspoon chili powder

    Salt and ground black pepper

2   teaspoons baking powder

    Vegetable oil

FOR SERVING

Pita bread, warmed

Pickle spears

Pickled turnips

Sliced green bell peppers

Sliced or diced tomato

Chopped fresh parsley

Thinly sliced onions

Tahini Sauce (recipe follows)

1. Soak the chickpeas in 3 cups water at least 12 hours or overnight. (Be sure chickpeas are always covered with water. If necessary, add more.) Drain and rinse.

2. In a blender or food processor, grind the beans in batches until almost smooth.* Transfer to a large bowl. Add the parsley, cilantro, onion, green pepper, and chile (if using) to the blender. Blend until almost smooth. Add to the bowl with chickpeas and stir until well combined.

3. Add the cumin, garam masala, chili powder, and salt and black pepper to taste. Stir until well combined.

4. No more than 15 minutes before you cook the falafel, add the baking powder and stir well to combine.

5. Form into patties, using about 2 tablespoons of the mixture per falafel.

6. In a large deep skillet, heat about 2 inches of vegetable oil over medium-high heat. Cook falafel 5 or 6 at a time until golden brown on both sides. Drain on a paper towel–lined plate.

7. To serve, place the falafel in the middle of a pita bread. Add desired toppings and drizzle with Tahini Sauce. Fold and serve.

TAHINI SAUCE: In a small bowl, whisk together 6 tablespoons tahini, 1 clove minced garlic, juice of 1 lemon, ¼ cup water, and 1 tablespoon chopped fresh parsley. Season to taste with salt and pepper. Add more water if necessary to achieve desired consistency.

***NOTE:** You want the texture to be somewhere between couscous and a paste. If you don't grind the chickpeas enough, the falafel won't hold together, but if you overgrind, you will wind up with hummus.

WILD RICE WITH BACON, LEEKS, MUSHROOMS & BLUEBERRIES

Since the arrival of the Ojibwe people in the 1600s from the present-day northeast United States, wild rice, found naturally in northern Minnesota, has held immense spiritual, cultural, and nutritional value. Harvesting manoomin ("good berry" or "wondrous grain") from the region's lakes and waterways is done in late summer and early fall, traditionally from a canoe. One person stands in the canoe, pushing it through the tall plants using a long pole, while another knocks the ripe grains into the craft using wooden sticks. Grains that hit the water will become next year's crop. Traditionally, the green rice is then parched or roasted over an open fire, then threshed by being stepped or danced on to loosen and remove the outer hull. Finally, the rice is tossed up in the air from a birch bark tray so that the hulls blow away, leaving the nutty, delicious grains behind.

The forces of colonization, including loss of land, discrimination, the introduction of destructive technologies, and restrictions on traditional foodways—the means by which any group of people feeds themselves through hunting, gathering, cultivation, and industry—led to the decline of the health and well-being of many Indigenous communities. In recent years, Ojibwe in Minnesota have led programs to establish food sovereignty, including protecting the wild rice resources and reinvigorating traditional methods of harvesting and consuming this nutrient-dense, sacred food. This recipe is a modern interpretation of a traditional preparation that features both native and nonnative Minnesota ingredients.

SERVES 4 TO 6

1¼ cups wild rice

½ cup dried wild blueberries

¾ cup hazelnuts

4 ounces bacon, chopped

2 tablespoons butter

1 medium leek, halved lengthwise and sliced ¼ inch thick

Salt and ground black pepper

8 ounces chanterelle or morel mushrooms, cleaned and coarsely chopped

2 tablespoons finely chopped fresh mint

1. In a medium saucepan, bring 5 cups water to a boil. Add the wild rice and blueberries. Cover and cook over medium heat until tender, about 1 hour. Drain well.

2. Meanwhile, preheat the oven to 350°F. Spread the hazelnuts on a rimmed baking sheet and toast for 15 minutes, stirring once, until fragrant. Transfer to a clean kitchen towel to cool, then rub off the skins. Coarsely chop the nuts. Set aside.

3. In a large, deep skillet, cook the bacon over medium heat until crisp. Transfer to a paper towel–lined plate to drain. Pour off most of the bacon fat. Set aside.

4. Add the butter to the skillet. When melted, add the leek. Season with salt and pepper to taste, and cook for 4 to 5 minutes. Add the mushrooms and cook until tender but not mushy, about 3 to 4 minutes.

5. Add the drained rice to the skillet. Stir in the leek and mushroom mixture, hazelnuts, and mint. Season to taste with salt and pepper.

6. Transfer to a serving dish and sprinkle with the bacon.

THE SOUTHWEST

The states of the Southwest—Arizona, Texas, and New Mexico—are geographically big and culturally diverse. Texas, the largest state in the country, is home to Houston—the most culturally diverse city in the United States. The food of the region has appropriately big, bold, and varied flavors, based on the foundation of the cuisines of its Indigenous peoples and proximity to Mexico. Chiles, first cultivated in Central America and Mexico 6,000 years ago, reign supreme, bringing heat and fiery flavor to everything from tacos to Texas barbecue to Viet-Cajun boil, a testament to the ever-changing landscape of American food.

Arizona: Navajo tacos/fry bread

One of the most symbolic foods of the Navajo (Diné) people of Arizona has a complicated history. Navajo tacos (also called Indian tacos) and the fry bread used to make them are simultaneously celebrated and derided by Indigenous communities because they represent both perseverance and oppression. Between 1864 and 1866, the U.S. government conducted 53 forced marches of the Navajo people between 250 and 450 miles from tribal lands in northeastern Arizona and northwestern New Mexico to the Bosque Redondo Reservation in east central New Mexico. This became known as The Long Walk, and the land at the end of it was not conducive to cultivation of their traditional diet of vegetables and beans. The government provided canned goods, as well as white flour, processed sugar, salt, baking powder, powdered milk, and lard. Community members used the government-provided ingredients—many of which did not reflect or align with their traditional food culture and thus were part of a "colonial diet"—to create new dishes, fry bread among them. Fry bread and Navajo tacos are always two of the biggest draws at powwows, intertribal gatherings that were prohibited by the federal government throughout the 19th century. According to the *Navajo Times*, fry bread was first turned into a taco sometime in the mid-1960s at the tribally owned Navajo Lodge, a motel and restaurant in Window Rock, Arizona. A cook took a piece of crispy fry bread and topped it with beans, red and green chiles, and salad for a single hungry customer one night

◄ The fry bread on which Navajo tacos are made is a source of both pain and pride—as a symbol of survival—of the Navajo (Diné) people.

and within days was making as many as 75 each day. Today, a traditional Navajo taco is topped with beans, seasoned ground or shredded beef, lettuce, tomato, cheese, green chile, and sour cream. While there is a growing movement within Indigenous communities to decolonize unhealthy diets based on the commodity foods provided by the U.S. government—to return to Indigenous food knowledge—there are those who will likely always look at fry bread as something more than food. Leonard Chee, who grew up on the Navajo Nation, told *Smithsonian Magazine* in 2008 that when he says "fry bread is Navajo life," he is not glorifying his childhood poverty, but accounting for a shared experience of adversity. "Fry bread," he says, "connects tribes."

Texas: Viet-Cajun boil

In America—and in most of the world throughout history, actually—there is never complete stasis in any one type of cuisine. The diets of communities, countries, and continents are ever-evolving due to immigration, migration, and the cultural cross-pollination that results. The Viet-Cajun crawfish boil is a perfect example of this phenomenon. Unlike so much of food history, there's little argument that it originated in Houston, a fusion of two traditions that have their own separate histories. By the summer of 1975, just a few months after the Vietnam war ended, more than 120,000 Vietnamese refugees entered the U.S., many of whom were resettled along the Gulf Coast. There they encountered Louisiana's "boiling points," outdoor spots where vendors sold hot crawfish and cold beer. They

were reminiscent of the quán nhau—outdoor beer-and-snack joints that sold fresh seafood—back home. Crawfish are not indigenous to Vietnam, but both cultures—Cajun and Vietnamese—share the influence of French cooking. While the traditional Cajun crawfish boil consists of crawfish boiled in Cajun spices and served straight up in huge piles with corn and potatoes on the side, the Viet-Cajun boil takes it a step further, adding ingredients popularly used in Vietnamese cooking. The cooked crawfish are immediately cooled, then tossed in garlicky butter flavored with lemongrass, roasted onions, and orange wedges, and served with a dipping sauce

of salt, pepper, and lime. Until 2005, the Viet-Cajun boil existed in Houston, but primarily in the backyards of the Vietnamese community. Then, after Hurricane Katrina hit, many Vietnamese from New Orleans evacuated to Houston and stayed, turbocharging the trend. Viet-Cajun restaurants began popping up, and one of the most popular dishes was the Viet-Cajun boil. In 2018, Trong Nguyen, chef-owner of Crawfish & Noodles, was named a James Beard Award semifinalist, largely for his Viet-Cajun crawfish, which can be ordered regular, mild, medium, or spicy.

▲ Viet-Cajun boil was created by Vietnamese immigrants who arrived in Houston after the Vietnam War.

STACKED RED CHILE ENCHILADAS

While enchiladas are popular all over the Southwest, there is an assertion in some quarters—particularly in New Mexico and some parts of West Texas—that they should be stacked, not rolled. New Mexico stacked enchiladas feature chile-sauced corn tortillas layered with fillings—sometimes just cheese, sometimes meat, poultry, or fish. This recipe comes from the Diaz family, formerly of the 1600-acre Diaz Farms near Deming, New Mexico, where, among other things, they grew both red and green chiles. Ruben, the patriarch of the family, emigrated from Jalisco, Mexico, in 1947 at the age of 19. Gradually he learned the farming trade and acquired equipment and 100 acres of rented land, which was the start of Diaz Farms. You'll finish this dish, the family says, with your *"panza llena y corazon contento"* (stomach full and heart content). While using rehydrated chiles in the sauce is more traditional, this recipe calls for chile powder—both work equally well.

SERVES 2

FOR THE SAUCE

- 2   teaspoons all-purpose flour
- ¼   teaspoon dried oregano (preferably Mexican)
- 1   teaspoon ground cumin
- ½   cup New Mexico red chile powder*
- 2   teaspoons vegetable oil
- 1   tablespoon minced white onion
- 1   clove garlic, minced
-     Salt

FOR THE ENCHILADAS

-     Vegetable oil
- 6   corn tortillas
- 1   cup shredded Monterey Jack cheese
- ¼   cup finely diced yellow onion
- 2   large eggs
- 1   cup shredded lettuce
- ⅔   cup chopped tomato
-     Cooked pinto beans and rice, for serving

1. **FOR THE SAUCE:** In a small bowl, stir together the flour, oregano, and cumin. In a medium bowl, whisk together the chile powder and 2½ cups water until smooth. Set both aside.

2. In a medium saucepan, heat the vegetable oil over medium heat. Add the onion and garlic, and sauté until the onion is translucent, about 5 minutes. Whisk in the flour mixture and cook, whisking constantly, until the flour begins to turn a light golden brown, 3 to 4 minutes.

3. Remove from heat and slowly add the chile mixture, whisking constantly. Return to medium heat and bring to a boil, stirring constantly, until bubbles form.

4. Reduce heat. Cover and simmer for 2 to 3 minutes, whisking occasionally to catch any lumps that begin to form.

5. Remove from heat and cool completely. When cool, add salt to taste.

6. **FOR THE ENCHILADAS:** Preheat the oven to 350°F.

7. In a medium skillet, heat 1 tablespoon oil over medium-high heat. Quickly dip 1 tortilla in the hot oil to soften. Dip in the chile sauce and place in a baking dish. Top with a generous 2 tablespoons cheese and 1 tablespoon of the onion. Repeat with another tortilla, 2 tablespoons cheese, sauce, and 1 tablespoon onion, adding more oil to pan as needed.

8. Heat a third tortilla, dip in sauce, and place on the stack. Top with additional sauce and another generous 2 tablespoons cheese. Repeat with the remaining ingredients to create two enchilada stacks. Heat in the oven until cheese melts, 5 to 6 minutes.

9. Meanwhile, fry the eggs to desired doneness.

10. Top stacked enchiladas with the fried eggs and additional sauce. Top with the lettuce and tomato. Serve with pinto beans and rice.

*****NOTE:** The names New Mexico chile powder and Hatch chile powder are often used interchangeably, and they both come in mild, medium, and hot varieties. Use a type—or a combination of types—that suits your taste.

Recipe reprinted with permission of the Diaz family in memory of Eddie Diaz.

A TASTE OF PLACE | 69

THE MOUNTAIN WEST

The terrain of this region is among the most diverse in the country, ranging from rugged mountains whose thickets are ripe with wild berries, to rivers and streams teeming with fish, to vast expanses of grasslands conducive to grazing cattle, to high desert. It is a land of big skies and wide-open spaces and otherworldly rock formations that has retained a strong cultural presence of the Indigenous peoples—the Shoshone, Paiute, Apache, and Nez Perce, among many others—despite their displacement by white Americans who moved west to establish farms, ranches, mines, and religious communities.

Colorado: Rocky Mountain oysters

The first thing to establish about this regional specialty is that they have nothing to do with bivalves. Also called prairie oysters, cowboy caviar, and mountain tenders, among cruder nicknames, plainly speaking, they are the testicles of mammals—specifically those of bulls, bison, pigs, and sheep. They can be found at bars, restaurants, and festivals that celebrate them as their primary focus. They can be prepared a number of ways but are most commonly deep-fried. After various tissues and membranes are removed, they're sliced and pounded flat, seasoned, dredged in flour or dipped in batter, and fried until crisp and golden brown and served with any number of dipping sauces. Bruce's Bar in Severance, Colorado—in addition to oysters harvested from bulls—goes so far as to offer those from grass-fed bison and lamb. The practice began as white Americans moved west in the mid-19th century, toting the principle of Manifest Destiny, as they forcibly took lands from Native people. Although the white ranchers who moved into the American West may have modeled their "nose-to-tail" approach from the Native people they encountered, it is most likely they began incorporating cooked-over-the-coals testicles into their diet because they had to make use of every last bit. Additionally, castrating young bulls before they reach sexual maturity is an established practice of animal husbandry that reduces aggression and also has the beneficial side effect of producing more marbled, tender meat. The taste of Rocky Mountain oysters has been variously described as akin to venison, calamari, liver, gizzard, and yes—bison in particular—chicken.

Nevada: Prime rib

Wolfgang Puck opened a satellite of his L.A. eatery, Spago, in Las Vegas in 1982. He was the first celebrity chef to open a restaurant there, but many others followed, including Thomas Keller, Giada de Laurentiis, Jöel Robuchon, and Bobby Flay. And while the influx of celebrity chefs changed the culinary scene of the city, one thing has not changed in almost 80 years: its obsession with prime rib.

In 1942, The Last Frontier—the second resort built on what came to be called the Strip—opened and began advertising "juicy rich prime ribs of Eastern steer beef, cooked in rock salt, served from the cart at your table with Idaho baked potato with chives, tossed salad, rolls, and coffee" for $1.50. Hotel casinos began selling prime rib dinners at a loss as a means to draw customers in to gamble—and leave them with enough cash to do so. Today, there are upward of 100 restaurants in the city with prime rib on the

▼ Cheap prime rib dinners were first offered by Las Vegas casinos trying to lure gamblers through their doors.

menu. Those with names such as Primarily Prime Rib and Bacchanal Buffet join the ranks of celebrity-chef steakhouses. Diners can get prime rib dinners at everything from white-tablecloth spots to coffee shops. It can be ordered on eggs Benedict for breakfast, on nachos, in macaroni and cheese or chili. H.D. Miller, a professor of history at Lipscomb University in Nashville who blogs at eccentricculinary.com, devoted an issue of his self-published magazine, *Travelling Shoes*, to Las Vegas in 1997 and included a piece in it called "The Cult of Prime Rib." "The marquee of every hotel, every casino, and every . . . juke joint in town touts a low-cost prime rib meal. And if we can believe those marquees, prime rib isn't just for dinner anymore," he writes. "Instead, the erstwhile glutton can now enjoy prime rib . . . in every possible culinary permutation and combination, at every possibility."

▶ Basque croquetas are crisp little morsels filled with thick and creamy fillings, most traditionally with béchamel and salt cod or Spanish ham.

Idaho: Basque croquetas

The Basque Country—officially the Basque Autonomous Community, called *Euskadi* in the Basque language—is a region made up of three provinces in northern Spain and three in southwest France, in the western Pyrenees. It has a language and culture that is distinct from either country—in fact, the language, Euskera, has no known link to any other language and may be the oldest in Europe. In the late 1800s, Basques began immigrating to America. The largest concentration came to Idaho, where they found work in mining, ranching, and—most significantly—sheepherding.

The rugged landscape felt like home, and sheepherding didn't require them to speak English. The state is now home to the largest population of Basques outside of the Basque Country. That community has a tremendous impact on the culture of Idaho's largest city, Boise, where at restaurants, bars, markets, and numerous festivals, Boiseians enjoy the tradition of *pintxos* (PEEN-chos), or Basque tapas. Some of the most popular include tortilla, a quiche-like omelet of potatoes, onions, and pimiento peppers; *bocadillos*, a selection of mini sandwiches; and perhaps the best-loved one of all, *croquetas*, breaded and fried morsels that have thick and creamy fillings such as chicken and cheese with piquillo peppers, or béchamel combined with

salt cod or chopped Ibérico or Serrano ham. While similar in form to classic French croquettes, which are potato-based, classic Basque croquetas rely on a thick white sauce to form small balls or cylinders that are rolled in bread crumbs and deep-fried. The resulting bites—a hot and crispy exterior that yields to a rich, creamy, flavorful center—are irresistible.

Utah: Funeral potatoes

"Funeral potatoes. Such a sad name for a food that makes people so happy," writes Aleah Ingram in the *LDS Daily*, the online newspaper of the Mormon Church. That sentiment sums it up for those who love this dismally named but supremely delicious dish. In its purest form, funeral potatoes are a

side dish that consists of frozen hash browns (or "sometimes fresh ones, if you're fancy like that," writes Jenn Rice in *Food & Wine* magazine) combined with shredded cheese, melted butter, mushroom or chicken soup, and sour cream in a casserole that's topped

Every year, the Utah State Fair holds a funeral potatoes cook-off. One winner—deemed "not your mama's funeral potatoes" by *The Salt Lake Tribune*—contained pepper Jack cheese, salsa, and crushed tortilla chips.

with more cheese and buttered cornflakes and baked until hot and bubbly. Some cooks switch it up by adding ingredients such as bacon or jalapeños. It's cheesy, creamy, crispy, and comforting—so it's no surprise it has mystical bliss-inducing powers. How it got its name and affiliation with the Church of Jesus Christ of Latter-day Saints is no mystery. It's been in

the repertoire of the Relief Society, the Mormon women's auxiliary organization in charge of providing meals and other forms of help for the many births, weddings, and funerals that take place in a community of generally large families, since the 1950s. At that time, many Americans were turning to cooking with processed foods. Funeral potatoes are easy to make, can be made in large quantities, and have broad appeal. They are an anticipated presence at funerals, but also other church gatherings. "No matter what your favorite recipe is, most everyone has one," Ingram writes, "and if you go to any ward potluck you'll find at least five kinds to try." Funeral potatoes are such a part of the food culture of the state, that when Salt Lake City hosted the 2002 Olympics, one of the traditional lapel pins exchanged by the athletes was a dish of them (the other was a dish of green Jell-O).

Wyoming: Trout

Wyoming has almost 110,000 miles of rivers and streams, about 27,000 of which are fishable. Combine those with 67 lakes and that adds up to a lot of opportunities for fishing. While there are 22 game fish species swimming in

Wyoming waters, there is one that anglers most associate with the state: trout. There are six primary species of trout in Wyoming, including rainbow trout, golden trout, brown trout, brook trout, lake trout, and cutthroat trout—which has four subspecies. Trout populations vary widely, depending on the flushing flow, quality of the spawning habitat, and reproduction. The Wyoming Game & Fish Department gives a "blue ribbon" designation to streams that have more than 600 pounds of trout per mile. There are several on the list—including (but not limited to) sections of the Bighorn, Shoshone, Snake, Salt, and Wind rivers—but one dwarfs the 600-pound criterion. The Grey Reef section of the North Platte River consistently hits astonishingly high numbers, as many as 8,000 fish per mile. What to do with all of that trout? Grill, pan-fry, or bake it. The Game & Fish Department collects recipes on its website to inspire home cooks. Restaurant preparations range from the classic, such as trout amandine—with toasted almonds, brown butter, and lemon—to the cutting-edge. Establishments in Jackson Hole offer dishes such as trout served with pancetta, black garlic, and citrus vinaigrette; smoked trout served on pommes Anna with trout eggs, sorrel, and caraway cream; smoked trout cakes topped with pickled fennel and onion relish; and trout crudo (raw) topped with salmon roe, jalapeño, yuzu, and shisho salt. When in Wyoming, eat trout. "I don't even like trout," said one restaurant patron in an online review, "but it was great here."

▲ Six primary species of trout swim in Wyoming's 110,000 miles of rivers and streams. Preparations range from traditional trout amandine to cutting-edge recipes.

BISON MEATBALLS WITH HUCKLEBERRRY SAUCE

An ingredient with deep and contentious roots in the Mountain West, the use of bison reflects a long history of tensions between community members and governing bodies in Montana. Bison in Montana were pushed to the brink of extinction by hunters and a campaign by the U.S. Army to eliminate this primary food source for Native people in order to drive them into reservations. By 1889, there were just more than 1,000 bison left, down from a peak of about 30 million. The American Bison Society was founded by private citizens in 1905 to lobby the U.S. government to set aside land to protect and restore bison. In 1908, President Theodore Roosevelt established the National Bison Range—an 18,500-acre parcel of land in western Montana carved out in the middle of the Flathead Indian Reservation—without tribal consent. In 2021, after decades of advocacy by community members, management of the range was turned over by the U.S. Fish and Wildlife Service to the Confederated Salish and Kootenai Tribes. Some ranchers are now raising grass-fed bison, making it more widely available all over the country.

SERVES 4

FOR THE SAUCE

1 tablespoon olive oil

2 tablespoons minced red onion

2 tablespoons minced fresh sage

2 cups fresh huckleberries or blueberries, plus more for garnish

¼ cup sugar

⅔ cup red wine vinegar

⅔ cup dry red wine

Salt and ground black pepper

FOR THE MEATBALLS

¼ cup olive oil, divided

2 shallots, minced

3 cloves garlic, minced

½ cup fresh bread crumbs

3 tablespoons whole milk

1 large egg, beaten

2 teaspoons chopped fresh thyme leaves

1 teaspoon salt

½ teaspoon ground black pepper

¼ teaspoon ground allspice

1¼ pounds ground bison

1. FOR THE SAUCE: In a medium saucepan, heat the oil over medium heat. Add the onion and sauté until softened and starting to turn golden, 3 to 4 minutes. Add sage and cook, stirring, for 1 minute.

2. Add the huckleberries, sugar, vinegar, and wine. Bring to a boil, then reduce heat and simmer until thickened, stirring occasionally, about 15 minutes. Season with salt and pepper to taste.

3. FOR THE MEATBALLS: In a medium skillet, heat 2 tablespoons of the olive oil over medium heat. Add the shallots and sauté, stirring frequently, until softened and translucent, about 5 minutes. Add the garlic and cook, stirring, 1 minute; cool.

4. In a large bowl, combine the bread crumbs, milk, egg, thyme, salt, pepper, and allspice. Add the bison and shallot mixture. Mix until blended, then roll into 1¼-inch balls.

5. In a large nonstick skillet, heat remaining 2 tablespoons olive oil over medium heat. Cook the meatballs, in batches, until browned on the exterior and cooked through (an instant-read thermometer inserted into the center should be 160°F). Transfer the cooked meatballs to a serving platter and cover lightly to keep warm. (The interior of the meatballs will look redder than beef due to the leanness of bison.)

6. To serve, drizzle the meatballs with sauce. Garnish with fresh huckleberries.

THE FAR WEST AND PACIFIC

Although this region is divided into three subregions—California, the Northwest (Alaska, Oregon, and Washington), and the Hawai'ian Islands—all are geographically touched by the Pacific Ocean, and the food culture of each state is impacted in some way by the enormity of it. Its waters provide seafood. The temperate coastal climate of the northernmost area of it is conducive to growing berries. And then there is California, which produces more than one-third of the vegetables and two-thirds of the fruits and nuts consumed in the United States. Of course, the people of the region—its original inhabitants and those who arrived here over the centuries—have had as much influence on the food as the terrain.

Alaska: Reindeer dogs

Approximately 750,000 caribou range over the state of Alaska, so it's not surprising that a commonly eaten meat there is caribou or reindeer. Caribou and reindeer are the same animal (*Rangifer tarandus*). In North America, the animals are referred to as caribou if they are wild, and as reindeer if they are domesticated. Reindeer evolved to be slightly shorter and stockier than their wild cousins, making them preferred as meat sources by the Indigenous peoples who herd them, including the Cup'ig people of Nunivak Island off the southwest coast of Alaska. There are between 2,000 and 2,500 head in the Nunivak herd—the largest source of reindeer meat sold commercially in the state—which is managed by some of the 200 residents of the village of Mekoryuk. Some of that meat winds up in reindeer hot dogs. Reindeer dogs are not made with 100 percent reindeer meat. Because the meat is lean, it is usually blended with pork and/or beef. The sausages are traditionally split down the middle, grilled, and served in a steamed bun. One of the classic toppings—pioneered by M.A.'s hot dogs in Anchorage in the 1990s—is Coca-Cola-glazed grilled onions, but different vendors serve them in a variety of ways. One tops the dogs with onion, sauerkraut, and mustard; another with spicy mustard, cheese, sautéed onions, and jalapeños; and another with sautéed onions and chipotle sauce. Some make it "Seattle style" with a squeeze of cream cheese on top. A saloon in Juneau offers a reindeer corn dog. Reindeer dogs have enough of a following that they have migrated to the lower 48, where they can be ordered in cities such as Portland and Denver.

Hawai'i: Spam musubi

Residents of Hawai'i—a population of about 1.4 million—consume nearly 7 million cans of Spam a year, much of it in Spam musubi, a ubiquitous snack that can be found in gas stations, supermarkets, delis, convenience stores, and local restaurants. Spam musubi reflects a fusion of cultures, and as beloved as it is, also a fraught history. Hawai'ians of Japanese descent make up nearly 17 percent of the population. The roots of Spam musubi lie in a Japanese snack called *onigiri* (also called *omusubi*)—sticky rice to which a salty and umami ingredient such as salmon, tuna,

▼ Spam musubi is a ubiquitous snack in Hawai'i, where it was created by a nutritionist and entrepreneur of Japanese descent.

or pickled plum is added before being wrapped in nori. The Hormel Foods Corporation first made Spam—a mix of pork, salt, water, sugar, and sodium nitrate—in 1937. It was provided by the U.S. government as part of the rations for troops sent to the Pacific during World War II, and also to the more than 120,000 Japanese Americans who were forced into American incarceration camps from 1942 to 1945. Some of these Japanese cooks allegedly began topping rice with seasoned slices of Spam and baking it. During this same period, Spam began to find its way into Hawai'ian dishes. In the early 1980s, Barbara Funamura of Po'ipu, Kaua'i, a nutritionist and entrepreneur, created a traditionally triangle-shape *onigiri* with Spam, and it began selling big at a restaurant in a local mall. Soon it was all over the islands. Funamara quickly realized it was much faster to make—and it came out much more uniform—if it was made in a mold in a rectangular shape, its current and classic form.

Washington: Geoduck

Just as Colorado's Rocky Mountain oysters have nothing to do with bivalves, Washington's geoduck ("gooey duck") has nothing to do with waterfowl. It is, in fact, a bivalve—an enormous one—with a simple but occasionally blush-inducing anatomy. Its neck, a protuberance called a siphon, can range from 6 inches to 3 feet long. It emerges from a shell that holds the mantle, or breast. Both the siphon and mantle are edible and highly prized as something of a delicacy. The geoduck is the world's largest burrowing clam, meaning it is usually found 2 to 3 feet deep in mud, sand, or gravel. Although it ranges from Alaska to Baja California,

it is most often found in subtidal and intertidal waters like those of Puget Sound. Some food historians believe that the current-day pronunciation of geoduck derives from Europeans' misinterpreted and reinterpreted pronunciation of the Nisqually word for burrowing clams. The average weight of a geoduck is about 2 to 2½ pounds at harvest. After careful cleaning, the giant clams can be prepared in a variety of ways, including stir-fried or sautéed, cooked in chowder, or ground up and turned into fritters.

Many geoduck fans, however, believe its sweet, delicate flavor is best experienced raw, in sushi or sashimi. Seattle's restaurants have offered up such inventive dishes as geoduck crudo with celery and crispy quinoa and sashimi with sesame-ginger-lime dressing. "It's a raw clam," Seattle-based chef Ethan Stowell told *Eater*, "and it's as sweet as it gets for something that comes from the ocean."

▲ Geoduck ("gooey duck"), a bivalve found in Puget Sound, is most often eaten raw, in dishes such as sashimi and crudo.

CALIFORNIA

CHICHARRÓN PUPUSAS

A civil war in El Salvador that started in 1979 and lasted through the entire decade of the 1980s spurred hundreds of thousands of Salvadorans to flee the violence. Many of them came to California, and to Los Angeles in particular. In fact, more El Salvadoran-born people live in L.A. than in any other city in the United States. So it's not surprising that by 1981, the first *pupuseria* opened in that city, and as Salvadorans continued to arrive through the 2000s, a profusion of them popped up—taking the form of anything from a street stand to a food truck to a sit-down restaurant. A much-beloved street food that is considered to be the national dish of El Salvador, a *pupusa* is a masa corn cake stuffed with a variety of fillings, such as cheese, beans, *chicharrón* (ground seasoned pork), spinach, shrimp, squash, and *loroco* (an edible flower prevalent in Central America). Masa dough is patted out, filled, and shaped into a round sealed pocket, then cooked until golden brown on a griddle. It is traditionally eaten with a condiment called curtido—a pickled slaw made of cabbage, carrots, and onion that cuts through the richness of the filling and heaviness of the bread—and sometimes a tomato salsa.

MAKES 24 PUPUSAS

FOR THE MEAT

- 1½ pounds pork shoulder, cut into 2-inch cubes
- 1 teaspoon salt
- 1 bay leaf
- 1 teaspoon ground cumin
- 2 cloves garlic, peeled
- ½ pound tomatoes, coarsely chopped
- ½ red onion, coarsely chopped
- ½ green bell pepper, stemmed, seeded, and coarsely chopped
- ¼ teaspoon ground cloves
- 1 tablespoon vegetable oil

FOR THE BEANS

- ½ pound El Salvadoran red beans or pinto beans, soaked overnight, drained
- ½ tomato, chopped
- ¼ white onion, chopped
- ½ green bell pepper, chopped
- Salt
- 2 tablespoons vegetable oil

FOR THE DOUGH

- 4 cups instant masa harina
- 2 teaspoons salt
- 3 cups lukewarm water

FOR THE PUPUSAS

- 1½ cups grated mozzarella
- Salvadoran or Mexican crema (optional)
- 1 recipe Curtido (recipe follows)
- 1 recipe Tomato Salsa (recipe follows)

1. **FOR THE MEAT:** Place the meat in a large pot and add water to just cover. Add the salt, bay leaf, cumin, and 1 of the garlic cloves. Bring to a boil. Reduce heat and simmer, uncovered, until water evaporates, allowing the meat to fry in its own fat, about 1 hour.

2. When the meat is browned and tender, transfer to a food processor. Discard bay leaf. Add the tomatoes, red onion, green pepper, remaining 1 clove garlic, and cloves. Pulse until everything is combined and the mixture has the consistency of a coarse paste.

3. In a large skillet, heat the vegetable oil over medium-high. Add the meat mixture and cook, stirring occasionally, until vegetables have softened, about 6 to 8 minutes. Set aside.

4. **FOR THE BEANS:** In a medium pot, combine the beans, tomato, onion, and green pepper. Cover with about 4 inches of water. Bring to a boil. Reduce heat and simmer, uncovered, until very soft, about 2 to 2½ hours. Add salt to taste.

5. In a blender or food processor, blend the bean mixture, including liquid, until very smooth. In a large skillet, heat the oil over medium. Add the beans. Cook, stirring frequently, until thick, about 15 minutes. Set aside.

6. FOR THE DOUGH: In a large bowl, whisk together the masa harina and salt, then add the water. Use your hands to mix until a clay-like dough forms.

7. FOR THE PUPUSAS: Place the cheese in a medium bowl. Knead with your hands until it has a soft consistency, adding a little Salvadoran crema, if necessary, to bring it together. Set aside.

8. To assemble the pupusas, fill a small bowl with water and a little bit of vegetable oil. (Wet your hands with the mixture to keep the dough from sticking to your hands.) Take a golf ball–size piece of dough. Roll into a ball, then flatten into an even round. Top with about ½ tablespoon of the meat mixture, 1 teaspoon of the beans, and 1 teaspoon of the cheese. Fold the dough over the filling until it's completely sealed. Pat the ball between your hands to form a flat cake that is about ⅜-inch thick. (If dough cracks open when shaping, add a little more water.) Repeat with the remaining ingredients.

9. Heat a large pan or a griddle over medium heat. Brush with vegetable oil. Cook 2 or 3 pupusas at a time until bottoms are golden brown, about 2 to 4 minutes. Flip and cook on the other side until golden brown and heated through. Keep warm in a 200°F oven in a single layer on a large baking sheet.

10. Serve hot, topped with Curtido and Tomato Salsa.

CURTIDO: In a medium bowl, combine ½ head green cabbage, grated; 1 carrot, grated; ½ small red onion, grated; 1 teaspoon dried oregano; and ½ teaspoon salt. Toss to combine. Stir together 1 cup water and ¼ cup white or apple cider vinegar. Pour over the cabbage mixture. Toss to combine. Cover and chill in the refrigerator for at least 3 hours. Drain before using. (This is best chilled overnight.)

TOMATO SALSA: In a blender or food processor, combine 5 tomatoes, coarsely chopped; ½ white onion, coarsely chopped; 1 jalapeño pepper, stemmed; 1 clove garlic; and salt and black pepper to taste. Blend until smooth. In a large skillet, heat 2 tablespoons vegetable oil over medium heat. Carefully add mixture to pan. Cook, stirring frequently, until slightly thickened and darker in color, about 6 to 8 minutes. (This can be made ahead. Bring to room temperature before using.)

Recipe courtesy of Ana Herrera.

OREGON

MARIONBERRY PIE

The pride of all of the produce grown in Oregon is also the smallest—a juicy, perfectly balanced, and exclusively Oregonian fruit called the Marionberry. The berry was developed by USDA researcher George F. Waldo at Oregon State University in Corvallis in the 1940s. He crossed the flavorful Olallie and high-producing Chehalem blackberries in 1945 and began testing the new fruit in Marion County in 1948—hence the name. The berries underwent testing until 1956, when they were released commercially. They are beloved by Oregonians for their perfectly balanced flavor of sweetness to acidity and tiny, almost undetectable seeds. In season for a fleetingly brief four weeks starting just after the beginning of July, they're too soft to be shipped fresh out of state, but every year upward of 30 million pounds are produced—mostly in the fertile Willamette Valley—and there are no shortage of takers. Berries that aren't eaten fresh are frozen and brewed into beer or processed into soaps, candles, lotions, sauces, jams, and of course, pie filling—one of the most popular ways to use the berries. The results have been superb ever since the berries were first introduced and then tested for quality and flavor in the Food Technology Department at Oregon State, which named them the best tasting berry in 1954.

SERVES 8

¼ cup cornstarch

1 cup granulated sugar

1¾ pounds (6½ cups) fresh or frozen marionberries

Pastry for Double-Crust Pie (recipe follows)

Egg wash (1 egg beaten with 1 tablespoon milk)

Coarse white sanding sugar

1. In a large bowl, whisk together the cornstarch and sugar. Add the berries and any juices, and toss to coat. Set aside.

2. On a lightly floured surface, roll out one portion of dough into a 12-inch circle. Ease into a 9-inch pie dish. Arrange the berry mixture evenly in pie shell.

3. For a top lattice crust, roll the remaining dough portion into a 12-inch circle on a lightly floured surface. Using a pastry wheel or knife, cut into ½-inch-thick strips. (Use a ruler for the straightest strips.)

4. Place one pastry strip horizontally across the top of the filling (use the longest strips for the center of the pie and the shorter strips on the edges). Lay the next strips vertically on top of the first. Continue placing the strips on the filling, alternating strips horizontally, then vertically, to create a woven pattern.

5. When all of the strips have been placed on the pie, trim the ends even with the edge of the bottom pastry. Press the strip ends into the bottom pastry to seal.

6. Fold the bottom pastry ends over the ends of the lattice strips. Crimp the edge as desired. Chill pie in refrigerator for 30 minutes.

7. Preheat the oven to 375°F. Brush the pie with egg wash and sprinkle with coarse sugar. Bake until the filling bubbles and the pastry is golden in the center, 55 to 60 minutes for fresh berries, or up to 1½ hours for frozen berries. If crust begins to overbrown, cover lightly with foil.

8. Let cool on a wire rack until room temperature, at least 3 hours.

PASTRY FOR DOUBLE-CRUST PIE: In a large bowl, whisk together 2½ cups all-purpose flour and 1½ teaspoons kosher salt. Add 6 tablespoons cold cubed unsalted butter and ¾ cup chilled vegetable shortening. Using a pastry cutter or two forks, cut the butter and shortening into the flour until it resembles coarse meal (a few pea-size bits are fine). Drizzle ½ cup cold water into the mixture, 1 tablespoon at a time, stirring with a rubber spatula or wooden spoon after each addition. Stop adding water when dough begins to form large clumps. (If air is dry, you may need to add a little more than ½ cup, but add no more water than you need to.) Transfer the dough to a lightly floured surface. Using floured hands, fold the dough into itself until the flour is fully incorporated into the fat. Form into a ball and divide in half. Flatten each piece into a 1-inch-thick disk. Wrap tightly in plastic wrap and refrigerate for at least 2 hours (and up to 5 days).

THE MARK OF HISTORY

Between 1892 and 1954, almost 12 million immigrants entered the United States through Ellis Island, bringing profound changes to the American way of eating.

Across time and cultures, foodways are not static. They are moved and changed by social, political, and environmental forces. Enslavement, immigration, legislation, war, social movements, and economic realities have all had profound effects on the American table. The diversity and disparities of the American experience are undeniable, but through food, we can perhaps begin to connect, gain an understanding of the experiences of our fellow citizens, and build a shared sense of belonging.

ENSLAVED BLACK COOKS

From cooking methods such as deep-frying and barbecuing to the introduction of ingredients such as melons, okra, yams, and black-eyed peas, enslaved people brought here from West Africa foundationally changed what we eat today.

In any country or on any continent, native foods become part of the culture, familiar and comforting. They're also a matter of survival, as local populations have adapted and assimilated them. The enslaved people transported in chains on ships across the Atlantic from West Africa to North America brought with them seeds and plants perhaps as a way of retaining culture but mostly to feed them and increase their chances of survival. They planted their own fruits and vegetables to supplement their scant plantation rations, tending their own gardens at night after long days in the fields. And it wasn't just ingredients such as okra and the kola nut—the signature ingredient in Coca-Cola—or sweat-inducing hot peppers. They also brought and adapted dishes to the American colonies,

including jambalaya and gumbo, which are thought to have their origins in West Africa. Even the method of braising mustard or collard greens in broth, sometimes with ham hock, has its roots in the cooking of enslaved Africans.

Indeed, most of what is regarded as Southern cooking has its origins there. Revisionist history born of white supremacy erased the culture and food traditions enslaved Blacks brought with them, a development not to be counteracted until the Black Power movement of the 1960s and the coining of the term "soul food."

In the South, pork was king. While plantation owners and their families ate "high on the hog," their human property learned to waste nothing, eating feet, head, ribs, fatback, and organs, usually rationed to three pounds or less per person each week. For the plantation owners, they slaughtered and butchered animals, salted and dried the cuts, and smoked them over low, indirect heat: barbecue. They used whatever wood was plentiful in the region, be it hickory, pecan, oak, or, in parts of Texas, mesquite. These woods imparted distinct flavors in the finished barbecue.

Enslaved African cooks also learned to alter or even conceal the flavor of their lesser rations, making sauces with hot peppers from their gardens mixed with vinegar.

Adaptation of a New World Food
A native crop domesticated by the Indigenous peoples of North America and adopted by European colonists became a staple of the enslaved people who labored on the plantations. It was a common ration—a staple consumed in some form at almost every meal. Native Americans

▼ The kitchen where enslaved cooks prepared meals for their white owners at Somerset Place plantation in Creswell, North Carolina.

had long cultivated and used corn, and enslaved people borrowed some of their cooking traditions, making dough of meal, salt, and water, covering the dough with collard leaves, and cooking it in hot ashes. The result was called cornbread, corn pone, or hoecakes. In their quarters, the people often crumbled cornbread over boiled vegetables and the vegetable stock or pot liquor.

In the end, it was the enslaved Africans' reliance on salt and fat, particularly pork fat, that got them through grueling days in the fields—but their long-term impact was greater than that. Their way of cooking came to define the cuisine of the South and far beyond.

Countless Black plantation cooks—relegated to 16-foot-wide kitchen cottages that doubled as living quarters and whose hearths burned 24 hours a day with a 1,000°F fire—weren't just providing labor, but were creating and crafting what would become the American way of eating.

VOL. XII.—No. 68.—M   THE COOK

WASHINGTON'S BLACK CHEF

One of the enslaved people who lived on George Washington's estate, Mount Vernon, was a man named Hercules Posey. He was Washington's cook, a charismatic figure whose kitchen skills and meticulousness were legendary. "Under his iron discipline, wo[e] to his underlings if speck or spot could be discovered on the tables or dressers," wrote George Washington Parke Custis, Washington's stepgrandson, "or if the utensils did not shine like polished silver."

When Washington moved to Philadelphia in 1790 to assume the presidency, he had Hercules sent from Mount Vernon to the presidential mansion to cook and run the kitchen. Hercules requested that his son, Richmond—the eldest of three—accompany him to serve as a kitchen assistant.

In the spring of 1796, at the end of Washington's second term, his wife Martha's maid, Ona Judge, ran away. When Washington returned to Philadelphia in the fall, he left Hercules and Richmond behind in Virginia, where they were reassigned from the kitchen to hard labor outdoors.

On February 22, 1797—Washington's 65th birthday—Hercules self-emancipated, running away from Mount Vernon to New York, where he worked as a laborer and cook until his death at the age of 64, likely from tuberculosis.

Hercules was gone, but the impression he made in the minds of those who had eaten his food remained. Custis described Hercules as "a celebrated artiste . . . as highly accomplished a proficient in the culinary art as could be found in the United States."

◀ An image of an enslaved cook at a house in Amherst County, Virginia, drawn by illustrator David Hunter Strother in the 1850s.

JOLLOF RICE

If you want to start a lively debate among West Africans or those with West African roots, bring up jollof rice. A dish whose origins go back as far as the 14th century, it was adapted by enslaved Black cooks and is thought to be a progenitor of jambalaya. This fiery red rice is a regular at celebrations and family gatherings. Most devotees would agree that it's made with white rice that's cooked in a saucy mixture of tomatoes, chile peppers, onion, and spices. Each country, and each cook, customizes it from there, creating an ongoing competitiveness. Nigerians use parboiled rice while Ghanaians prefer basmati. Some cooks add seafood while others prefer braised goat or lamb, or even opt for a vegetarian version. This version replicates the popular "party jollof rice," which boasts a smoky flavor created by cooking it over an open flame until the bottom essentially scorches, creating a layer of crispy rice.

SERVES 6

- 1   large yellow onion, chopped
- ¼   cup cooking oil (such as canola)
- 1   teaspoon dried thyme, crushed
- 1   teaspoon curry powder
- 1   teaspoon paprika (hot or mild)
- 1   teaspoon ground ginger
- ½   teaspoon salt or garlic salt
- 2   bay leaves
- 1   to 2 tablespoons tomato paste (optional)
- 1   (14.5-ounce) can fire-roasted diced tomatoes, drained, or 4 Italian-style plum tomatoes, chopped
- 3   red poblano peppers or 2 large red bell peppers, seeded and coarsely chopped
- ½   of a Scotch bonnet or habanero pepper, seeded and coarsely chopped
- 3   cups organic chicken broth or vegetable stock
- 2¼ cups converted long-grain rice, rinsed and drained
- 1   tablespoon butter
- 1   to 2 cups cooked peas, cooked corn, and/or shredded cooked chicken (optional)

1. Reserve ½ cup onion and set aside. In a large saucepan, cook the remaining onion in hot oil over medium heat for 3 minutes or until tender, stirring frequently. Stir in the thyme, curry powder, paprika, ginger, salt, and bay leaves. Cook about 3 minutes more or until onion is tender and just starting to brown, stirring occasionally. Stir in tomato paste.

2. Meanwhile, in a blender combine the drained tomatoes, reserved onion, poblano peppers, and Scotch bonnet pepper. Add 1 cup of the broth and blend until smooth. Stir the tomato-pepper mixture into the cooked onion mixture in the saucepan. Bring to boiling. Reduce heat and simmer, uncovered, for 20 minutes or until sauce is reduced by about half, stirring occasionally. Stir in the remaining 2 cups broth and bring to boiling. Stir in the rice. Cover the pan with foil and a lid.

3. Reduce heat to low and simmer for 30 minutes. Uncover; remove the bay leaves and stir in the butter. Season to taste with additional salt and ground black pepper. If using, stir in the peas, corn, or chicken. For a traditional "smoky" flavor, turn heat to medium and let the rice cook a few minutes longer until it starts to stick on the bottom and turn brown (but not totally burned).

EARLY AMERICAN BEER BREWING

Beer has played a pivotal role in American life and culture since the days of European colonization—and even among some groups of Indigenous people living in North America when the first colonists arrived on its shores.

It's almost impossible to overstate the importance of beer at the time of colonization. Archaeological evidence indicates that Indigenous communities throughout North America made fermented beverages with corn, fruits, and tree saps. European-style beer—ales brewed with barley and hops—proliferated following colonists' arrival. They brought beer as rations on their ships, to nourish and hydrate them. In some ways, beer was no less essential than food and shelter. In addition to it having calories—it was often called liquid food or liquid bread—beer was safer to drink than untreated water, which could be lethal.

In modern terms, many of these early American beers were low-alcohol "small beer," meant to be drunk throughout the day by children and adults alike. Beer can be brewed using most any grain containing starch—sorghum, rice, corn, wheat, and, most commonly, barley—that can be

▲ A pewter tankard made in 1802 in Germany is part of the Cultural and Community Life: Domestic Life collection at the Smithsonian's National Musem of American History.

▶ The brewhouse at Monticello, where Peter Hemings—Thomas Jefferson's enslaved Black chef—brewed beer, including his signature persimmon wheat beer.

converted to fermentable sugars in a boil, which yeast then consumes to produce alcohol. The very first colonists often built breweries adjacent to their homes to contain the potential damage from fire. Decades later, professional breweries sprang up in places like Philadelphia, New York, and Baltimore to serve growing numbers of colonists. Brewing beer was challenging, however— especially in comparison to the production of distilled spirits and apple cider—and Americans continued to import beer from Europe well into the 1800s.

Beer Was Here from the Beginning

Brewing was heavy, hot, hard work. Often, white male colonists were not the primary brewers in a community. Rather, it was enslaved men and women and servants who brewed beer, baked bread, cooked, and did other household work. Bondspeople and servants also tended crops like barley and hops. Historians have found records of enslaved people in Virginia who sold their hops to nearby brewers to earn money.

Beer played a role in the Revolutionary War. When George Washington assumed command of the Continental Army, he decreed each of his troops receive a quart of spruce beer daily. As the war dragged on and supplies became scarcer, Washington fought for and won the right to his soldiers' ration, arguing that beer was vital to seeing the war to a successful end.

As American settlements grew, demand for commercially brewed beer surpassed what could be reliably supplied from England, leading farmers to plant more barley fields and hops. Cider made from apples that thrived in the temperate climate was another popular beverage and was actually more prevalent than beer because it was easier to produce and required much less land. No new settlement of any size was without a tavern, and their proprietors were among the most prosperous in town.

THE BLACK BREWMASTER OF MONTICELLO

At Thomas Jefferson's Monticello estate, beer was considered a "table liquor," served at dinner. While Jefferson's wife, Martha, had successfully brewed some beer in the 1770s and Jefferson himself brewed a batch in the spring of 1812, he usually stocked up by the gallon or cask in Williamsburg or Philadelphia. Then Peter Hemings, Jefferson's enslaved chef, took over. In 1812, Jefferson was visited by Captain Joseph Miller, formerly a London-based brewer and maltster who agreed to train Hemings in the art and science of brewing. Hemings took his newfound knowledge and ran with it, experimenting and perfecting the process. He became known for his innovative recipes, one of which was a persimmon wheat ale. In 2020, Avery Brewing Company, based in Boulder, Colorado, released a revival of this unique beer, inspired by an 1822 recipe found at Monticello. Travis Rupp, Avery's research and development manager and beer archaeologist, described the process of unraveling Hemings' recipe in a February 2020 blog post. "Forced to be the silent hero," Rupp wrote, "Monticello ale achieved high praise once [Hemings] took over."

While British traditions emphasized ales and ciders, central and eastern European immigrants— from present-day Germany and the Czech Republic—brought techniques for making lager-style beers to the United States. By 1830 or so, the speed of travel between Europe and North America had quickened enough to allow for lager yeast to survive the journey. Distinct from ales, lagers must be fermented and stored in cool conditions. They require more time to make and a more carefully calibrated environment. The result is a clear, crisp, refreshing beer, served cold. A Bavarian brewmaster named John Wagner is credited with making America's first lager in Philadelphia in 1840.

THE RISE OF THE CHINESE AMERICAN RESTAURANT

In even the smallest towns across America, there is usually at least one Chinese restaurant. The reasons for this proliferation counterintuitively lie in anti-Asian racism—and the adaptations Chinese cooks made to traditional dishes to draw white Americans in the door again and again.

▲ The fortune cookie is associated with Chinese restaurants, but it actually began its life as a Japanese cracker.

▼ A man cooks in the kitchen of a Chinese restaurant in San Francisco's Chinatown in 2011.

The love of your life is right in front of your eyes.

In 1849, Chinese laborers began migrating in large numbers to the United States, most of them from the southern Chinese port city of Canton, to work in gold mines, agriculture, and factories, and most famously, to build railroads in the west. The entrepreneurial among them started businesses, including restaurants—the first of which was Canton Restaurant, with seating for 300, which opened in San Francisco in 1849.

Beginning in the 1870s, white Americans began venturing into Chinatown to experience what they thought to be exotic, but they took a dim view of both owners and clientele. "Most of the visitors viewed the Chinese as barbaric rat and dog eaters who ate with sticks," writes Grace Young in her James Beard Award–winning book, *Stir-Frying to the Sky's Edge*, "shoveling rice and pungent alien foods into their mouths."

In the 1870s, the country was hit by an economic downturn, and the approximately 100,000 Chinese living here began to experience resentment and worse—beatings and lynchings by white Americans who felt threatened by their willingness to work for lower wages. Beginning in 1882, the Chinese Exclusion Act barred immigration from China and disallowed those who were already in the United States to visit and return. The law was repealed in 1943, but in that period the country experienced explosive growth in the number of Chinese restaurants. The reason was a loophole in the law.

Beginning in 1915, the Chinese owners of certain types of businesses could obtain a special visa that allowed them to go to China and return to the U.S. with employees. Restaurants were on that list. From 1910 to 1930, the number of Chinese restaurants quadrupled in America. There was a catch to the availability of the visa, though. It was only for high-end restaurants, so those who became the beneficiaries of it lavished their interiors with ornate finishes and gilded ornamentation. Going out for Chinese food was considered a luxurious affair.

In journalist Louis Beck's 1898 book, *New York's Chinatown: An Historical Presentation of Its People and Places*, he describes the restaurants as being housed in "gorgeously decorated and illuminated buildings" with Chinese lanterns "suspended in reckless profusion from every available point." Shark fins could be had for $2, fried duck's web for 75 cents, and chop suey for 15 cents. Beck notes that Black Americans "were among the earliest fans of eating Chinese."

There were also, of course, the more spare spots that offered up a bare-bones atmosphere and affordable food. By the late 1800s in New York City, the hipsters and bohemians of the day were venturing out to Chinatown to expand their culinary worlds. These "chop suey houses" spread all over the city and eventually across the nation.

Adaptation Is a Two-Way Street

In 2009, there were more than 45,000 Chinese restaurants in the country—more than all of the McDonald's, KFC's, Pizza Huts, and Wendy's put together at the time. Then, in March 2020, at the beginning of the Covid-19 pandemic as anti-Asian bias soared, CNN reported that 59 percent of Chinese restaurants had ceased their credit and debit card transactions and that in total 233,000 Asian American businesses closed in spring of that year. Despite this, the impact Chinese Americans had and continue to have on America's food culture is undeniable.

"While the Chinese restaurant business helped shape the American diet, Chinese food was at the same time being shaped, transformed, and altered by American popular taste," wrote Haiming Liu, author and professor of Asian American studies at California State Polytechnic University in a 2009 research paper.

"In this case," he wrote, "adaptation was a two-way process."

▼ Orange Garden is Chicago's oldest Chinese restaurant, opened in 1932 by the Chen family.

THE MODERN CHINESE MENU

What Julia Child did for French food in America, Cecilia Chiang did for Chinese cuisine. Chiang came to San Francisco from China in 1959 to visit her widowed sister, who lived on the edge of Chinatown. Some friends wanted to open up a Chinese restaurant, and Chiang helped them negotiate the deal—and also made a $10,000 investment. When they pulled out last minute, she was left with a $26,000 lease.

In 1961, as something of an accidental restaurateur, she opened up The Mandarin on Polk Street, with hot-and-sour soup, mu shu pork, tea-smoked duck, pot stickers, and Peking duck on the menu. Business was slow at first, until *San Francisco Chronicle* columnist Herb Caen wrote a glowing piece about the food. It wasn't long before the restaurant was packed and Chiang's style of food became the standard-bearer at Chinese restaurants across the country.

SIU MAI

While the most familiar Chinese American restaurants in cities and towns throughout the country serve up dishes such as moo goo gai pan, cashew chicken, and sweet-and-sour pork, those with large Chinese American populations are often home to dim sum restaurants as well. Dim sum is an assortment of steamed and pan-fried dumplings, savory and sweet buns, fritters, fried specialties like spring rolls and shrimp balls, sweet puddings, cakes, tarts, and delicate glutinous rice desserts. Servers circulate through the dining room with carts carrying their offerings. Diners stop them as they pass and request what they want—then pay at the table for everything they've consumed.

MAKES ABOUT 40 DUMPLINGS

3   dried shiitake mushrooms

8   ounces ground pork

4   ounces large shrimp, peeled, deveined, and minced

3   tablespoons minced water chestnuts

1   scallion, trimmed and minced

1   teaspoon minced fresh ginger

1   clove garlic, minced

1   tablespoon oyster sauce

1   teaspoon Shaoxing wine, Chinese rice wine, or dry sherry

1   teaspoon toasted sesame oil

¼   teaspoon salt

⅛   teaspoon ground white pepper

½   teaspoon granulated sugar

1   large egg white, beaten

40 siu mai wrappers*

Finely minced carrot

Soy sauce, for serving

1. Rinse the dried mushrooms under cool running water. Place in a small bowl and add warm water to cover. Allow to soak for 20 to 30 minutes or until softened; drain. Remove the stems and discard. Mince the caps.

2. In a large bowl, combine the mushrooms, pork, shrimp, water chestnuts, scallion, ginger, garlic, oyster sauce, wine, sesame oil, salt, pepper, sugar, and egg white. Mix thoroughly to combine. Cover and chill in the refrigerator for 4 hours.

3. To assemble the dumplings, hold a wrapper flat on one hand. Place about 2 teaspoons of the filling in the center of the wrapper. Bring the wrapper up around the filling, pressing lightly to adhere it to the filling while gently rotating to create "pleats" around the edge. Use the back of a spoon to pack the filling in tightly. Lightly squeeze the dumpling around the "waist" to keep the filling intact during steaming. Gently tap the bottom of the dumpling on the counter to flatten it so it will stand upright in the steamer. Top with a little bit of the minced carrot. Set aside and repeat with remaining wrappers and filling, being sure to keep the wrappers covered with a damp towel to keep them from drying out as you work.

4. Line a steamer basket** with parchment paper that has several small holes poked in it (to allow the steam to come through) or cabbage leaves to keep dumplings from sticking. Fill the bottom of the pot with water, being careful that it comes close to but doesn't touch the bottom of the basket. Place just enough dumplings in the basket so that there is at least ½ inch between them. (Dumplings will stick to each other if they touch.) Bring the water to a boil, then add the basket to the pot. Cover and steam until the filling is cooked through, 5 to 8 minutes. Repeat with the remaining dumplings, adding more water as necessary.

5. Serve with soy sauce.

*NOTE: Siu mai wrappers are available at most Asian food markets. The standard size is 3 inches, which is what you will need for this recipe.

**NOTE: If you would like to use a traditional bamboo steamer—widely available at Asian markets—place it in a wok or other pot that will allow it to sit level and secure and above the water line.

JEWISH FOOD IN AMERICA

America is home to the largest population of Jews in the world—roughly 7.5 million people—followed by Israel with 6.7 million. The long history of Jewish migrations around the world, whether to flee discrimination or seek new opportunities, is reflected in Jewish food in the United States and is not easily defined.

▲ Chewy, tuggy, boiled-then-baked bagels were brought to America by Polish immigrants. Lox originated in Scandinavia. The two came together—with cream cheese—in New York in the early 20th century.

▼ A pushcart market on Manhattan's Lower East Side, circa 1915. Jewish immigrants operated these mobile businesses as their first enterprises.

Taken as a whole, Jewish food is a diasporic cuisine, meaning it embodies influences from all over the world in places that Jews have lived during the diaspora, or the dispersion of the Jewish people outside of Palestine or modern Israel. Even within the Jewish community, defining it can be difficult and contentious.

Jewish food in this country is perhaps more varied than most Americans realize, reaching beyond borscht, blintzes, and brisket—even if those are the first foods that come to mind. Although Naama Shefi, founder of the Jewish Food Society, defines it more broadly, conceding in a 2019 interview with the Israeli newspaper *Haaretz* that "The term 'Jewish food' is still identified in the American consciousness with Ashkenazi food."

There are three primary groups within world Jewry—Ashkenazi, Sephardi, and Mizrahi. Which group people fall into is essentially based on their geographic and historical origins. *Ashkenazi* is the Hebrew word referring to Jews whose roots lie in Central and Eastern Europe, including Germany, Poland, Lithuania, and Hungary, as well as Russia. Globally, about 80 percent of the Jewish population is Ashkenazi. *Sephardic* refers to Jews with origins in Spain and Portugal. *Mizrahim* are descendants of Jews from the Middle East and North Africa.

The largest and most impactful wave of Jewish immigration to the United States—at least as far is food is concerned—was the influx from Eastern Europe. Between 1880 and 1924, more than 2 million Jews from Russia, Austria-Hungary, and Romania arrived, often settling in big cities—New York, Boston, Baltimore, Philadelphia, and Chicago.

Eastern European Cuisine Dominates

Because of their sheer numbers, Jewish food in America has historically been defined by Ashkenazi traditions—the aforementioned borscht, blintzes, and brisket, as well as smoked fish, lox, gefilte fish, bagels, pickles, and chicken soup with kreplach (dumplings). The classic Jewish deli (from the German *delikatessen*, a shop that sells prepared foods)—with its pastrami on rye, corned beef, chopped liver, pickles, and breads—also rooted in Ashkenazi cuisine, became a center of Jewish life in these cities.

Jewish food in this country is tremendously more varied and reflective of the whole diaspora. The concept of "Mizrahi food," which originated in Israel, is defined by the Middle Eastern and Mediterranean origins of its people—fresh meats, poultry, and fish, lots of fresh vegetables and olive oil, rice instead of potatoes, and dishes featuring all manner of legumes and bulgur. High-profile American-Israeli chefs such as Michael Solomonov of Zahav have raised the profile of both Mizrahi and Sephardic foods.

Because of the fraught history of the Jewish and Arab peoples in the Middle East, ascribing regional dishes such as hummus, falafel, bourekas, and shakshuka to one culture or another is a highly sensitive subject, and the discussion about how to approach this is ongoing in the Jewish community.

▲ What is now Katz's Deli in Manhattan was established in 1888. It's known for its pastrami on rye, considered among the best in the city.

Jeffrey Yoskowitz, co-author with Liz Alpern of *The Gefilte Manifesto,* admits to feeling "complicated" about declaring foods shared by many faiths and cultures as explicitly Jewish.

Because of the increasingly central role Israel plays in American Jewish life, he says, over time the Jewish community has come to identify foods such as hummus and falafel as their own. "But then again, in New York," he told *Haaretz,* "sour garlic-dill pickles are considered a Jewish food. Try telling that to a Polish person."

In a June 2020 webinar hosted by American Jewish University to explore what defines modern American Jewish food culture, Yoskowitz and Alpern concluded that "There may, in fact, be no such thing as 'Jewish cuisine,' but rather many amazing and diverse cuisines that all share the same umbrella."

A NEW LOOK AT OLD LAWS

"Kashrut" refers to a set of Jewish dietary laws that directs how food should be prepared and consumed. Foods that may be eaten are deemed kosher, from the Hebrew term *kashér,* or "fit." As Joan Nathan writes in *King Solomon's Table,* "Jews in different times and places have had differences in understandings of the dietary laws, and many Jews have adhered to them in varying degrees of strictness, in and outside of their homes."

A movement known as eco-kashrut—which layers a consciousness about keeping kosher with that of humanely raised and slaughtered meat, supporting local agricultural programs, and reducing carbon footprints—is seen not just as a reflection of that movement within the larger population but as an outgrowth of Jewish values.

"What can we learn by renewing the ancient text?" writes Rabbi Arthur O. Waskow on *My Jewish Learning.* "For shepherds and farmers, food was what they ate from the earth. For us, it is also coal, oil, electric power, paper, plastics that we take from the earth. For shepherds and farmers, kashrut was the way of guiding their eating toward holiness. For us, eco-kashrut should do the same."

MATZOH BALL SOUP

Matzah, matzo, matzoh balls—the spellings vary for these Jewish soup dumplings as much as the recipe itself. The original matzoh balls (known as *knaidlach*, *knodel*, or *knaidel*) were mostly a European Ashkenazi dish. Leftover matzoh, the brittle unleavened bread eaten during Passover, was crushed into meal and mixed with egg, chicken fat, and seasoning to make round dumplings served in chicken broth. In 1888, Russian American baker and rabbi Dov Behr Manischewitz opened a small matzoh bakery in Cincinnati, the most important economic, culinary, and cultural center for German Jews at the time. The company expanded and eventually opened plants in New Jersey, producing matzoh ball mix and premade matzoh ball soup, among other kosher foods.

SERVES 10

- 1 medium chicken (preferably organic and/or free-range), cut up
- 1 large onion, chopped
- 6 carrots, sliced
- 6 stalks celery, sliced
- 4 cloves garlic, minced
- 1 tablespoon kosher salt
- 1 tablespoon apple cider vinegar
- ¼ cup peeled and finely chopped fresh ginger
- 1 tablespoon fresh lemon juice (optional)
- 1 tablespoon chopped fresh parsley
- 1 recipe Matzoh Balls (recipe follows)

1. Cut the chicken into pieces. Cut the chicken breast meat from the bone in large pieces and refrigerate, covered, until needed. In a large pot, bring 2½ quarts (10 cups) water and the remaining chicken pieces to boiling. With a spoon, skim off any foam from the surface. Add the onion. Reduce heat and simmer for 1 hour. Stir in carrots, celery, garlic, salt, and if using, vinegar. Bring to boiling; reduce heat and simmer, uncovered, 1 hour more. Add the reserved chicken breast, ginger, and if using, lemon juice. Simmer, uncovered, 30 minutes more.

2. With tongs, remove all chicken from broth and let stand until cool enough to handle. Using two forks, pull the chicken from the bones in bite-size pieces and shred the boneless chicken breast.* Remove layer of fat atop soup with a spoon and, if desired, reserve for matzoh balls. Return the chicken to broth. Discard the chicken bones and skin. Stir the parsley into broth. Season to taste. Add Matzoh Balls and heat through.

*****NOTE:** To make ahead, cool the broth to room temperature, cover, and chill for up to two days. Remove solidified fat and, if desired, save fat for matzoh balls. Continue as directed.

MATZOH BALLS: In a medium bowl, beat 4 eggs with a fork. Stir in 1 cup matzoh meal, ¼ cup rendered chicken fat (schmaltz)** or vegetable oil, ¼ cup chicken broth or water, 1 tablespoon chopped fresh parsley, and 1 teaspoon salt. Mix with a fork until combined. Cover and refrigerate 30 minutes or up to 24 hours. Fill a Dutch oven two-thirds full of water and 1 tablespoon kosher salt; bring to boiling. Meanwhile, shape the matzoh mixture into 1-inch balls using wet hands (mixture will be sticky). Drop the matzoh balls into boiling water; reduce heat and simmer for 30 to 40 minutes or until just tender but not falling apart. Remove with a slotted spoon.

******NOTE:** You can purchase a jar of chicken schmaltz or use the fat removed from the surface of homemade chicken soup. Vegetable oil works as a substitution but will not have as much flavor.

MASS IMMIGRATION FROM EUROPE

Few historical events have had more impact on the fabric of American food than immigration. From the second half of the 19th century into the early 20th century, waves of immigrants from Europe made their mark.

Between 1850 and 1913, close to 30 million people immigrated to the United States from Europe—one of the largest episodes of immigration in history. By 1900, nearly 14 percent of the population was born outside of the United States. Their reasons for coming were diverse—crop failure and famine, a lack of jobs, land shortages due to traditional systems of inheritance, rising taxes, and religious and ethnic persecution—but there was a common thread: a general lack of freedom and opportunity they thought could be remedied by crossing the Atlantic Ocean.

The first to come in great numbers were the Irish. As early as the 1840s, fully half of the immigrants to the United States had come from Ireland, in large part due to the Great Famine, a period of mass starvation and disease from 1845 to 1849. At a time when the world economy was largely booming, a blight struck potatoes across the land and made a staple of the Irish diet scarce. More than a million Irish died.

For much of the late 19th century, most European immigrants arrived through East Coast facilities—most notably the Castle Garden depot at the tip of Manhattan, which became known as the "Golden Door." Then, on January 1, 1892, the federal government opened Ellis Island. The first immigrant to be processed at Ellis Island was Annie Moore, a teenage girl who sailed from County Cork with her two younger brothers to reunite with their parents, who had arrived two years earlier.

Between 1920 and 1930, nearly 5 million Irish arrived to the United States, most of whom settled in Boston, New York, and other East Coast cities—though a substantial portion moved west to Chicago.

An Open-Door Policy, for a Time

The failure in the mid-19th century of revolutions to establish democracy in present-day Germany caused thousands to flee to America in the following decades. One of these was Adolphus Busch (1839–1913), who left in 1857 and landed in St. Louis, where he married the daughter of a successful brewer. By 1890, nearly 3 million German-born immigrants lived in the United States, settling primarily in Milwaukee, Cincinnati, and St. Louis. Street vendors began offering pretzels and sausage, including the frankfurter. To this day, Milwaukee has a vibrant German food culture, with beer halls, schnitzel, bratwurst and knockwurst, pork shanks, and pretzels.

The next group that began immigrating en masse were the Italians. Between 1880 and 1924, more than 4 million Italians arrived, the vast majority from the south of the country. Most settled in large cities and because of poverty and the discrimination they faced, they tended to congregate in large numbers in poor neighborhoods.

Italians—and the cuisine they adapted to their new surroundings—had a huge impact on

▼ A 1904 painting-style photograph depicts Adolphus Busch, who immigrated from present-day Germany in 1857 to St. Louis, where he married the daughter of a successful brewer and eventually formed Anheuser-Busch.

American food as a whole. Most Italian immigrants came from the comparatively poorer south and Sicily, but the American abundance of foodstuffs and cheap prices allowed them to eat far more luxuriantly than *la cucina povera* (the "cooking of the poor" or "peasant cooking")—a diet largely made up of grains, legumes, and vegetables—that they were used to.

Much of what they fashioned here wouldn't have been recognizable as Italian food to their relatives back home. Consider spaghetti and meatballs. The meatballs may have been an iteration of *polpette*, a bready version served without sauce in Italy, but here, they could be made mostly of meat. Pasta was considered an appetizer in Italy; in America, it became a main dish. The sauce ladled on top was based on widely-available canned tomatoes. Non-

continued on page 102

▲ The main building of the Ellis Island immigration reception station in New York Harbor in 1919.

◄ Newly arrived European immigrants often operated food carts such as this New York City hot dog cart, pictured in 1936.

THE MAN ON THE CAN

There is a story behind the image of the smiling, mustachioed fellow in a stately chef's hat on this label that explains a bit about how America fell in love with pasta with tomato sauce. The character—Chef Boyardee—was a real chef named Ettore "Hector" Boiardi.

At the age of 16, he left his home in northern Italy and sailed to America, arriving at Ellis Island in 1914. He had been working as an apprentice chef since the age of 11, and he immediately went to work at New York City's Plaza Hotel, where his older brother was a maître d'. By 1917, he had moved to Cleveland to run the kitchen at the Hotel Winton, and by 1924, he had his own restaurant—*Il Giardino d'Italia* ("Garden of Italy"). His customers could not get enough of his signature spaghetti with tomato sauce and tangy Parmesan cheese, and began clamoring for a take-home version they could make themselves.

Boiardi began putting together meal kits of dried pasta, cheese, and marinara sauce stored in clean milk bottles. Eventually, the take-out business overtook the dine-in business. He and two of his brothers opened a small processing plant and launched the phonetically named Chef Boyardee Food Company in 1928. The first product was a packaged pasta dinner that included a box of spaghetti, a jar of pasta sauce, and a can of Parmesan cheese.

continued from page 101

Italian immigrants embraced this hybrid cuisine as enthusiastically as the Italians who had created it, cheerfully sitting down to spaghetti and meatballs, lasagna, linguine with pesto, and, of course, an Americanized interpretation of pizza.

Central and Eastern European Jews also immigrated in great numbers—more than 2 million between 1880 and 1920—particularly after the widespread pogroms in the Russian Empire. Orthodox Jews who observed kosher dietary rules tended to settle where kosher foods were available, which was in larger cities on the East Coast—or they opened kosher groceries or delis on their own. The first Jewish deli is believed to have opened in about 1880 in New York, but it wasn't until the 1920s that these now-classic institutions became a center of Jewish life in larger cities. American delis sold bread and fresh-sliced cheeses and meats, particularly favorites such as pastrami, corned beef, and kosher salami.

While the first wave of European immigrants had been from Northern Europe, most of the later arrivals came from Italy, Poland, and elsewhere in Southern and Eastern Europe. Americans' racist responses to these immigrants at the turn of the 20th century, coupled with the political isolationism that followed World War I produced decades of severe restrictions on immigration throughout the mid-20th century. It would not be until 1965 that immigration reform would undergo another dramatic shift.

This period of mass immigration had a profound effect on the fabric of American food. Just as new dishes brought to the West Coast by Chinese immigrants who arrived in the mid-19th century to work on the railroads eventually spread across the country, so too did new foods brought by these immigrants from Europe. Over the century that followed this period—particularly in the second half of it—Americans embraced curries from India, pad thai from Thailand, phở from Vietnam, doro wat from Ethiopia, and so much more.

◄ Immigrants arrive at Ellis Island in 1905.

MACARONI AND CHEESE

The earliest known recipe for what could be called macaroni and cheese, which calls for sheet pasta to be cut into squares then layered in a casserole with cheese and baked, appears in *Liber de Coquina*, a 14th-century Italian cookbook. And although the 4 million Italian immigrants who arrived between 1880 and 1924 certainly brought their beloved *maccheroni* with them, it was actually members of the enslaved Hemings family who introduced this dish to America. When Thomas Jefferson served as Minister of France from 1784 to 1789, he took James, his chef, with him, who trained at an elite French cooking school. Somewhere in Europe—either France or Italy—both encountered a luxurious dish of noodles baked in a creamy, cheesy sauce. When they returned to Philadelphia, James bartered his freedom from Jefferson with the stipulation he would train someone in the kitchen. That someone happened to be James' younger brother, Peter, who traveled to Washington with Jefferson when he became president in 1801. In 1802, Peter famously prepared a dish called "macaroni pie" for a state dinner. By 1824, recipes for the dish began appearing in early American cookbooks, including a layered and baked version in Mary Randolph's *The Virginia Housewife* in 1824. The Antebellum South embraced an ultra-creamy, baked version as a cultural staple that's still expected on the holiday table. This recipe calls for sharp cheddar, but feel free replace half the cheddar with American cheese for a milder, creamier result.

SERVES 4 TO 6

- 9 ounces elbow macaroni (2½ cups)
- 3 tablespoons butter, plus additional for buttering baking dish
- 2 tablespoons finely chopped onion or green onion (optional)
- 3 tablespoons all-purpose flour
- 2½ cups milk (preferably whole milk)
- 3 cups shredded sharp cheddar*
- ⅛ teaspoon ground black pepper and/or cayenne pepper
- ⅛ teaspoon smoked or sweet paprika (optional)
- Bread Crumb Topper (optional; recipe follows)

1. Preheat the oven to 375°F. Cook the macaroni according to package directions. Drain and set aside. Butter a 2-quart baking dish.

2. For the cheese sauce, in a large saucepan, melt the 3 tablespoons butter. If using, add the onion and cook about 2 minutes, until tender but not brown. Stir in the flour; cook and stir 1 minute. Whisk in the milk all at once. Cook and stir over medium heat until slightly thickened and bubbly. Add 2½ cups of the cheese, the pepper, and if using, paprika. Stir until the cheese is melted. Gently stir the cooked macaroni into the cheese sauce. Transfer to the buttered baking dish. Sprinkle with Bread Crumb Topper, if using.

3. Bake, uncovered, 25 to 30 minutes or until bubbly and heated through. Makes 4 to 6 main-dish servings.

*NOTE: For a milder, creamier macaroni and cheese, substitute 1½ cups of the sharp cheddar cheese with shredded American cheese or mild cheddar.

BREAD CRUMB TOPPER: In a small skillet, melt 1 tablespoon butter. Stir in ¾ cup fresh bread crumbs. Cook and stir 1 minute. Sprinkle on top of the macaroni and cheese just before baking.

MEXICAN MIGRATION

Mexicans and Americans have been mingling along the southern border since long before it existed as it does today. The blending of cultures and ingredients created one of the most popular cuisines in the world.

The first Spanish missions in what is modern-day Texas sprang up in the 1600s, possibly as early as 1632. In the centuries that followed, Mexicans migrated north from rural areas in search of stability and jobs, but the decade-long Mexican Revolution that began in 1910 and spasms of political instability in the country that followed led to waves of migration that had a profound impact on the political, cultural, and culinary landscape of the American Southwest and beyond.

These new arrivals brought recipes and chile peppers with them. El Charro Café—founded in 1922 in downtown Tucson, Arizona, lays claim to being the oldest Mexican restaurant in continuous operation by the same family in the country.

Its menu features a take on *carne seca*—dried salted meat whose origins lie in ancient Central and South America—as well as classics such as guacamole, fajitas, tacos, burros, nachos, chile rellenos, and enchiladas that most Americans define as Mexican food. In reality, the cuisines of the interior of Mexico are highly regionalized, and what has come to be known as Mexican food in this country is in fact a regional development of its own—an American borderland cuisine that has its roots in the culinary culture of the Tejano people, Hispanic people who live in Texas and are descended from Spanish-speaking settlers from the northern Mexican states, which include Baja California, Sonora, Chihuahua, Coahuila, Nuevo León, and Tamaulipas.

The term "Tex-Mex" was first used to describe it in the mid-1940s. The popular perception of Tex-Mex is that it's rice, refried beans redolent of lard, and enchiladas topped with sauce and yellow American cheese. Diana Kennedy, one of the most influential Mexican food authorities of the latter 20th century, drew the line, saying Tex-Mex was not authentic Mexican food. Proprietors of Mexican restaurants in the U.S. took umbrage at Kennedy's exclusionary edict. Kennedy had a point, however. The Mexican food she studied and celebrated in the interior of Mexico bore little resemblance to the offerings at thousands of Mexican restaurants in the United States.

Birth of a New Cuisine

Moreover, many Tex-Mex foods were invented in the U.S. or very close to the border. These include chili con carne, the Texas state dish; fajitas, which debuted at Ninfa's in Houston in 1973; and nachos, whose origin—like many American foods—is the result of improvisation.

What Americans recognize as burritos made with tortillas almost the size of a dinner plate first appeared in California in the 1960s. Chimichangas—fried burritos—first appeared in Tucson in the years following World War I. This may also have happened at El Charro, although other places take credit for it too.

The cuisine that developed out of this cross-pollination along the border is its own kind of authentic, then, precisely because it can't be

▲ A Mexican woman and her children stand with bundles of their belongings on the edge of the Rio Grande River, circa 1910.

▼ This wood-and-steel tortilla press, one of several in the Smithsonian collections, was made in Mexico and used in Napa, California.

pinned to one single region in Mexico—or to any of the American states that border it.

Journalist, columnist, and author Gustavo Arellano addressed this in his book, *Taco USA: How Mexican Food Conquered America.* "We must consider the infinite varieties of Mexican food in the United States as part of the Mexican family—not a fraud, not a lesser sibling, but an equal," he writes in the introduction. "As I've driven and flown across the country and come across a mild salsa, a mutated *muchacho* . . . and other items I immediately wanted to decry, I remembered the concept of what the legendary Chicano scholar Américo Paredes deemed Greater Mexico: that the influence of Mexico doesn't cease at the Rio Grande. Wherever there is something even minutely Mexican, whether it's people, food, language, or rituals, even centuries removed from the original mestizo source, it remains Mexican."

▼ El Charro, the oldest continuously operating Mexican restaurant run by the same family, opened in 1922 in Tucson, Arizona. "Charro" refers to the horsemen of the province of Salamanca.

THE ETYMOLOGY OF NACHOS

The origin story of nachos became more widely known in 1988, thanks to Adriana P. Orr, a researcher at the *Oxford English Dictionary* tasked with tracing the etymology of the word "nacho." Armed with new knowledge that "Nacho" was a diminutive for the name Ignacio, she tracked down a quote from the 1954 *St. Anne's Cookbook* from the Church of the Redeemer in Eagle Pass, Texas—which included a recipe for *Nachos Especiales*—and the tale of how they came to be.

In 1943, a group of women whose husbands were stationed at the army base at Eagle Pass crossed the border to Piedras Negras, Mexico, to eat at a restaurant called the Victory Club. They reportedly asked the chef, Ignacio "Nacho" Anaya, to whip up something new for them. He tossed together elements he found in the kitchen and called them *Nachos Especiales*. The dish caught on—on both sides of the border.

CHICKEN TAMALES VERDES

Dating to pre-Hispanic times in Mexico, Indigenous people crafted edible, portable bundles for hunting or other excursions by wrapping ground corn masa filling with corn husks for steaming. When Spaniards brought pigs to Mexico, lard was added to the masa filling to lighten it and add flavor—one of many future adaptations to this Mexican dish. While the filling and even the wrappers vary regionally, it is almost universally women who are responsible for making tamales. Because they are so labor-intensive, tamales are considered a special food reserved for weddings, religious holidays, and social gatherings. The fillings range from savory to sweet and include other ingredients besides masa, such as meat, chiles, cheese, or even fruit. Tamales crossed the border with Mexican immigrants and still have a spot at family gatherings and community celebrations and on restaurant menus. Eat them warm and usually without sauce, unwrapped and enjoyed like presents.

MAKES 16

- 16 dried cornhusks (each about 8×6 inches)
- 1½ cups shredded cooked chicken
- ½ cup salsa verde
- 1 tablespoon chopped fresh cilantro
- ½ cup lard, slightly chilled
- 1 teaspoon baking powder
- ½ teaspoon salt
- 2 cups masa harina (about 1 pound)
- ¾ cup chicken broth, room temperature
- ⅓ cup bottled roasted red pepper, cut into thin strips
- ½ cup crumbled queso fresco or feta cheese

1. Soak the cornhusks in enough hot water to cover for 30 minutes or until soft; drain and pat dry.

2. For filling, in a bowl, combine the shredded chicken, salsa verde, and cilantro; set aside.

3. For dough, in a large bowl, beat the lard, baking powder, and salt with an electric mixer on medium for 1 minute or until smooth and fluffy. Alternately add the masa and broth, beating until mixture is the consistency of paste.

4. To assemble, starting with the tapered end of a cornhusk toward you, spread 2 rounded tablespoons dough in a 3×4-inch rectangle, leaving a border on all sides (about 1½ inches on tapered side near you). Spoon a heaping tablespoon of filling down the center of the dough. Top with a couple strips of red pepper and some of the cheese. Bring the long sides of the cornhusk up and over the dough, overlapping to enclose the filling. Fold the tapered end up to close and loosely tie with a strip of cornhusk or 100 percent cotton kitchen string. Repeat with the remaining husks, dough, filling, peppers, and cheese.

5. To steam, stand the tamales upright (open ends up) in a steamer basket, filling the space but not packing too tightly. Fill any empty spaces with balls of foil to keep the tamales upright. Pour at least 1½ inches water into bottom of a steamer or Dutch oven. Place the basket in the steamer over the water. Bring to boiling; cover. Reduce heat to medium-low. Steam about 1 hour or until the dough pulls away from the cornhusks and has a spongy texture. Check the water level occasionally and add hot water to the steamer if needed.

A NATION GOES DRY—OR NOT

The temperance movement that began even before the colonies gained their independence culminated in Prohibition, which lasted, such as it was, from 1920 to 1933. It did not go well.

▲ A "Celebrate the Century: 1920s" souvenir postage stamp issued by the USPS in 1998 depicts men emptying a barrel of wine into a sewer as an act of enforcing Prohibition.

▼ Izzy Einstein, left, shares a toast with his partner, Moe Smith, in a New York bar in 1935, after the repeal of Prohibition. In the 1920s, the two were the most effective team of Prohibition agents, using disguises to arrest bootleggers, close speakeasies, and confiscate liquor.

On January 16, 1919, Nebraska became the 36th state to ratify the 18th Amendment. A headline in the *Washington Post* the next day read, "Given One Year of Grace." For those who could afford it, there was a run on any existing alcohol to stockpile for the new dry reality. Beginning January 17, 1920, it would be illegal to make, transport, or buy alcohol. Production of beverages containing more than one-half of 1 percent alcohol was outlawed, meaning almost all distilleries, wineries, and breweries went out of business.

Ale and cider had been staples since the time of the pilgrims—and were often safer than water to drink. But the consumption of strong drink such as whiskey and rum became a source of worry even before the American Revolution, as women saw their husbands drink up the family wages. By the early 19th century, the temperance movement dovetailed with religious revivalism.

By the early 20th century, temperance societies—particularly the Woman's Christian Temperance Union—were a political force, with local chapters in many if not most communities. The Anti-Saloon League, formed in 1893, worked with the WCTU to ensure that the 1916 election resulted in achieving the two-thirds majorities in Congress necessary to initiate what became the 18th Amendment.

There were very legitimate concerns surrounding the nation's alcohol consumption during this era. Anyone over the age of 15 could drink, and in the years between 1900 and 1915, the average adult was consuming about 2.5 gallons of pure alcohol per year—about 13 standard drinks per week.

The impact on the nation's health, however, was not the the only factor in the temperance movement. The country was in the middle of a huge wave of immigration from Europe, and not everyone was keen on the influx. "The historical narratives of Prohibition and the anti-immigration movements in America are intimately intertwined," writes Molly Banta in a July 2015 issue of *The Wilson Quarterly*. "Following relatively lax immigration laws in the United States at the beginning of the 20th century, the Prohibition movement considered immigrants—many of whom came from cultures with more permissive attitudes toward alcohol, and who, in the United States, formed the backbone brewing industry—as the primary obstacle to a dry and morally sound nation."

The Bootlegging Begins

Prohibition had limited intended effect, and enforcement was problematic from the beginning. Drunkenness declined but alcohol consumption dropped only by about one-third as liquor was smuggled from Canada, the Caribbean, and elsewhere. Domestically, bootleggers and moonshiners made their own in secret and tried to keep a step ahead of federal authorities. Speakeasies offering bathtub gin and other potables were an open secret in cities. By 1925, in New York City alone there were between 30,000 and 100,000 speakeasies.

There were exceptions to the rule. Wine could be used for sacramental purposes, and federal regulations allowed Americans to make up to 200 gallons of "non-intoxicating" wine per household for personal use. With a wink and a nod, California vineyards produced "raisin cakes," dried grape bricks packaged with a label warning, "Caution: will ferment and turn into wine."

▲ Authorities hang up a poster advising the public in 1922 that a building has been shuttered for a year for breaching the National Prohibition Act.

By the early 1930s, most Americans agreed that Prohibition was creating more problems than it was solving, and with the Great Depression throwing millions out of work, government saw an opportunity to create jobs and raise tax revenues by again legalizing liquor.

In 1932, Franklin Roosevelt ran for president on a platform calling for Prohibition's repeal. In February 1933, Congress introduced the 21st Amendment—the only case of one amendment repealing another. It gained ratification quickly.

CARRY AND HER HATCHET

The most celebrated, feared, and reviled temperance activist was Carrie Nation (sometimes spelled Carry) , a reformer who believed she was on a mission from God—"a bulldog running along the feet of Jesus," as she put it—to eradicate demon liquor.

She became known for what she called her "hatchetations," literally taking a hatchet to saloons. "I ran behind the bar, smashed the mirror and all the bottles under it; picked up the cash register, threw it down; then broke the faucets of the refrigerator, opened the door and cut the rubber tubes that conducted the beer," she wrote of her raid on a Kiowa, Kansas, bar, in her 1904 book, *The Use and Need of the Life of Carry A. Nation*. Not surprisingly, bars began to hang signs on their doors that read, "All nations welcome—except Carrie."

FRENCH 75

This cocktail—which hearkens back farther than Prohibition but became widely known after its publication in Harry MacElhone's *ABC of Mixing Cocktails* in 1919—is said to have gotten its name because it had as much kick as a 75mm French field gun from World War I. It features gin—one of the most popular types of illicit alcohol during the era—with lemon and simple syrup, topped off with a splash of Champagne.

SERVES 1

- 1 lemon
- 2 tablespoons (1 ounce) gin
- 1 tablespoon (½ ounce) Simple Syrup (recipe follows)
- 1 cup ice cubes
- ¼ cup (2 ounces) dry sparkling wine, such as Champagne, chilled

1. Using a zester or paring knife, slice the peel from the lemon in a long, thin spiral. Set aside.

2. Cut the lemon in half and juice on a citrus juicer.

3. In a cocktail shaker, combine the gin, 1 tablespoon (½ ounce) of the lemon juice, Simple Syrup, and ice cubes. Shake vigorously for 20 seconds. Strain into a chilled Champagne flute or coupe, and top with the sparkling wine.

4. Curl the lemon peel around your finger to create a twist. Garnish the drink with the twist and serve immediately.

SIMPLE SYRUP: In a medium saucepan, combine 1 cup granulated sugar and 1 cup water. Bring to boiling, stirring until sugar has dissolved. Cool completely. Store in a tightly sealed container for up to 1 month.

THE GREAT DEPRESSION

The 1929 stock market crash and subsequent Great Depression triggered a fundamental shift in what Americans eat, how they think about nutrition, and the government's role in helping to feed the nation.

▲ A postage stamp issued in 1998 features the iconic image of "Migrant Mother," taken in 1936 by photographer Dorothea Lange.

▼ Men stand in a New York bread line. The sign reads "Paid Up to this Point, Every Dollar pays for 20 More Meals." Men ahead of the sign are assured of a meal that costs 5 cents.

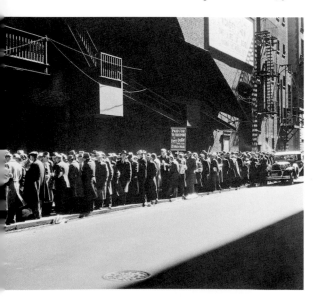

President Herbert Hoover had grown up in privation as an orphan in Iowa and had been instrumental in alleviating hunger in Europe after the First World War. But he was recalcitrant when it came to providing stateside relief, claiming Americans' reliance on self-sufficiency would see them through. He remained steadfast even as, by 1931, unemployment approached 25 percent. In a radio address that year, Hoover said, "The spread of government destroys initiative and thus destroys character." Drought, dust bowls, and floods devastated rural America. Children in Oklahoma claimed as adults they were five or six years old before they saw their first rain.

The crisis was no less acute in cities. In New York, bread lines distributed 85,000 or more meals every day. Franklin Roosevelt unseated Hoover as president in a 1932 landslide, but he was similarly ambivalent about the federal government providing wholesale hunger relief, arguing the primary responsibility was on local and state entities.

The government eventually stepped in, creating the Federal Emergency Relief Administration in 1933, a precursor of the Works Progress Administration. A branch of the Department of Agriculture was tasked with reaching out to homemakers with tips on how to stretch their families' food budgets. Housewives across the country listened to "Aunt Sammy" instruct them on a radio program called *Housekeeper's Chat* about the nutritional benefits of beans and other foodstuffs being distributed.

Bland Is Better

The emphasis during this era was not on flavor but rather what had been determined at the time was the science of good nutrition. In fact, good taste was seen as a dubious quality. Spices and garlic were considered stimulants, which would only increase hunger. Government-supplied food was deliberately bland because it was believed blandness would spur the recipients to find a job and earn money to buy seasonings. "When they were handing out relief boxes, they deliberately didn't add such things as mustard and vinegar with the relief boxes because they didn't want people to become too happy with receiving food relief," Andy Coe, co-author of *A Square Meal: A Culinary History of the Great Depression*, told NPR in 2016. And while obesity and rampant food waste are among the modern era's defining issues, real hunger and vitamin deficiency were hallmarks of the Depression. Food fortification, which began around 1920, expanded during the Depression to supplement ingredients that had been reduced or eliminated during processing. Iodine was added to salt, folic acid to flour and cereal.

A research team of home economists at Cornell University developed a fortified food product called Milkorno (as well as two others called Milkwheato and Milkoato). All were blends of grain flour and skim milk. Milkorno, a blend of cornmeal, powdered skim milk, and salt, was touted as being able to feed a family of 5 for less than $5 a week. A 5-pound bag sold for 20 cents.

A family consisting of a mother, a father who worked construction, two boys aged 10 and 16, and a 13-year-old girl was given a $5 bill and had 16 cents left over after a week of supplementing their diets with Milkorno. A sample menu included Milkorno with brown sugar and milk along with bread and butter for breakfast; baked beans with chopped suet, scalloped potatoes, buttered carrots, whole wheat bread and butter, and fried Milkorno mush with syrup and milk for dinner; and scrambled eggs, coleslaw, biscuits and butter, and baked Milkorno custard for supper.

"The purpose of these foods," Professor Flora Rose, who directed the research, said at the time, "is to bring about desirable nutritional changes through unconscious practice in using food with widespread nutritional values."

▼ A man sleeps on a dock in New York City, circa 1930. The three-piece suit he wears under his worn overcoat indicates his previous white-collar employment.

HOOVER STEW

During the Depression, President Herbert Hoover had the ignominious distinction of having a variety of things named for him. A "Hoover blanket" was a newspaper used to stay warm. "Hoover flags" were empty pants pockets turned inside out. "Hoover leather" was cardboard used to fix shoes. Then there were Hoovervilles and Hoover stew. Hoovervilles were shanty towns that sprang up after hundreds of thousands of people were evicted from their homes. These Hoovervilles were often located near soup kitchens, where "Hoover stew" was a regular meal on the menu.

Hoover stew was a concoction of broth, cooked macaroni, sliced hot dogs, stewed tomatoes, and canned corn. It was all simmered together then served up in bowls. It wasn't exactly the "chicken in every pot" promised by Hoover's Republican supporters in the 1928 election, but it sustained thousands through a very difficult time.

THE USDA SCHOOL LUNCH PROGRAM

Every year, more than 30 million public school children consume almost 5 billion school lunches. That's a lot of lunch. The 1946 National School Lunch Act made it all possible—from every scoop of canned peas to each pint of milk.

▼ Teenage girls line up at the cafeteria counter of Woodrow Wilson High School in Washington, D.C., October 1943.

Whether your school lunch tray was loaded with Fish Shortcake (1940s), Barbecue Wieners with Mashed Potatoes and Buttered Green Beans (1970s), or a Scrambled Hamburg on Bread (1980s), you were a beneficiary of the federally funded school-lunch program that since the Truman era has sought to provide the nation's schoolchildren with a full belly to fuel them through the school day.

For most of the 19th century, schoolchildren were responsible for their own midday meals. Those who lived in cities went home for lunch. Those who lived in rural areas far from home brought their own lunches in a "pail," something cold or soup in a pint jar that could be heated in a big pot of hot water on the schoolroom stove.

An influx of immigrants from Europe in mid- to late century—most of whom were fleeing poverty in their home countries— could not immediately escape it here. By the 1870s, an estimated 12 percent of school-age children in New York City were homeless, and those who were housed were often crammed into filthy tenements. Then, a 1904 book titled *Poverty* by sociologist Robert Hunter describing the lives of working-class people in Chicago and New York galvanized reformers. An anonymous writer asserted in an issue of *The School Journal* at the time that healthy school lunches could improve "the physical vigor of the urban population."

Teachers noticed that undernourished children tended to be lethargic and unable to concentrate. As far back as the 1850s, a patchwork of local organizations was stepping in to provide or subsidize school lunches. At the turn of the 20th century, the Women's Educational and Industrial Union in Boston prepared hot lunches in a central kitchen and distributed them throughout the city to an average of 5,500 students a day. A sample menu from 1912 lists Beef and Barley Soup for 4 cents, a Lettuce or Cheese and Olive Sandwich for 3 cents, and Sponge Cake for 2 cents.

A report in *The Journal of Home Economics* in 1910 notes that "the teachers [in Boston] are unanimous in the belief that the luncheons are helping the children both physically and mentally."

An Evolving System

This cobbled-together and localized way of feeding schoolchildren largely remained until the Great Depression, when farmers faced financial ruin when prices collapsed, creating surpluses of commodities such as wheat flour and beef. People were out of work, and hunger and malnutrition were increasing sharply.

The solution: a federal school lunch program. With provisions in FDR's New Deal, the federal government bought surplus foodstuffs from farmers and hired thousands of women to cook and serve hot lunch to hungry students.

▲ A girl prays over her school lunch, circa 1937. At the time, meals were subsidized by the Federal Surplus Commodities Corporation.

By 1941, there were federally funded school meal programs in all 48 states. The system was signed into law by President Harry S. Truman with the National School Lunch Act in 1946. In 1966, the Child Nutrition Act established a free breakfast program as well.

School lunch has seen changes through the decades. In the 1980s, the Reagan Administration sought to cut millions of dollars from the program, resulting in the infamous declaration of ketchup as a vegetable. In the 1990s, the federal government allowed fast-food giants such as McDonald's, Taco Bell, and Little Caesar's to set up shop in the schools. A program that had begun in a nation suffering from childhood malnutrition now had a different problem—childhood obesity.

In 2010, Congress passed the Healthy, Hunger-Free Kids Act, which allowed the USDA to revise school meals to include more whole grains, fresh fruits, and vegetables.

School lunch will undoubtedly continue to evolve, but one thing is unlikely to change: the expressions of delight and inevitable groans as that day's offerings are read during morning announcements.

SEGREGATING SUSTENANCE

In 1951, three years before the desegregation of the nation's schools, the USDA released a report, *Participation of Negro Children in School Lunch Programs,* in which teachers and school administrators from Black schools in the South issued reports on the impact of the National School Lunch Program on their students and communities.

In many cases, the community and Parent-Teacher Associations had to help raise funds or gifts in kind to renovate and equip the schools.

Schools planted gardens, and children and their mothers canned produce in school kitchens.

The school lunchrooms became centerpieces of the community. "Proof of what the program means to the community is a recent incident that occurred," says the report from Antioch, Alabama. "Somehow, a rumor started that there would be no lunchroom next year. One father made a trip to the county seat to see about it. When the superintendent informed him that the rumor was ill founded, he was satisfied, but just before leaving, turned and said with emphasis, 'We couldn't do without our lunchroom.'"

THE GREAT MIGRATION

Over a period of six decades in the 20th century, more than 6 million Black Americans fled poverty and segregation in the rural South for city living in the North, Midwest, and West. The impact on the country at large was sweeping, culinarily and otherwise.

▲ The first barbecue stand in Kansas City was opened by Henry Perry in 1908.

▼ Passengers disembark the *City of New Orleans* train in Chicago in 1953.

White supremacy reigned in the post–Civil War Jim Crow South. The Ku Klux Klan, which saw itself as a necessary correction to Reconstruction excesses, routinely used harassment, intimidation, rape, and lynching to keep Southern Blacks "in their place." Blacks struggled to make a living by sharecropping, and a boll weevil epidemic at the end of the 19th century made life even more difficult.

As had happened before, war presented opportunity for those willing to pick up stakes. The Great War halted steady European immigration, and industrial laborers were in short supply in the North. Factories put out the word, advertising in Black newspapers, particularly the influential *Chicago Defender*. Some 1 million people relocated in the first three years of the Great Migration, which began in 1916 and ended around 1970.

"They left as though they were fleeing some curse," wrote journalist Emmett J. Scott of the early days of the migration. "They were willing to make almost any sacrifice to obtain a railroad ticket, and they left with the intention of staying."

Black populations exploded by as much as 500 percent in cities such as New York, Detroit, Chicago, and Philadelphia. The children of the Great Migration—either directly or by their descendants—include Richard Wright, John Coltrane, Zora Neale Hurston, Miles Davis, Jackie Robinson, Ralph Ellison, James Earl Jones, Tupac Shakur, Prince, Michael Jackson, Venus and Serena Williams, and countless others.

The work the migrants found might have been a step up from sharecropping, but it was still oftentimes arduous. They worked in foundries, slaughterhouses, and factories, often in dangerous conditions. The influx of migrant women created a robust competition for domestic worker positions.

Bringing Barbecue North

Of course, these newcomers brought their food traditions with them, as their enslaved ancestors had brought theirs from Africa. One need look no further than the establishment of Kansas City and Chicago as epicenters for barbecue—the creation of formerly enslaved cooks on Southern plantations—for the profound effect the Great Migration had on the American table.

The first barbecue restaurant was established in Chicago in the 1930s, a direct result of migration from the Mississippi Delta. The origin of Kansas City barbecue goes back further, to Henry Perry— known as the "father of Kansas City barbecue."

Perry, a native of Memphis, Tennessee, worked on steamboats on the Mississippi and Missouri rivers before moving up to Kansas City in 1907. In 1908, Perry opened a barbecue stand in the Garment District selling meats smoked over oak and hickory and wrapped in newsprint for 25 cents. He later moved to an old trolley barn a few blocks away and operated from there through the 1930s. It was the progenitor of the now-famous Arthur Bryant's.

The Black church was the center of life in the South and influenced the development of what's now called soul food. Special occasions such as Emancipation Day and Juneteenth were cause for lavish communal celebrations, with fried chicken or fish, slow-cooked greens, sweet potato pie, and watermelon. For most of the year, however, Blacks—particularly in rural areas—ate as their enslaved elders had: variations on cornbread, seasonal vegetables from their gardens, and little meat.

Food was cheaper and more plentiful in the North, but cramped tenements with meager kitchens made the kind of home cooking Black families ate in the South a challenge. Religious relief groups, Black churches, street vendors, and Black-owned or Black-friendly restaurants filled the void, and once-special-occasion foods became more everyday fare.

This trend was enhanced by a newfound prosperity. As these families had more disposable income, they enjoyed these foods more often. After World War II, when economic fortunes further improved, many Black families moved to homes that had space to garden and kitchens with modern appliances. They also had more disposable income to buy groceries. "This growing prosperity," writes Adrian Miller, author of the James Beard Award–winning *Soul Food: The Surprising Story of An American Cuisine, One Plate at a Time*, "incubated an enduring culinary tradition—Sunday dinner with extended family, with a table full of special-occasion foods."

▶ A group of Florida migrants stops near Shawboro, North Carolina, in 1940 on their way to Cranberry, New Jersey, to pick potatoes.

THE HARLEM RENAISSANCE

No city neighborhood benefited more culturally from the Great Migration than Harlem. A few middle-class Black families had moved there even before the migration, but when migrants came in waves, whites fled. Harlem became to New York City what the Left Bank was to Paris—a magnet for novelists, poets, intellectuals, musicians, actors, painters, and entrepreneurs.

Aside from the Black church, the integrated Cotton Club, which had two bandstands, was the place to be. In this creative stewpot, it wasn't just the arts that flourished. Migrants who moved to Harlem from the American South encountered immigrants from other places—particularly the Caribbean, where people fled political upheaval and revolution during the 19th century. The result was a mixing and melding of food traditions from many places of the Black Diaspora.

"In what it eats," noted a 1928 article in the *New York Times*, "Harlem shows itself off less a locality than an international rallying cry."

SOUL FOOD EVOLUTION

Although the term "soul food" took hold in the 1960s, it had been used in various applications from the 1940s to denote Black cooking as separate from Southern cooking. It is a tradition with strong roots in the African American community that continues to evolve.

Soul-food scholar Adrian Miller asserts that while all soul food is Southern, not all Southern food is soul food. Soul food is related to Southern cooking, but because it flows from the cooking of enslaved West Africans, it's richer, spicier, saltier, and sweeter. Miller defines soul food as those foods primarily of the interior Deep South, mainly Georgia, Mississippi, and Alabama. It grew out of the rations enslaved people were given each week—five pounds of a starch such as cornmeal, rice, or sweet potatoes; a few pounds of dried, salted, or smoked beef, fish, or pork; and a jug of molasses—plus anything they were able to hunt, fish, or grow in their gardens. Soul food evolved to incorporate foods such as fried chicken and catfish, hush puppies, and sweet potato pie after adoption of special-occasion foods by the Black church after emancipation during special celebrations.

But soul food is not just the story of leftovers or economic expediency, asserts culinary historian and educator Michael W. Twitty. It is, he writes in a 2013 article for *The American Prospect*, "no ailing culinary bastard. It is the cuisine of Du Bois' 'double consciousness,' edible jazz, the most surreptitious means of preserving African culture."

During the 1940s, Black jazz artists faced unequal treatment compared to white artists who received better gigs and higher pay despite the art form originating among African American musicians. Tired of the unequal treatment, African American jazz artists began to experiment with the musical traditions of the Black church. "So these jazz artists say, 'We're taking this music to a place where we don't think white musicians can mimic the sound,'" Miller told *Epicurious* in a 2016 interview. "And that's the sound of the Black church in the rural South. That gospel sound they started fusing into jazz, they described as 'soul' and 'funky' in the late '40s. And soul started becoming a label for almost all aspects of Black culture: soul music, soul brothers, soul sister, soul food."

In the 1960s, Miller writes in a 2015 blog post on *First We Feast*, "Black power advocates seeking to unify African Americans across class, geography, and varying experiences with oppression saw cultural totems like food as a powerful connector."

Malcolm X used the term "soul food" in his 1965 *The Autobiography of Malcolm X*, which helped summon the rise of the Black Power movement. The Black culinary traditions migrants brought north with them during the Great Migration came to be known as soul food, an empowering term at a time of strong and growing Black cultural identity.

Everything Old Is New Again

Cuisines adapt and evolve. A cuisine born of necessity, the oldest traditions of soul food date to pre-slavery West and Central Africa. Dominant white Southern culture adopted these techniques and dishes of soul food partly because enslaved cooks incorporated their food traditions into the food they prepared on Southern plantations. The culinary skills of an enslaved cook were particularly vital to the creation of Southern food.

▼ Malcolm X used the term "soul food" in his 1965 *The Autobiography of Malcolm X* as a term of cultural pride. Today, soul food goes beyond the traditional foods (such as fried okra, above) and includes vegan and vegetarian fare.

▲ Sylvia's Restaurant on Lenox Avenue in Harlem.

Poor whites who weren't landed gentry also adopted these traditions.

Although revered for its rich history and taste, some members of the Black community have criticized soul food for its high amounts of starch, fat, and calories, leading to high rates of hypertension, type 2 diabetes, clogged arteries, stroke, and heart attacks among Black Americans.

Many young Black chefs and home cooks are returning to the roots of the largely vegetarian diets of their ancestors, who lived primarily on grains, legumes, and fresh vegetables from their gardens.

"The most creative energy within soul food right now is within the vegan and vegetarian culinary genres," Miller writes in a *First We Feast* post. "After all, it's really the seasoning that sets soul food apart from Southern food. Vegan and vegetarian soul food are often cast as a complete departure of the traditional cuisine, but the focus on vegetables closely aligns with how African Americans ate during slavery and Reconstruction. It's not a culinary farewell—it's really a homecoming."

AT HOME AT SYLVIA'S

In 1962, Sylvia Woods, born and raised in Hemingway, South Carolina, opened her eponymous restaurant in in a former luncheonette in Harlem. It had six booths, 15 stools, and a menu featuring ribs, hot cakes, cornbread, fried chicken, and black-eyed peas and rice.

Sylvia's became what the *New York Times* called the "de facto" social center of Harlem. It was a place where expatriate Black Southerners such as restaurateur and opera singer Alexander Smalls—who came from South Carolina in 1977—could find familiarity and comfort.

Going there, he told the *Times*, he knew he was going to have "fried chicken and candied yams and mingle and run into folks who made you feel like you were back home, south of the Mason-Dixon line . . . You hear the roar of history, . . . a flash of civil rights and marches, Sylvia standing out front during a press conference and being the mother of whatever the movement was, an anchor that anchors this great community."

COLLARD GREENS

The practice of boiling leafy greens, including collards, is a historically popular African cooking technique. In the South, some enslaved people were allowed to grow vegetables to supplement their food rations, including greens. They slow-simmered pungent collards, a member of the cabbage family, with pork fat and seasonings. A bonus was the savory pan juices that collected in the pot, known as pot likker (or pot liquor). In keeping with the practice of dipping starches into saucy African meat-and-vegetable dishes, pot likker was mopped up with cornbread, Today collards are touted for their bountiful nutritional offerings including vitamin A, which is thought to be more readily absorbed by the body when paired with a little fat.

SERVES 6 TO 8

1 medium onion, chopped

2 tablespoons cooking oil or olive oil

2 cloves garlic, minced

1 teaspoon salt

½ teaspoon black pepper

¼ teaspoon crushed red pepper or hot sauce

1 meaty smoked ham hock or about 1 pound cured and smoked pork shoulder, rinsed

2 pounds collard greens (about 2 bunches)

1 tablespoon apple cider vinegar or red wine vinegar

Granulated sugar (optional)

1. In a Dutch oven, cook onion in hot oil for 2 minutes. Add the garlic, salt, black pepper, and crushed red pepper; cook 1 minute more. Add 2 quarts (8 cups) water and ham hock. Bring to boiling; reduce heat and simmer, uncovered, for 1 hour.

2. Meanwhile, trim the stems from the collard greens and the tough center vein that runs through the larger leaves and discard. Wash the greens thoroughly in several changes of water; drain and pat dry. Stack the leaves and roll them into a cylinder. Cut crosswise into ½ inch strips. Add to the mixture in the Dutch oven, pushing down with a spoon to cover. Bring to boiling; reduce heat and simmer, uncovered, 30 to 40 minutes or until greens are tender but not mushy. Stir in vinegar. Remove from heat.

3. Transfer the hock to a cutting board, and let stand until cool enough to handle. Remove the meat from hock and coarsely chop. Add the desired amount of meat back to the greens. If needed, heat through. Season to taste with additional salt and black pepper. If bitter, add a couple pinches of sugar. Transfer to a serving dish along with desired amount of cooking liquid.

WOMEN IN WORLD WAR II

The traditional role of women as homemakers was challenged during World War II. Some went to work outside the home. Others continued to manage the homefront exclusively. Both did so under new circumstances that impacted how they fed their families.

American women have always worked, whether inside or outside the home or both. But the arrival of World War II transformed the nature of women's work in the United States: who was working for pay, where they were working, and the kinds of jobs they were accomplishing. The number of women in the American workforce during World War II grew by some 6.5 million. They comprised more than 35 percent of the civilian workforce, and their numbers grew by 50 percent between 1940 and 1945. More than 22 percent of all married women worked outside the home. The most dramatic growth was in defense-related industries, where female employment grew by more than 460 percent. Women were hired in droves to fill empty factory positions to help the war effort.

Whether a woman worked outside the home or not, though, she—as the culturally appointed preparer and provider of meals at the time—was subject to rationing instituted by the Office of Price Administration, established in August 1941.

The government promoted planting Victory gardens and canning as a source of fresh fruits and vegetables. Nearly 20 million Americans planted gardens in backyards, empty lots, and even rooftops. Even so, a study showed households were spending an additional 20 percent on food between 1942 and 1944.

Rationing was complex and ever-evolving. Each individual received a coupon book of colored ration points—red for meat, butter, and other fats, canned fish, or canned milk; blue for canned and bottled foods. Housewives could pool the whole family's points and budget them accordingly to have more control over the family diet.

Black-Market Beef

A campaign by the federal government touting the notion that soldiers engaged in physically demanding and dangerous work on the front needed significantly more food than those at home convinced many homemakers that in cooperating with rationing, they could do their part to ensure a successful end of the war. However, not everyone was on board. Some who could afford it frequently participated in a black-market trade to supplement their stocks, particularly meat. Fully 20 percent of all meat during this period was sold on the black market.

Rationing of nonfood items also had an effect on the types of foods that were available to Americans. Canned goods were often scarce because so much steel was diverted to the war. Rubber and gas rationing meant some fresh produce was unavailable because it couldn't be transported from the regions where it was grown. With prime cuts of meat off the table, housewives got creative. Magazines aimed at women promoted alternative proteins such as liver, heart, fish, cheese, and legumes, particularly soybeans.

▼ The iconic image of Rosie the Riveter by J. Howard Miller appeared on posters in 1942 for Westinghouse as a way to encourage women to support the war effort by joining the workforce. A copy of the original poster is housed at the Smithsonian's National Museum of American History.

Local newspapers printed ration-friendly recipes such as "Magic Spread," which extended butter with gelatin and evaporated milk.

A recipe from the May 15, 1943 edition of *The New York Age*—a prominent Black newspaper of the time—featured an article titled "Baked Peanuts A Meat Substitute." The recipe called for soaking peanuts overnight, then cooking them with canned tomatoes, molasses, sugar, and spices similarly to Boston baked beans. "The canny housewife takes advantage of other foods which offer the same nutritive values [as meat]", the article reads. "And she starts with the lowly legumes—the kidney bean, soybean, or peanut—which, the Foods Laboratory shows, are rich in most of meat's food values."

Housewives were already charged with meal planning, budgeting, shopping, cooking, and cleaning. Now they had to go to the store with alternatives in mind if what they wanted wasn't available. Before the war it was common for women to shop daily, but as more of them went to work their time was more valuable. They used their refrigerators and freezers much more. Some left their lists with the grocer and picked up their foods the following day. Children were often drafted to stand in line for food while their mothers worked or shopped elsewhere.

The editors of *Good Housekeeping* magazine made it one of their missions during the war to provide support to homemakers dealing with the new reality.

They took the position that ". . . life in American homes must go on and will go on; and for that sake of the generations to come we must not lose sight of that—never, not for a single day, because it is home life, and all it implies, that we are now defending."

LIVING ON "C-RATS"

While Americans who remained at home during World War II were devising new and creative ways to cook organ meats, legumes, and game meats such as deer and muskrat, American soldiers in Europe and the Pacific were dining on rations of a different sort.

A dinner or supper C-ration created for combat troops was typically composed of a canned main dish such as pork and beans, canned fruit, chewing gum, a chocolate bar, instant coffee and sugar tablets, processed cheese and biscuits, cigarettes, and a matchbook. Lighter and less bulky K-rations could be carried in a pocket and were designed for paratroopers and messengers.

Although the 2,900-calorie daily menus provided the soldiers fuel, from a gustatory standpoint, they left much to be desired.

▶ A woman purchases canned goods with ration coupons in a neighborhood grocery store in New York City in the 1940s.

PROSPERITY IN THE POSTWAR 1950s

Economic prosperity and an end to food rationing after World War II encouraged conspicuous consumption while an explosion in processed foods proclaimed to liberate American housewives from the drudgery of daily meal-making.

▲ Poppy Cannon published *The Can-Opener Cook Book* in 1951.

▼ An ad in the March 1955 *Family Circle* magazine touts the flavor, convenience, and economy of canned tuna.

Ramping up production during World War II had two beneficial effects for the American economy. It pulled it out of a depression and created a system that could produce goods demanded by the young families created when the G.I.s came home and began marrying, having children, and buying homes—many of which were funded by the G.I. Bill of Rights—in unprecedented numbers.

All of this spending was about more than accumulating material goods for enhancing everyday life. It became a point of patriotism as well, a way to contribute to the advancement of the American way of life. "The good purchaser devoted to 'more, newer, and better' was a good citizen," Harvard University historian Lizabeth Cohen told PBS' *American Experience*, "since economic recovery after a decade and a half of depression and war depended on a dynamic mass consumption economy."

Much of the technological innovation was put forth in the service of food production and preparation, and it had a huge impact on what and how postwar Americans ate. Appliance and food manufacturers advertised on television and published pamphlets encouraging women to embrace the newest technologies to make the kitchen not a place of endless toil and drudgery but one of convenience and cheer. With the establishment of the Interstate Highway System, Americans were traveling more, which meant less time at home.

Canned goods came roaring back. Families moved to the suburbs and shopped not at the neighborhood grocer but at new "supermarkets." Between 1948 and 1958, the number of such markets doubled to more than 2,500, with most of them in new suburbs or planned developments.

The Birth of the Cutting-Edge Kitchen

A kitchen with cutting-edge technology came to symbolize postwar affluence. Electric ranges, combination refrigerator-freezers, washers and dryers, and even small appliances like electric skillets and blenders moved in. Between 1945 and 1949, Americans bought 20 million refrigerators and 5.5 million stoves, a trend that continued into the next decade.

It wasn't all extravagance and conspicuous consumption, though. Products like Saran Wrap and Tupperware encouraged thrift and reusing leftovers, which were often made at least partially with convenience products such as canned soup, canned hamburgers, and canned macaroni and cheese.

In 1951, Poppy Cannon, who was by turns the food editor for *Ladies' Home Journal* and *House*

Beautiful and the author of several cookbooks, published *The Can Opener Cook Book*, which encouraged women to make sophisticated cuisine in a hurry by doctoring up the contents of cans. A recipe for Casserole à la King called for canned chicken à la king, canned macaroni in cream sauce with cheese, cheese, bread crumbs, butter, and parsley or watercress. The method included layering the chicken and macaroni in a casserole dish, sprinkling with cheese, bread crumbs, and dots of butter, then baking until hot and bubbly. To finish, garnish with parsley and "Serve from its own dish."

"At one time a badge of shame, hallmark of the lazy lady and the careless wife, today the can opener is fast becoming a magic wand," Cannon wrote, "especially in the hands of those brave, young women, nine million of them (give or take a few thousand here and there), who are engaged in frying as well as bringing home the bacon."

All manner of foods were in abundance during this period, and most white Americans had more money in their pockets—older and Black Americans did not share equally in the prosperity—than they had since the Great Depression. Beef consumption rose steadily until, by the 1970s, every American was consuming more than 100 pounds of it annually, often in the form of the juiciest, best-marbled steaks they could find. The health repercussions of that would come to light at the beginning of the decade, but during the 1950s and '60s, the nation was in the grip of a kind of meat madness.

It was all part of achieving what Americans perceived as the "the good life," the *American Experience* piece asserts. "With the things that defined 'the good life' within economic reach," the writer says, "working-class people could achieve the upward mobility they craved."

▶ Between 1945 and 1949, Americans bought 20 million refrigerators and 5.5 million stoves, a trend that continued into the next decade.

FIFTIES FOODS WE STILL EAT

The 1950s saw an explosion of processed foods, many of which are still very much embraced by the buying public today. Boxed cake mixes have been around since the 1930s but fell out of favor in the 1950s, until manufacturers began making ready-made frosting and packaged decorations. Kraft Foods introduced the ubiquitous individual slices of mild, long-lasting processed yellow American cheese, which is still the classic cheese of choice for cheeseburgers and grilled cheese sandwiches.

Diet soda—originally developed for and marketed to diabetics—was repurposed as "diet" soda, and it became increasingly popular with health- and weight-conscious consumers, particularly women.

And in 1958, inventor Momofuku Ando began marketing instant ramen noodles in Japan. In 2019, the U.S. consumed 4.6 billion servings of instant noodles.

FOOD IN ADVOCACY

From the lunch counter of a Greensboro, North Carolina, Woolworth's to the Black Panthers' community breakfast to countless marches, food helped fuel the Civil Rights Movement.

Because all humans have to eat, food is a useful lens to examine the entirety of culture—politics, gender, economics, and race. And food, as much as the tireless pursuit of a more perfect union, helped to fuel the Civil Rights Movement in the 1960s.

Sometimes it was a symbolic demonstration the brave activists knew was doomed to fail. Such was the case of four Black students from North Carolina A&T College who, on Feb. 1, 1960, sat down at the segregated Woolworth's lunch counter in Greensboro and asked for four coffees. They could shop at the store, but they couldn't get served a simple cup. They sat there passively until the store closed.

The nonviolent example set by the four young men—David Richmond, Ezell Blair Jr., Franklin McCain, and Joseph McNeil—inspired other sit-ins and similar actions throughout the segregated South. These actions weren't spontaneous.

Activists and civil rights leaders gathered in Black-owned restaurants to eat, organize, and strategize. These included Paschal's in Atlanta—one of Martin Luther King Jr.'s favorites—Dooky Chase's in New Orleans, and the Lassis Inn in Little Rock, Arkansas—the city where the battle to desegregate schools captured the nation's attention.

Many Black restaurateurs provided more than meeting rooms and free sustenance: they wrote checks to the Southern Christian Leadership Conference and other civil rights groups to support the movement.

The restaurant where the most important meetings were held was almost certainly Paschal's, where King, Ralph Abernathy, Andrew Young, John Lewis, and others met repeatedly with the aim to bend the arc of history toward justice. At one of the few white-tablecloth restaurants that seated Blacks in the South, they enjoyed fried chicken and catfish, collards and fried green tomatoes, and macaroni and cheese. Lewis, who was beaten nearly to death during the "Bloody Sunday" march in Selma, Alabama, and who later became a congressman from Georgia, remembered that Paschal's was where decisions were made that changed the country.

Freedom Through Food

King and other largely religious and committed nonviolent activists took one approach to the movement. The Black Panther Party on the West Coast—particularly in Oakland, California—took another. The Panthers, founded by Huey P. Newton and Bobby Seale in 1966 in part to end police brutality in Oakland, grew out their Afros, wore black leather jackets, and—taking advantage

▼ Civil rights activists such as Martin Luther King Jr. and Andrew Young frequently held meetings at Paschal's, a Black-owned restaurant in Atlanta. "Most of the [B]lack leaders lived on that side of town, and they stopped there on their way to work," Young told the *Washington Post* in 2011. "If you wanted to know what was going on, that's where most of the discussion was going on and where much of the planning was taking place."

▲ Bill Whitfield serves free breakfast to children before school in Kansas City in April 1969. The Black Panthers provided breakfast to children as one way to fight poverty and encourage solidarity and self-determination. Local merchants donated the food.

of open-carry laws—carried rifles in public. They did not disavow violence but viewed armed self-defense as necessary for protection and even survival. While much of the white establishment saw it as threatening, the militant component of the Black Panthers was just one facet of the organization, which also called for housing cooperatives, medical care, and the "power to determine the destiny of our Black and oppressed communities," as detailed in their 1966 Ten-Point Program guidelines.

In addition to embracing Black Power and self-determination, the Panthers also worked to support Black and marginalized people in their neighborhoods. Part of that strategy was to start

continued on page 130

THE FBI FIGHTS FREE BREAKFAST

FBI head J. Edgar Hoover was no fan of the Panthers' effort to feed and empower their communities, calling their work "potentially the greatest threat to efforts by authorities to neutralize the BPP and destroy what it stands for." Hoover's edict essentially gave federal officials and local police authority to destroy the effort.

In San Francisco, parents were told their children's Panther breakfast was infected with venereal disease. Elsewhere, FBI agents went door to door, telling parents the Panthers would teach their children to be racist. And in Chicago, the night before the first Panther serving of breakfast could begin, police broke in, destroyed the food, and urinated on it.

continued from page 129
serving free breakfast to the children in their communities before school, soliciting donations from friendly businesses.

The first free breakfast—a spread of chocolate milk, eggs, meat, cereal, and oranges—was held in January 1969 at an Episcopal church in Oakland. In just a few weeks, the number of children served went from the hundreds to the thousands. From 1969 into the early 1970s, the Black Panthers' Free Breakfast for School Children Program fed tens of thousands of hungry children, whose performance at school rapidly improved after getting a nutritious meal—with the help of dietitians—before starting class.

"The school principal came down and told us how different the children were," Ruth Beckford, a parishioner who co-founded the program, told Nik Heynen, a University of Georgia professor of anthropology and author of an article about the subject in a 2009 issue of *Annals of the American Association of Geographers*. "They weren't falling asleep in class," she told him, "they weren't crying with stomach cramps, how alert they were and it was wonderful."

The program spread across the country to a peak of 45 locations. The Panthers had other social programs, but free breakfast had long-lasting impact, helping lead to free or reduced-price school breakfasts to this day. In addition to helping Black schoolchildren thrive, the program demonstrated the Panthers' commitment to education, community organizing, and food justice.

▼ The Greensboro Four—Ezell Blair, Jr., David Richmond, Franklin McCain, and Joseph McNeil—all students at North Carolina Agricultural and Technical College—stage a sit-in at a Woolworth's lunch counter on February 1, 1960 to protest the store's segregationist policies.

GEORGIA GILMORE

One of the lesser-known heroines of the Civil Rights Movement—particularly the Montgomery, Alabama, bus boycott—was a woman named Georgia Gilmore. Gilmore started out selling chicken sandwiches to Black Americans participating in the boycott and ended up mobilizing a platoon of like-minded women who sold food to fund an alternative transportation system for those who refused to ride Montgomery city buses until they were desegregated.

The Rev. Martin Luther King Jr. and other civil rights leaders organized the boycott after the arrest of Rosa Parks for her refusal to move to the back of a city bus. Though a few women and girls had been arrested before Parks for defying the order to move to the back of the bus, civil rights leaders chose the Rosa Parks case to launch the boycott in December 1955. What King and his lieutenants might not have imagined was that city officials were so resistant to change that the boycott would drag on for more than a year before they buckled.

Gilmore started small, selling sandwiches and other fare at meetings of the Montgomery Improvement Association at Holt Street Baptist Church in Montgomery. Whatever profits she made she funneled back to the movement.

Pie for Progress: An Invisible Army
Still, one woman's efforts and relatively small monetary contributions couldn't sustain a long campaign. Soon, Gilmore mobilized other activist friends to sell more food—greens, sweet potato pies, and more—at businesses all over the city. The profits helped pay for fuel and other expenses incurred as a daily caravan of vehicles carried Black workers who didn't have cars of their own to and from work.

She called her loose coalition The Club from Nowhere because, with a wink and a nudge, it was said the money to fund the continuing boycott came from nowhere. The Black women in Gilmore's army didn't dare risk letting their white employers or landlords know where the money was going for fear of getting fired or evicted.

About three months after the boycott began and quickly became the focus of national attention, a county grand jury indicted King on a charge of conspiracy. Although Gilmore worked as a midwife, a vocation known to attract the kindly and compassionate, Gilmore could also be fierce and was known not to suffer fools. Called as a witness at King's trial, she lambasted a driver who had kicked her off a city bus, saying her money was as good as any white person's.

Although she was celebrated in the local Black community for her outspoken testimony, she likely had a strong feeling her courtroom candor would cost her her

▶ Georgia Gilmore adjusts her hat for the photographers after she testified as a defense witness in the bus boycott trial of the Rev. Martin Luther King Jr. on March 21, 1956 in Montgomery, Alabama. "When you pay your fare and they count the money," Gilmore testified, "they don't know the Negro money from white money."

job as a cook at a firm called the National Lunch Company. It's not clear whether she was indeed fired or quit, knowing she soon would be.

King suggested Gilmore go into business for herself and she did. Although her kitchen had already been a hub for organizing and strategizing, soon enough it became an informal back-door restaurant. King loved holding court there, inviting Robert Kennedy and Lyndon B. Johnson to dine with him.

IMMIGRATION ACT OF 1965

After John F. Kennedy's assassination, Lyndon Johnson assumed the presidency with a reformer's agenda. The sweeping Immigration and Nationality Act of 1965 opened up a world of flavors to the country at large.

The bill abolished the National Origins Quota System, established in 1921, that aimed to preserve America's racial homogeneity by encouraging immigration from Northwestern Europe and actively discouraging it from Africa, Southern and Eastern Europe, and Asia.

Prior to the implementation of the law, tens of thousands of people from Northern and Western Europe were granted visas each year while countries in Asia, Africa, and the Middle East were hardly allocated more than 100 slots each.

While the 1965 law still had quotas—a total of 290,000 total immigrants per year, including 170,000 from the Eastern Hemisphere, 120,000 from the Western Hemisphere, and a numerical cap of 20,000 on immigrants from any single country—it was largely based on family connections in the U.S. and the skills immigrants could offer, rather than their country of origin.

"A nation that was built by immigrants of all lands can ask of those who seek admission, 'What can you do for our country?'" Johnson said in his 1964 State of the Union address. "But we should not be asking, 'In what country were you born?'"

It was a seismic change in immigration policy, driven in part by the global perception that America systemically discriminated based on one's country of origin or the color of their skin. Johnson and others who were lobbying for passage of the law argued that it was largely symbolic and was not, he said, "revolutionary."

"The bill will not flood our cities with immigrants," Senator Ted Kennedy (D-Mass)—a leading supporter of the bill—told the Senate during debate. "It will not upset the ethnic mix of our society. It will not relax the standards of admission. It will not cause American workers to lose their jobs."

But it did change the face of America. In 1965, 84 percent of the population of the United States was non-Hispanic white. In 2015, that number was 62 percent. According to the Pew Research Center, 51 percent of those who have immigrated to the United States since 1965 have come from Latin America alone.

A Demographic and Culinary Revolution

"More than any other piece of legislation in the nation's history, the Act transformed the ethnic and racial makeup of the United States," writes Geraldo L. Cadava, professor of American and Latin American history at Northwestern University, in a 2015 article for *The American Historian*. "We live in a country that looks a lot different today than it did fifty years ago, largely because of the law."

Of course, this led to a food revolution in America. Mexican or Tex-Mex food was well-established by the time the legislation passed. Chinese food could be found in large cities beginning in the late 19th century. Even a handful of Indian or so-called "Hindu" restaurants were operating in the 1910s, although they were regarded as rare and fascinating curiosities.

Then in 1965, with World War II and its privations and active discouragement of anything but mostly bland food just 20 years in the past,

▼ After the Immigration and Nationality Act of 1965 dramatically increased the numbers of immigrants allowed into the United States from places such as India, Pakistan, Thailand, Japan, Korea, the Middle East, and Africa, their vibrant, flavorful cuisines arrived along with them.

intensely flavored foods began flooding in: Curries from India and Pakistan. Spicy coconut-based tom kha kai from Thailand. Wasabi from Japan. Kimchi from Korea. Szechuan peppers from China. Kibbeh from Lebanon. Adobo from the Philippines. Doro wat from Ethiopia. All of these flavors and dishes had been in the U.S. before, but their proliferation was far more limited. The old quota system had in large part locked out the wide world of tastes and dishes.

▲ President Lyndon B. Johnson signs the immigration act surrounded by Vice President Hubert Humphrey, Lady Bird Johnson, Muriel Humphrey, Sen. Edward Kennedy, Sen. Robert F. Kennedy, and others on Liberty Island on October 3, 1965.

This demographic shift will continue into the foreseeable future. By 2043, the Census Bureau predicts that the U.S. will become a "majority-minority" country, which means that no racial group comprises more than half of the population.

"Perhaps we can say that the 1965 Act may have hastened the pace of demographic change, led to change on a greater scale than had been seen before, introduced new communities that now have their own historians," Cadava writes in the piece for *The American Historian*. "But more than a moment of rupture, a break from the past, we might also see it as a law that made possible the continuation of a kind of pluralism that has defined America from the beginning."

THE EVOLUTION OF "ETHNIC" FOOD

Beginning in the 1950s, says Krishnendu Ray, author of *The Ethnic Restaurateur* and chair of the food studies program at New York University, the term "ethnic" referred to any food associated with a newly arrived group of people, as a way of marking "a certain kind of difference—difference of taste, difference of culture," he told the *Washington Post* in 2016. "You see it in the grocery store. Food that isn't associated with whites will be called ethnic."

The term evolved from "foreign," which was used from the mid-19th century to the beginning of the 20th century to denote the foods of recently arrived immigrants. "In an increasingly multicultural society, the term 'ethnic food,' . . . is now starting to take on an offensive character," writes Maria Goody in an NPR article featuring Ray, "lumping all nonwhite people and their cuisines together in a category of 'other.'"

Thankfully, that mindset is changing. "Opening our mouths to each others' foods," Goody writes, "can become a gateway to opening our minds to each others' cultures."

BUTTER CHICKEN

This Indian curry dish, *murgh makhani* (chicken in butter), has become known in the United States simply as butter chicken. It's a regular (and favorite) menu item for many Indian restaurants and originated as a practical solution to leftover tandoori chicken. In the 1920s, Indian chef and restaurateur Kundan Lal Gujral created his successful tandoori chicken in Peshawar by cooking seasoned chicken in a clay tandoor oven, typically reserved for baking bread. Gajral brought his tandoori chicken to Delhi in 1947, which made the Moti Mahal restaurant famous and contributed to the popularity of Indian cuisine globally. Gujral also created the famous butter chicken, a technique for reviving day-old tandoori chicken by stirring it into a rich, buttery tomato curry. This version calls for marinating chicken in seasoned yogurt to infuse it with the flavors of tandoori chicken before braising it in the tomato-cream sauce.

SERVES 6

- 1 cup plain whole-milk or Greek yogurt
- 1 tablespoon lemon juice
- 4 teaspoons garam masala
- 4 teaspoons cumin seed, crushed
- 1 teaspoon ground turmeric
- 6 bone-in chicken thighs, skin on or removed
- 1 stick butter (4 ounces), at room temperature
- 1 medium onion, chopped
- 2 tablespoons finely chopped fresh ginger
- 4 cloves garlic, minced
- 1 (2-inch) cinnamon stick
- ¼ teaspoon cayenne (optional)
- 1 (14.5-ounce) can fire-roasted diced tomatoes with green chiles
- ¾ cup heavy cream
- Salt and black pepper
- Hot cooked basmati rice
- ¼ cup chopped fresh cilantro

1. In a large bowl, stir together the yogurt, lemon juice, half of the garam masala, half of the cumin, and the turmeric. Add the chicken and coat on all sides with the marinade. Cover and refrigerate for 2 to 8 hours, turning chicken once.

2. In a large pan over medium heat, melt half of the butter. Cook the the onion in hot butter over medium heat until tender. Add the remaining 2 teaspoons garam masala and cumin seed, the ginger, garlic, and cinnamon stick; cook 2 minutes more, stirring frequently. Stir in the undrained tomatoes. Using tongs, add the chicken to the pan (pieces will still have marinade on them); discard the marinade.

3. Bring the mixture to boiling. Reduce heat and simmer, uncovered, for 25 minutes, stirring occasionally and spooning the sauce over the chicken. Stir in the cream and simmer 2 minutes more. Season to taste with salt and pepper. Remove from heat and stir in the remaining 4 tablespoons butter. Serve over rice and sprinkle with the cilantro.

THE RISE OF KOREAN CUISINE

An economic slowdown in South Korea in the 1970s and '80s propelled immigration to the United States. From Koreatowns on the coasts, bulgogi, bibimbap, and, most recently, sweet-and-spicy fried chicken have taken hold across the country.

▲ Kimchi—a spicy, pungent condiment of fermented vegetables—has found its way into cocktails, grilled cheese sandwiches, and even pizza.

▼ West 32nd Street is the main artery through Manhattan's Koreatown. Korean immigration to the United States spiked during the 1970s and '80s.

Despite the opportunity for immigration opening up after the Immigration and Nationality Act passed in 1965, massive numbers of Koreans weren't eager to come to America until their home country's economy stagnated.

During the 1970s and '80s—a time of economic difficulty in South Korea—Korean immigration to the United States spiked. In 1960, there were just 11,000 Korean immigrants living in the country. By 1980, that number had increased to 290,000—a 2,500 percent increase. As of 2017, there were just over 1 million Korean immigrants in the U.S., and only about 25 percent arrived after 2000. Most of them settled on either coast, in California, New York, and New Jersey. To this day, almost half of all Korean immigrants live in those three states.

As is the case with many new arrivals, they were drawn to neighborhoods in major American cities where fellow Korean immigrants had taken up residence. One of the most significant of these was a strip in Midtown Manhattan. They began opening up businesses, including bookstores, and of course, restaurants.

Immigrant Korean restaurateurs weren't quite as eager to cater to American palates as their Chinese, Japanese, and Thai counterparts. Japanese chefs offered a fresh take on traditional sushi rolls by playing with cream cheese and avocado. Nearly every Thai restaurant in America offered a version of pad Thai that is far sweeter than what is traditionally served in Thailand. Korean restaurants, on the other hand, initially catered mostly to Koreans.

"Korean restaurants, at first, were more of a clubby environment, for Koreans, by Koreans," said Matt Rodbard, co-author of *Koreatown: A Cookbook*, in a 2014 interview with *Serious Eats*. "There wasn't really much of an effort to draw in non-Korean guests."

Bulgogi and Beyond

Koreatowns popped up all over the country, from New York to Houston to Los Angeles. These offered alcohol, karaoke, and restaurants that stayed open late. Many of the first non-Koreans to venture to K-towns were restaurant workers coming off their late shifts and looking for something their own establishments didn't offer. The answer was often bulgogi, thinly sliced marinated and grilled beef; *tteokbokki*, a stir-fried dish of spicy rice cakes; bibimbap, a rice-based dish with meat, seafood, vegetables, and sauces;

and *makchang*, grilled beef intestine. Korean fare was uncompromising—intensely flavored kimchi is an acquired taste for many. If it was going to be discovered, it would be on its own terms.

Eventually, trailers and brick-and-mortar stores serving Korean barbecue and fried chicken opened.

Sit-down Korean barbecue is a carnivore's delight and an experience meant to be shared communally, with meats such as bulgogi, *galbi* (flanken-cut beef short ribs), and pork belly cooked on tabletop grills until smoky and charred.

Bulgogi—at its simplest thinly sliced, marinated, and grilled beef—is thousands of years old. Ribeye is frequently used because it's tender and marbled with fat, but brisket and sirloin are also popular. The marinade usually contains some combination of soy, garlic, sugar, green onion, and Asian pear. (Asian pears contain an enzyme called *calpain*, which further softens and sweetens the razor-thin slices of meat.) Another favorite is spicy pork *jeyuk bokkeum* (also called dwaeji bulgogi) in a marinade heavy on Korean chili powder.

All of this meat is accompanied by *banchan*, side dishes such as seasoned soybean sprouts, sautéed spinach or watercress, spicy cucumber or radish salad, stir-fried zucchini or cucumbers, steamed eggplant, pickled vegetables, and of course kimchi. Soju, an astringent liquor distilled from rice, is typically drunk in shots.

Although the country's introduction to Korean food was slow to start compared relatively to the rate of immigration, it is decidedly here to stay.

"Korean food was eventually going to be discovered," chef Phillip Lee, owner of Kimchi Taco Truck and Kimchi Grill in Brooklyn, New York, told *Serious Eats*. "It was introduced in the U.S. before Thai and Vietnamese food, but it never caught on for various reasons . . . My goal is for everyone in America and the world to have a jar of [kimchi] in their refrigerator."

KOREAN FRIED CHICKEN

Ethereally crisp-skinned Korean fried chicken is a culinary gift that was introduced to Korea and given back to the world, recalibrated with different seasonings and cooking method.

Its roots lie in the Southern-style fried chicken Koreans began selling from stalls in Seoul and Busan when U.S. troops were stationed in South Korea in the late 1940s and early 1950s.

Korean fried chicken starts with smaller, more tender birds than American fried chicken. The chicken is usually seasoned with spices and salt and very lightly dredged in very fine flour such as cornstarch or rice flour. It's then double-fried in a method that renders all of the fat in the skin, creating a crackly, nearly transparent crust Chinese cooks refer to as "paper-fried chicken."

The chicken is then sometimes (but not always) hand-painted with a sticky, garlicky, sweet-and-spicy sauce.

▶ Beef bulgogi is among the most familiar Korean dishes in the U.S.

POSTWAR VIETNAMESE MIGRATION

The end of the Vietnam War in 1975 brought waves of Vietnamese refugees to the United States. A longing for the flavors of home—and for many, the need to make a living in a new land—resulted in an introduction of a cuisine that has, given the relatively short trajectory of Vietnamese migration, had tremendous impact on the culinary life of the country.

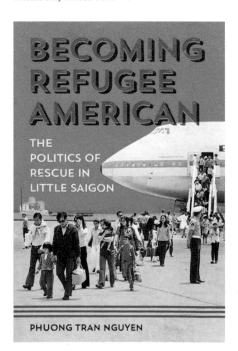

▲ Salty, savory fish sauce—made by fermenting anchovies—adds a rich umami flavor to many Vietnamese dishes.

▼ Phuong Nguyen, author of *Becoming Refugee American*, says that Vietnamese refugees often opened restaurants simply because they needed work.

BECOMING REFUGEE AMERICAN

THE POLITICS OF RESCUE IN LITTLE SAIGON

PHUONG TRAN NGUYEN

In 1980, there were 231,000 Vietnamese migrants living in the United States. By 2017, that number was more than 1.3 million, making them the sixth-largest foreign-born group in the country. Immediately after the war, many who came needed work. Opening a restaurant seemed the solution, "partly that's because how Asian culture is commodified in this country," Phuong Nguyen, author of *Becoming Refugee American: The Politics of Rescue in Little Saigon,* told writer Jean Trinh in an article in a November 2017 issue of the KCET Food online newsletter. "The beauty of a restaurant was that it required little formal training, almost no certification, or professionalization—at least in the short term."

Over a relatively short amount of time, non-Vietnamese Americans were introduced to rice vermicelli with grilled pork sausages, spring rolls, bánh mì, and, of course, phở.

The phở found in America is invariably of the South Vietnam variety, with lots of tableside garnishes like fresh herbs, fish sauce, and sliced chiles. In fact, phở originated in North Vietnam and migrated south when the country was partitioned in 1954. The war started the following year and ended with the fall of Saigon in 1975.

Regardless of their socioeconomic status back home, most migrant Vietnamese endeavored to find meaningful work to become economically self-sufficient in a new country. Through networking and family connections, many of them eventually migrated to large cities, most notably Los Angeles and San Jose, California; New Orleans; and Houston. Texas and Louisiana were popular destinations because of warm climates and the opportunity to work fishing jobs, which many had done in Vietnam, on the Gulf Coast. In particular, New Orleans became a destination because of refugee sponsorship by organizations such as Catholic Charities. The French-influenced architecture—even if it was a product of French colonialism—was a reminder of home.

A Taste of Home

Although Orange County, California, and Houston are both unquestionably meccas for Vietnamese fare, they offer very different menus. Southern California has broad representation of the food traditions from North Central and South Vietnam. Food from the North tends to be saltier and simpler—lots of fish sauce, fried fish or braised meat, and all manner of noodle soups. More common in the South are món nhâu, a kind of Vietnamese tapas and other snack-size offerings. Many of these items are wrapped in rice paper and

dipped in a sweeter, less salty fish sauce. Food from the South also incorporates coconut and sugar caramel, and those tastes are more common in Houston.

▲ The classic bánh mì sandwich includes grilled pork tenderloin, shredded carrot, cucumber, jalapeño pepper, and cilantro.

Whatever the locale, the first Vietnamese restaurants in the United States initially had little interest in catering to an American clientele. Their priority was creating a taste reminiscent of home, not Americanizing their cuisine. As Little Saigons cropped up and grew around the country, restaurants expanded from street food and home cooking–style fare to more sophisticated offerings. If phở once came with chicken gizzards and hearts as well as beef tendons and eggs, it's now not uncommon to find it with thin slices of pricey filet mignon or lean pork tenderloin. Also popular are fritters, often stuffed with sweet potatoes and shrimp, caramelized spare ribs, and whole fried fish with a bowl of tamarind soup topped with dill on the side.

BÁNH MÌ: A RECLAMATION

The bánh mì is a relic of the French colonization of Vietnam that has now spread all over the world. The classic—pâté, ham, and pork cold cuts layered on a baguette with mayonnaise, Maggi sauce, pickled vegetables, and thinly sliced chiles—is a creation that began with conquest and ended with reclamation.

Initially, only the French colonizers could buy bread. Wheat doesn't grow in Vietnam, and importing flour was expensive. That changed during World War I, when German-owned import companies were taken over by colonial authorities. When the French went off to Europe to fight, there was suddenly a surplus of French meats, cheeses, and breads. Now working-class Vietnamese began experimenting with them. Mayonnaise replaced butter, and by the 1950s, Vietnamese ingredients— pickled vegetables, cilantro, and chiles—were added.

BEEF PHỞ

Phở—the iconic Vietnamese noodle soup that's topped with a garden of fresh herbs, chiles, and sprouts—originated in Northern Vietnam as a simple breakfast dish sold by street vendors. Because of Vietnam's tropical climate, it made sense to enjoy hot soup early before the day heated up. Phở also provided nourishment to laborers, such as those headed to the rice fields. The soup migrated south in the 1950s and '60s when the country split, along with the almost 1 million people fleeing Communism in the north. The southern version took on more ingredients and vibrant flavors that are replicated in much of the phở prepared in the U.S. Phở arrived in America around 1975, along with the thousands of Vietnamese who fled after the fall of Saigon. America's current obsessions with global cuisine, healthier eating, and spicy food feed the growing interest in this restorative comfort soup.

SERVES 8

- 1 large onion, coarsely chopped
- 1 3-inch piece ginger, peeled and sliced
- 2 teaspoons cooking oil
- 1 (32-ounce) carton organic reduced-sodium beef broth
- 2 pounds meaty beef bones such as beef oxtails, short ribs, or knuckle
- 2 small carrots, sliced
- 1 tablespoon fish sauce
- 3 whole star anise
- 1 4-inch cinnamon stick
- 1 teaspoon whole peppercorns
- 5 whole cloves
- 2 cardamom pods
- 8 ounces thin rice stick noodles
- 1 pound beef sirloin, trimmed and very thinly sliced*
- 3 green onions, thinly bias-sliced
- 1 cup fresh bean sprouts

  Toppings such as lime wedges, sliced chile peppers, cilantro sprigs, mint sprigs, Thai basil sprigs, and/or sriracha sauce

1. In a large skillet, brown the onion and ginger in the oil over medium-high heat, stirring frequently. Transfer to a slow cooker. Add the broth, 1 cup water, the beef bones, carrots, fish sauce, star anise, cinnamon stick, peppercorns, cloves, and cardamom pods. Cover and cook on low 8 to 9 hours or high 4 to 5 hours.

2. Remove the bones and let stand until cool enough to handle. Remove any meat from the bones and shred; discard bones. Strain the broth through a sieve lined with 100-percent-cotton cheese cloth; discard the carrots and spices. Skim the fat from the broth** and return the broth to the cooker. Turn the slow cooker to high (if on low) and keep warm.

3. In a large pot, bring 2 quarts water to boiling; remove from heat. Add the rice noodles and let stand for 3 minutes; drain in a colander and immediately divide into eight bowls. Divide the shredded meat, sliced meat, green onions, and bean sprouts among bowls. Ladle seasoned broth atop and serve with desired toppings.

***NOTE:** Partially freezing the sirloin will make it easier to cut. Using a sharp knife, slice it very thinly across the grain. The meat is raw when topped with the broth. If you prefer the meat cooked more, dip the slices into the hot broth for a minute before placing in the bowls.

****NOTE:** To make ahead, you can cool the seasoned broth and refrigerate for up to 3 days or freeze for up to 3 months. Continue as directed except use a saucepan to thaw and reheat the seasoned broth.

FOOD-TRUCK REVOLUTION

There has long been a culture of street food in America, but it was given a boost by an unlikely event—the economic crash of 2008. The financial crisis caused many chefs to lose their restaurant jobs and to consider new and creative ways they could pursue their craft and make a living at the same time, while incurring far less overhead than a full-service restaurant requires.

Of course, street food and food trucks long predate the 2010s. Street vending was a vital source of food in colonial and antebellum cities across North America, and often served as a vital economic toehold for recent migrants who started street vending businesses to support their families. Some claim the first food truck in the United States was a wagon vendor Walter Scott parked in front of a newspaper office in Providence, Rhode Island, in 1872 to sell sandwiches and coffee to journalists and pressmen. Within a decade, Scott had close to 300 wagons all over the country.

Another precursor of sorts may be the chuck wagons stretching from Texas to California that fed hungry cowboys during the cattle drives that began after the Civil War. The U.S. Army has long used mobile canteens to feed troops on base.

"Roach coaches"—rundown vehicles that parked at construction sites in the 1970s and '80s and sold hamburgers, hot dogs, premade sandwiches, and bags of chips—were so named for their questionable sanitation practices. And *loncheras*—stationary food trucks owned and operated by Latinx entrepreneurs and serving Latin American staples—have long been a fixture at construction sites and factories.

The latter-day boom is represented by the rise of businesses like Kogi Barbecue, which began serving Korean short rib tacos from a trailer in front of a Hollywood nightclub late one night in 2008. Chef Roy Choi was soon getting national attention for his inventive and inexpensive food. His food was new and exciting. Others—peddling Indian dosas, grass-fed beef sliders, and goat cheese and dried cherry ice cream—followed. As a result of the emergent gourmet food truck scene, street food clientele expanded and diversified along with the food offerings.

Choi was one such casualty of the 2008 financial meltdown. The Dow Jones U.S. Restaurants & Bars Index dropped 13 percent that year, with casual dining businesses hit especially hard. In such a climate, restaurant owners saw it was a lot cheaper to operate a truck than to open a new brick-and-mortar restaurant—or sometimes even keep an existing one open.

Location, Location, Location

As trucks became fixtures on many city street corners, smartphones and social media grew exponentially, allowing trucks to let their customers know where they were going to be the next day and

▼ Food trucks have gone far beyond tacos. These modern mobile restaurants offer up fare such as Indian dosas, curry fries, grass-fed beef sliders, macaroni and cheese, and Ethiopian doro wat served with injera.

what the specials might be. The marketing budget for such an operation was almost nothing.

Food trucks remain popular more than a decade after the contemporary boom. Truck operators can be nimble, adapting to customers' changing needs and tastes, responding to food trends and cultural movements. There were enough of them in the U.S. by 2011 that Zagat added a category called "Food Truck Reviews" in its popular guides. In 2019 there were an estimated 23,000 trucks in the U.S. doing about $1 billion in business every year, with steady growth every year.

Trucks also filled a niche during the Covid-19 pandemic, serving hungry customers who were reluctant to dine inside. By April 2020, the restaurant business saw an $80 billion drop in revenues. By contrast, food trucks offered order-ahead options and worked with neighborhoods and homeowners' associations to deliver meals to customers' doors. The order-ahead option accounted for more than 50 percent of some operations' revenues. Customers could even sign up for text alerts to be notified where and when the trucks had arrived, preparing dishes fresh on location.

And during the racial justice protests of the summer of 2020, Los Angeles restaurant guide and food blog *The Infatuation* put out a list of Black-owned food trucks in the city as just one more way to support the movement.

THE FIRST TACO TRUCK

In 1974, 32-year-old Mexican immigrant Raul O. Martinez—who up to that point held jobs as both a Mexico City traffic officer and a Los Angeles dishwasher—had a vision: to sell authentic, high-quality soft-shell tacos from a renovated ice cream truck on the streets of East Los Angeles. While his friends were highly skeptical, on a summer night of that year, he parked his truck next to an East L.A. bar. He sold $70 worth of tacos that night and within weeks was taking in $150 in an evening. Within 6 months, he opened his first King Taco restaurant—now a multimillion-dollar chain of 22 brick-and-mortar locations in Los Angeles and San Bernadino counties.

▼ A lineup of food trucks in Atlanta offers potential customers a variety of fare. From the chuck wagon of the American West through the construction boom's "roach coaches," by 2015, American food trucks were a $1.2 billion industry.

KOREAN BEEF (BULGOGI) TACOS

Chef Roy Choi was one of hundreds of chefs who lost their restaurant jobs in the economic downturn of 2008. He fused his experience growing up eating Mexican food in Los Angeles with his Korean heritage to create the wildly popular Korean taco, which he sold—and still sells—from his fleet of Kogi Korean BBQ trucks on the streets of L.A. and elsewhere. In 2010, Choi was named one of the top ten "Best New Chefs" by *Food & Wine* magazine—the first food-truck chef to achieve that distinction—and in 2016, *Time* magazine put him on its list of the 100 most influential people in the world. This isn't his recipe, but it aligns with the spirit of combining flavors and culinary techniques from different cultures that is the hallmark of the post-2008 food truck scene.

SERVES 4 TO 6

FOR THE MEAT AND MARINADE

1¼ pounds flank steak

½ small pear, peeled and grated

¼ cup reduced-sodium soy sauce

2 tablespoons light brown sugar

2 tablespoons toasted sesame oil

3 cloves garlic, minced

1 tablespoon minced fresh ginger

1 tablespoon gochujang (Korean red pepper paste)

2 tablespoons canola oil, divided

FOR THE SLAW

1 cup shredded green cabbage

1 cup shredded purple cabbage

⅔ cup shredded carrots

¼ cup chopped fresh cilantro

¼ cup sliced scallions

3 tablespoons olive oil

1 tablespoon fresh lime juice

2 teaspoons honey

1 clove garlic, minced

Dash salt

FOR THE SAUCE

½ cup Mexican crema or sour cream

2 tablespoons fresh lime juice

1 teaspoon sriracha sauce

FOR SERVING

12 street taco–size corn tortillas

Lime wedges

1. **FOR THE MEAT AND MARINADE:** Wrap the meat in plastic wrap and freeze for 30 minutes. Unwrap and slice across the grain into ¼-inch-thick slices.

2. In a medium bowl, combine the pear, soy sauce, brown sugar, sesame oil, garlic, ginger, and gochujang. Whisk to combine. Place the meat in a large resealable plastic bag and pour the marinade over. Seal the bag and massage to thoroughly coat all of the meat. Marinate in the refrigerator for at least 2 hours or overnight.

3. **FOR THE SLAW:** In a large bowl, combine the green cabbage, purple cabbage, carrots, cilantro, and scallions. In a small jar with a lid, combine the olive oil, lime juice, honey, garlic, and salt. Shake vigorously. Pour over the cabbage mixture. Toss to coat. Cover and refrigerate until serving time.

4. **FOR THE SAUCE:** In a small bowl, whisk together the crema, lime juice, and sriracha. Cover and refrigerate until serving time.

5. To cook the meat, heat 1 tablespoon of the canola oil in a large cast-iron pan over medium-high heat. Working in batches, cook the steak in a single layer, turning once, until charred and cooked through, about 2 to 3 minutes per side. Repeat with the remaining oil and meat.

6. **TO SERVE:** Warm the tortillas on a hot griddle or skillet until pliable. Top with the meat and slaw. Drizzle with the sauce. Serve with lime wedges.

CONFLICT CUISINE®

Throughout history, war, conflict, and privation have forced people to move, taking their native foods with them. Sharing them gives refugees a way forward in their new land, increases cultural understanding, and bolsters the cause of peace.

Goat *karhai* from Afghanistan. Beef *tibs* from Ethiopia. *Pupusas* from El Salvador. *Ćevapi* from the Balkans. Although in the normal course of immigration and movements of people new foods are introduced to the countries in which they settle, war and political turmoil also mean that foods of a former homeland become sources of memory and connection to places that have been lost.

"Once upon a time it was common knowledge that you could always tell where the latest global conflict was taking place by looking at the list of new restaurant openings in Washington [D.C.]," writes Johanna Mendelson Forman in a January 2015 post on dcist.com. " . . . Today if you crave phở, doro wat, or pupusas, you may not realize that the proliferation of Vietnamese, Ethiopian, and El Salvadoran restaurants represent the hopes and dreams of people who fled their homelands with little more than memories of food they ate."

▲ Johanna Mendelson Forman, founder of Conflict Cuisine®.

▼ *Kabuli pulao*, a rice pilaf with meat, carrots, and raisins, is the national dish of Afghanistan.

These beloved and familiar foods help refugees and immigrants communicate their specific culture to the culture at large, even when they can't yet speak English.

Mendelson Forman, an expert on post-conflict transition and democratization whose past positions include Director of Peace, Security, and Human Rights at the United Nations Foundation, is the founder of Conflict Cuisine®, an organization that began as a course she teaches at American University's School of International Service "exploring how food of the diaspora communities in Washington reflected the state of conflicts around the globe, why food is a form of power that can be leveraged for good, as well as why it's a driver of conflict even in the 21st century."

Diplomacy Around the Table

What began as a single college course has grown into a resource whose stated mission is "to promote a greater understanding about differences in foodways (the cultural, social, and economic practices related to food) that may be a source of conflict.

"Through the study of diasporas—from refugees today to other immigrant populations who have settled in the United States and other parts of the globe—different foods have become borderless, yet tangible forms of culture that connect peoples no matter what their national origins.

"By gaining a deeper understanding of the culinary resources of a given culture it is possible to use food as a tool of conflict prevention and cross-cultural understanding.

"Conflict Cuisine® explores how food and the stories of those who prepare it can shift public perceptions about different cultures, while also

creating a means for newcomers to survive in their adopted homelands. It is often the case that food becomes an important means of bringing people together around the table in a way that promotes open dialogue."

From 1980, when the U.S. Refugee Admissions Program (USRAP) was established, to 2019, the United States accepted 3.7 million refugees and asylum seekers. From 2000 to 2019, the greatest numbers of refugees have come from the countries of Burma (Myanmar), Iraq, Somalia, Bhutan, the Democratic Republic of Congo, Iran, Ukraine, Cuba, Sudan, Russia, Liberia, Vietnam, Syria, Eritrea, and Afghanistan—all of which have seen conflict over this period.

Those numbers drove a corresponding boom in the varied fare available to Americans, particularly in urban areas—flatbreads, smoky grilled kebabs, falafel, and baba ghanoush from the Middle East; doro wat, slow-cooked fiery chicken stew from Ethiopia; arepas from Venezuela; and churrasco pupusas, tamales, and empanadas from all over Latin America.

Mendelson Forman believes food can be a tool for positive soft power—a phenomenon known as "gastrodiplomacy," or using the food cultures of different countries to aid cultural understanding, ease conflicts, and promote understanding and acceptance between cultures and nations. "Social gastronomy" is the use of food as a tool for social and humanitarian impact through culinary training and entrepreneurship to find a way forward in their new land.

"Social gastronomy uses food as a means rather than an end to ensure job training, integration into new societies for refugees, and [to] support gender integration into kitchens," she writes in an August 2020 post titled "What Is Gastrodiplomacy?" on ckbk.com. "Even if you cannot speak the language of a new homeland, through the kitchen you can make yourself understood. You can build common ground around a table."

TELLING THE STORY OF HOME

In Aurora, Colorado, Mango House—which advertises itself as "a shared space for resettled refugees and asylees," there are several food-court-style refugee-owned restaurants, including those serving Ethiopian, Syrian, Nepalese, Burmese, and Sudanese food. Diners can enjoy Burmese shan noodles, rice noodles in chicken soup topped with greens, peanuts, fried garlic, sesame seeds, and green onions; Syrian *kebah*, deep-fried breaded lamb, beef, and onion; or Sudanese *gurasa*, a thick naan-style pancake served with *dama*, spiced tomato and chicken stew—among many other dishes.

Mango House is not alone. There are similar setups elsewhere—Global Café in Memphis, Tennessee, and Emma's Torch in Brooklyn, New York, to name a couple. The Refugee Food Festival, a global initiative, has established events in New York and San Francisco.

The 56,000-square foot space—formerly a J.C. Penney store—was renovated in 2018 and 2019 by Dr. PJ Parmer, who has devoted his career to providing medical care to refugees.

Siri Tan, who opened Urban Burma—the first Burmese restaurant in Colorado—used to work with refugees but now serves up samosas, soups, noodles, stir-fries, and Burmese tea leaf salad to hungry diners.

"Our culture is very welcoming and hospitable. It's very beautiful," Tan said in an interview with the online *303 Magazine*. "People love to eat. When visitors come, [the Burmese] love to offer food. They love to feed you when you visit their house."

For Tan, the writer concludes, "making meals is all about telling the story of home."

CHAPTER 3

FOOD FADS & TRENDS

A 1952 illustration depicts gathering for a cookout. The "backyard barbecue" became popular with the post–World War II exodus of white families to the suburbs.

SMACKIN' FRESH!

While food is basic to survival, it is also subject to the vagaries of fashion. Some culinary practices have been born of necessity only to return as trends many decades later, while others emerge in response to a single moment in history. Still others are purely whimsical. After all, although a brown paper sack lunch would do just fine, isn't it more fun to eat from a lunch box emblazoned with your favorite superhero?

COFFEE OR TEA?

While much of the world's preferred stimulating beverage is tea, Americans are obsessed with coffee. It wasn't always that way, and the reason goes back to the American Revolution.

▲ "This is the kind of stuff I like to drink, by George, when I hunt bears," Theodore Roosevelt is quoted as saying as he sipped Maxwell House coffee in 1907.

▼ *The Destruction of Tea at Boston Harbor* by Nathaniel Currier depicts the 1773 Boston Tea Party.

English colonists and elsewhere brought the European tea tradition with them. But as momentum for a revolution built, tea came to be seen as a symbol of colonial oppression. Famously there was the Boston Tea Party in 1773, at which a group of colonists dressed as Native Americans dumped a lot of tea into the sea to protest what they saw as extravagant taxes levied by the crown.

That might have been an isolated act, but the protesters were far from alone in their sentiment, their use of tea as a focus for their loathing of the British. Even before he became America's second president and was still an English subject, John Adams wrote to his wife, "Tea must be universally renounced and I must be weaned, and the sooner the better." Many if not most colonists embraced a tea boycott as a means of protest. Tea drinkers were regarded as loyalists. And the alternative was at the ready. John Smith, founder of the Colony of Virginia, had become acquainted with coffee in his travels to Turkey and brought it with him to Jamestown in 1607. By the mid-1600s, coffee had replaced New York City's favorite breakfast drink: beer.

By the time the Revolutionary War ended in 1783, the revolutionaries had been boycotting tea for about a decade and at the same time developed a taste for coffee. Had the colonists not revolted, we likely would still be drinking more tea today.

"Good to the Last Drop"

As America's frontier expanded westward, coffee went along. Settlers and frontiersmen brewed it in open pots over campfires. Union and Confederate soldiers in the Civil War got a daily ration. Many veterans who hadn't been coffee drinkers before the war continued to enjoy it after its end, particularly in the morning.

By the beginning of the 20th century, Americans were drinking coffee more than ever. In 1900, R.W. Hills of Hills Brothers invented vacuum packaging, which kept the coffee fresher longer. Although it's something of a legend that Theodore Roosevelt pronounced Maxwell House "good to the last drop" on a 1907 visit to Andrew Jackson's home in Nashville, he probably didn't say exactly that. A contemporary account in the *Nashville Banner* newspaper did quote him saying, as he sipped a cup of coffee, "This is the kind of stuff I like to drink, by George, when I hunt bears." By the time the United States entered what came to be known as World War I, soldiers drank coffee to stay in drills and on the battlefield. The need to make the drink quickly in the field led to the first instant coffee that could be made simply by adding hot water.

THE DESTRUCTION OF TEA AT BOSTON HARBOR.

Employees of Seattle City Light—the city's public electric power utility—take a coffee break in the 1960s.

Even during the Great Depression, Americans were hesitant to give up the drink. Soup kitchens served the homeless and unemployed coffee and doughnuts, a pairing that lingers to this day. World War II rationing meant American households were limited to one pound of coffee per week.

In 1971, Jerry Baldwin, Gordon Bowker, and Zev Siegel opened the first Starbucks, modeled after coffee-roasting entrepreneur Alfred Peet's business in Berkeley, California—near Pike Place Market in Seattle. By 2019, it had more 14,000 locations across the country, a major player in the "gourmet" coffee revolution that took hold in the 1970s.

Today, coffee is the second most-traded legal commodity after oil. In 2016, about 150 million American adults—about half the total population—drank coffee daily.

Americans drink a little more than one and a half cups daily. More than 65 percent add cream or milk of some kind and/or sugar or other sweeteners. Coffee purists and health advocates frown on such adulterations, saying they can diminish the health benefits of black coffee, one of which is enhanced brain function—so maybe those coffee drinkers who claim to be at less than peak function before they've had their morning coffee are onto something.

A BRIEF HISTORY OF THE COFFEE BREAK

If you enjoy a coffee break or two during your work day, you likely have unions to thank. During the early 20th century, labor unions were successful in pressing factories to implement eight-hour workdays and prescribed rest times. As these mandated respites were instituted, many American workers refueled with coffee. As it happens, it was also about this time—right around 1900—that San Francisco-based Hills Brothers created a process for vacuum-sealing coffee grounds.

And while the coffee break was formally instituted by American businesses in the early 1900s, the citizens of Stoughton, Wisconsin—home of the annual Coffee Break Festival—lay claim to having invented it years before. In 1880, a tobacco warehouse located in the town hired Norwegian immigrant women to steam tobacco leaves. Because the warehouse was close to their homes, they could periodically step out to check on their children, prepare food, and yes, grab a cup of coffee.

EATS ON THE STREETS

Grab-and-go food is sold curbside and on street corners in every large city in the country. It is far from a modern phenomenon. In fact, street food in America goes back to the early 17th century, a tradition spurred by economic necessity, thrift, and convenience.

The range of street foods available in modern America is dizzying—burgers, pizza, tacos, burritos, hot dogs and other sausages, pretzels, falafel, caramel apples, ice cream, chile-and-cheese coated grilled corn, crab cakes, fried clams, kebabs, pastries, loaded fruits, vegan bao buns, warm and fragrant candied nuts. The one food you won't see much of these days was one of the very first street foods sold in the country: oysters.

When Henry Hudson arrived in what is now New York City in 1609, more than 220,000 acres of oyster beds sat on the harbor floor. The Europeans adopted the cooking method of the Lenape, the Indigenous people of the area, who wrapped oysters in seaweed and threw them in a fire to open the shells and cook the tender, succulent meat. Vendors began selling oysters from boats tied along the canals and from pushcarts in the streets.

As the sale of oysters moved indoors and they became something of a more rarified food, pushcarts peddling other types of foods became increasingly popular. Newly arrived migrants turned to selling their favored foods as a way to make ends meet. German vendors offered pretzels and sausages. Italians sold fruits and vegetables. And some of the 2.5 million Ashkenazi Jews who immigrated to New York City between 1880 and 1925 sold kosher dill pickles and knishes, a snack food that consists of a savory filling wrapped in dough and baked or deep fried.

The Street-Food Menu Expands

Elsewhere, the street food phenomenon took on the distinctive flavors of local populations. In early-19th-century Philadelphia, free Black women sold pepper pot soup on the city's streets. Across the country in Los Angeles, Mexican vendors were by the 1870s selling tamales from pushcarts or horse-drawn wagons to those who had come seeking gold or to work on the transcontinental railroad.

"By the 1890s, there were city government-sanctioned attempts to either severely limit or curb these tamaleros altogether, by restricting either their movements or their window for being able to sell," writes Farley Elliott in his 2015 book, *Los Angeles Street Food: A History from Tamaleros to Taco Trucks.*

This effort was spurred by several factors, including pushback from the owners of brick-and-mortar restaurants and the sensationalizing of any "fight, quarrel, or theft committed around the eateries, leading to a perception in polite circles that they weren't safe," wrote Gustavo Arellano in the *Los Angeles Times* in 2011. A typical headline of the times, Arellano writes, included "'Says the Tamale Wagon is a Nursery of Crime.'"

"Most efforts to crack down on the street vendors failed miserably because then, as now," Elliott writes, "Mexican street food simply proved too popular."

▲ Freshly baked soft pretzels served with cheese sauce or mustard are among the most poular and enduring street foods.

▼ A street vendor sells oysters and clams in New York City in 1903. Oysters were one of the first street foods sold in America. They became so popular that by 1820, the oyster beds around Staten Island were depleted.

Although for decades street tacos have certainly been having their moment in America, the most common street fare in the country remains the hot dog. The frankfurter itself is a constant, but the toppings vary. In Seattle, it may be grilled onions, cream cheese, jalapeños, and barbecue sauce. In Pennsylvania and New Jersey, the Texas Tommy is a split and fried or grilled frank served with bacon and plenty of cheese. Chicagoans are unequivocal about their native dog—a steamed or boiled all-beef frank on a poppyseed roll, topped with yellow mustard, bright green pickle relish, onion, tomato, dill pickle, sport peppers, and celery salt.

Street food remains popular because of its accessibility and diversity, offering some patrons traditional dishes and others cutting-edge flavor combinations and creative culinary styles.

The late food writer and chef Anthony Bourdain took it a step further. "Street food, I believe," he told a gathering at the inaugural World Street Food Congress in Singapore in 2013, "is the salvation of the human race."

NIGHT LUNCH WAGONS

Long before modern office workers and festival-goers began frequenting food trucks, nocturnally oriented Americans took sustenance at "night lunch wagons."

These horse-drawn wagons generally served food from 7:30 p.m. to 4:30 a.m., filling a gap left by brick-and-mortar restaurants, most of which closed by 8 p.m.

"Night owls of all classes," declared the *Boston Daily Globe* in 1893, "including workers, idlers, pleasure seekers, tramps and bums" could be found buying sandwiches, pie, and coffee at these mobile enterprises.

There is only one known night lunch wagon in existence today. When Henry Ford was a young engineer at Detroit's Edison Illuminating Company in the 1890s, he is said to have enjoyed a hot dog and coffee from the Owl Night Lunch Wagon nearly every day. In 1927, he purchased it and moved it to historic Greenfield Village, where it remains, often used for beverage service.

Food trucks in New York City in 2014. New York has a long history of street food.

GERMAN SOFT PRETZELS

Today Americans associate chewy, oversize pretzels with street vendors. Salt-studded and served warm with cheese sauce, soft pretzels are a budget-friendly fast food and a festival favorite. In Germany, the country known best for pretzels, this unleavened bread began as a Lenten food to be enjoyed by Catholics when meat, dairy, and eggs were prohibited. They were associated with luck and prosperity and even a symbol of marriage (tying the knot). After the Civil War in America, more and more Germans migrated to the States, becoming one of the largest immigrant groups in the 19th century. They brought their love of lager-style beer and pretzels, a pairing that stuck and is still a beer-hall tradition.

SERVES 10

4 to 4½ cups all-purpose flour

1 teaspoon instant yeast

1½ teaspoons salt

3 tablespoons butter, at room temperature

¼ cup baking soda

Kosher salt or coarse sea salt

Coarse-grain mustard or cheese sauce (optional)

1. In a large mixing bowl, stir together 3 cups of the flour, the yeast, and the 1½ teaspoons salt. Beat in the butter on low speed until it looks like coarse crumbs. Stir in 1¼ cups water on low speed until combined. Beat on high speed for 3 minutes. Beat in as much of the remaining flour as you can on low speed to make a moderately stiff dough, scraping down the sides frequently. (Or stir in as much of the remaining flour as you can with a wooden spoon.) Using the dough hook attachment on the mixer, knead until smooth and elastic, about 8 minutes. (Or turn dough onto a lightly floured surface and knead by hand until smooth and elastic, about 8 minutes, adding additional flour as needed.)

2. Shape dough into a ball and place in a lightly greased bowl. Cover; let rise in a warm place for 45 minutes or until dough is almost double in size. Punch dough down. Turn dough out onto a lightly floured surface. Divide dough into 10 equal portions. Cover and let rest for 15 minutes (this makes dough easier to shape). Line two baking sheets with parchment paper or lightly grease.

3. Working with one portion of dough at a time, roll into an 18-inch-long rope with tapered ends. Shape into a pretzel shape.* Transfer to a prepared baking sheet and continue with remaining dough portions. Cover pretzels with plastic wrap and refrigerate for 2 to 24 hours.

4. Preheat the oven to 425°F. In a large wide pot, bring 3 quarts (12 cups) water to boiling. Add the baking soda to the water, a spoonful at a time. Add three pretzels to the water, adding one at a time. Boil for 1 minute, turning once. Using a slotted spoon remove pretzels from water; drain on paper towels. Place pretzels about 1 inch apart on prepared baking sheets. Repeat with remaining pretzels. Sprinkle pretzels with kosher salt. Bake 16 to 20 minutes or until reddish brown. Transfer to wire racks. Cool completely. If desired, serve with coarse-grain mustard or cheese sauce. Makes 10 pretzels.

*NOTE: To shape pretzels, starting with one 18-inch-long rope of dough, form a loop and cross one end over the other about 4 inches from the ends. Twist once at the crossover point. Fold ends up and over the edge opposite side of the loop. Moisten ends and tuck them under the bottom ends of the loop. Press gently to seal.

THE COMMUNITY COOKBOOK

In a sense, community cookbooks were social media long before there was social media. They raised money and drove sweeping changes in both politics and culture that remain today.

Before there was GoFundMe or Crowdrise—or even door-to-door sales of caramel corn, Thin Mints, and discount coupon books—there was the community cookbook. These cookbooks—coveted by many collectors—were historically compiled by churches, synagogues, Junior Leagues and other women's groups, hospitals, garden clubs, local government, and entities such as police and fire departments as a way to raise funds for a local project or cause.

The first of these charity or community cookbooks was Maria J. Moss' *A Poetical Cook-Book*, published in 1864. A collection of her own recipes, Moss had the idea of using profits from the sale of her book to help pay for the medical care of Union soldiers wounded in the Civil War. The timing of the book's publication was key.

Moss sold her book at a "sanitary fair" being held in Philadelphia the year of its publication. These events were a type of bazaar or exposition that was organized by civilians and held to raise funds for the United States Sanitary Commission and other relief organizations supporting the Union cause.

A Poetical Cook-Book was a resounding success, and other community organizations took notice. Between 1864 and the early 1920s, more than 3,000 community cookbooks were published all over the country.

The advent of these types of books came at a time during which most women had no rights—no vote, no control over money, no place to meet outside the home. Putting together a cookbook for a cause was a way to exert some power.

In the beginning, they tended to be for a specific locale and reflected the cultural makeup of it. *The Landmarks Club Cook Book: A California Collection of the Choicest Recipes from Everywhere*, published in 1903, contained an entire chapter of "the most famous old Californian and Mexican dishes." The Village Improvement Society of Barnstable, Massachusetts, published *What We Cook on Cape Cod* in 1911. Soon enough, though, the cookbook was put to use to effect more widespread change.

Cooking for the Vote

The cause was suffrage for white women. The first, *The Woman Suffrage Cook Book*, published in 1886, was created by a group of progressive women in Massachusetts to raise money for the local suffrage campaign at the Boston Festival and Bazaar. In addition to raising money, the women also hoped the book would raise awareness for their campaign. Many of the contributors were emboldened enough to put the group's agenda right in the titles of their recipes. There was Mrs. Mary F. Curtiss' Rebel Soup, for example, along with Miss M.A. Hill's Mother's Election Cake.

White women have not been the only Americans to create community cookbooks. Black Americans, too, have come together to produce recipe collections that seek to raise funds for projects and programs that uplift their community and celebrate pride in their cooking heritage. In her James Beard Award–winning book, *The Jemima Code: Two Centuries of African American Cookbooks*,

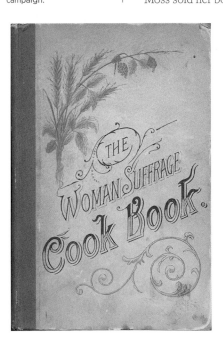

▼ *The Woman Suffrage Cook Book*, written by a group of progressive women in Massachusetts in 1886, was created to raise money for the local suffrage campaign.

Toni Tipton-Martin cites several of these, including *The Chef*, published in 1944 by the City Federation of Colored Women's Clubs of Tulsa, Oklahoma. The proceeds were used to pay off debts incurred to build the Colored Girls' Receiving Home, whose mission was to care for "neglected, abandoned, and delinquent minors at the hands of law enforcement officers" after the massacre of an estimated 300 Black citizens there in May of 1921.

While the golden age of community cookbooks is long over, the works themselves remain valuable relics studied by food historians and other academics and are popular on the rare books market.

"Laid end to end," Barbara Haber, former curator of books at the Schlesinger Library at Harvard University, told *Food & Wine* magazine, "they would form a history of America on a community level."

▲ Since their inception, community cookbooks have been created by towns, churches, civic organizations, police and fire departments, and private entities such as hospitals to raise money for a cause. The first community cookbook published in America, *A Poetical Cook-Book,* in 1864, raised funds to pay for the medical care of Union soldiers wounded in the Civil War.

GOING ONLINE

Printed and bound community cookbooks are rarer than they used to be, but digital or online community cookbooks are proliferating. There was a particular profusion of these types of community books during the coronavirus pandemic that began in 2020.

Baltimore artist and chef Krystal Mack created a digital cookbook called *How to Take Care* that raised money to help victims of domestic violence. The Valley Ranch Islamic Center in Irving, Texas, created a digital and print cookbook of recipes. The Seattle Ladies Choir created a digital community cookbook called *Comfort Food in Challenging Times* that reflects the diversity of the group. Recipes include *upma,* an Indian porridge, and Texas peach cobbler.

"These are cookbooks," Mack told the *New York Times*, "that put the power back into the people's hands."

THE BACKYARD COOKOUT

Postwar prosperity and explosive growth in the suburbs pushed Americans into their backyards to embrace cooking over fire. "There is no doubt about it," declared *House and Garden* in 1951, "America is barbecue minded."

▲ Americans eat 50 billion burgers per year. They—along with hot dogs, steak, and chicken—are the most popular foods to grill in the United States.

▼ Grilling enthusiast George Stephen, who worked at Weber Brothers Metal Works in Palatine, Illinois, welding half-spheres together to make buoys, created the kettle grill in 1952. The original is housed at Weber headquarters.

Cooking outdoors was nothing new in 1950s America. Native people cooked outdoors over open fire, as did generations of Black American pit masters. But the modern backyard cookout owes its popularity to the rise of suburbia.

The post–World War II exodus of white Americans to the suburbs was fueled by a desire to distance themselves from urban living and neighbors of color. Suburbs provided a sense of exclusivity, relaxed privacy, and modernity. Vast new supermarkets offered a bounty of fresh produce and juicy steaks, all under one roof. Suburbanites had houses with pastoral backyards—a perfect spot for a portable charcoal kettle grill, an outdoor hearth for family and friends to gather around.

Postwar affluence meant they could afford to eat a lot of meat—which, after the rationing of the war, they embraced heartily. More money in their wallets also allowed many Americans to travel, and they did—to places such as the Pacific Islands, Mexico, California, Hawai'i, Florida, and the Caribbean. The outdoor living and cooking the warm climates in these places afforded was enchanting. Upon returning home, travelers wanted to re-create a romanticized sense of relaxed living in their own backyards. The tiki boom was born. American suburbanites donned Hawaiian shirts to "barbecue" while sipping on sweet tropical cocktails.

The backyard grilling movement also hastened a modest adjustment in the culinary division of labor. Men donned aprons—some declaring they were "Daddio of the Patio" or saluting "Hail to the Chef"—and embraced their inner caveman, wielding tongs in one hand and a cold beer in the other, serving up hot dogs and burgers while women tended to the ambrosia salad in the comfort of their kitchens.

More Leisure Time, More BBQ

Many Americans had more leisure time after a provision of the 1938 Fair Labor Standards Act mandating a 40-hour workweek went into effect in 1940. That meant weekends and holidays were a perfect time to gather the neighbors in the cul-de-sac. There was a geopolitical component at play, too, an urge to flaunt the American way of life during the Cold War. As such, not firing up the grill on warm-weather holidays such as Memorial Day, Independence Day, or Labor Day was near-unpatriotic. Manufacturers such as Weber produced and marketed cookbooks to men with a primordial urge to cook meat over a hot fire.

There's some disagreement about the origin of the term "barbecue" so it's not surprising there's a distinction between barbecue and grilling. Suburbanites may have said they were barbecuing. They might have split the difference and said they had a barbecue grill. But true barbecue is cooked low and slow, usually but not always over indirect heat. Most of what Ward Cleaver, his neighbors, and their descendants did and are still doing is grilling: cooking fast over a hot, direct fire.

Although the backyard grilling craze slightly altered the gendered division of labor in cooking, it largely negated or at least ignored the African American and Afro-Cuban roots of true barbecue. Enslaved Black cooks had developed many of the recipes and techniques white backyard cooks used and

served their neighbors. Few postwar barbecue cookbooks acknowledged that this type of cooking had a long history among Native Americans and African Americans.

"It takes just one summer season to turn a caveman into an outdoor chef in full 1955 regalia," declared *Look* in "America Bit by the Barbecue Bug" from a July 1955 issue of the magazine. "A man takes over with a few more tools than a primitive hunter: a fire, a stick, or an old fork, some meat. After one bite of a frankfurter he has personally charcoal-charred, he is hooked as a cook. Spurred on by his family, he pores over grill ads, . . . voraciously collects barbecue recipes, and splurges on the fanciest cook-out equipment he can find . . . From little picnics, elaborate barbecues grow—and grow."

▲ The first portable grill made its appearance as early as the 1930s. The advent of a grill that could be folded up and toted to any picnic spot fueled the fire for grilling beyond the backyard.

FUELING THE FIRE

One of the first images that comes to mind when thinking of backyard grilling is the black Weber kettle grill. The design originated with harbor buoys cut in half. With the addition of vents for controlling temperature, the charcoal grill was born.

Of course, these grills needed fuel. In 1919, Edward G. Kingsford helped Henry Ford secure a stretch of timberland to supply Ford's auto plants. Ford, always on the lookout for ways to maximize profits and efficiency at his factories, began to press wood waste into blocks, the first charcoal briquettes. Ford marketed them under his own name, but the product was eventually renamed Kingsford Charcoal.

AMBROSIA SALAD

Named after the food of the Greek and Roman gods, ambrosia teeters between a loosely defined salad and a dessert. In the late 1800s, it appeared in American cookbooks as little more than oranges, usually sweetened, and grated fresh coconut—both luxuries at the time. Ambrosia took hold in the South in the 1900s as a festive and colorful Christmas dessert, which sometimes included fruit juice, pecans, and even sherry. With greater access to fresh fruit and convenience products, ambrosia took on new flavors. A sweet and kitschy ambrosia of colorful miniature marshmallows, mixed fruit, and coconut bound with whipped topping and/or sour cream joined the mix of recipes and became an iconic addition to 1960s backyard barbecues and family potlucks.

SERVES 6 TO 8

- 2 oranges, peeled
- 2 cups bite-size pieces fresh pineapple
- 1 cup pitted sweet cherries or seedless grapes, halved
- ½ cup grated fresh coconut or shredded coconut
- 2 tablespoons cream sherry, orange liqueur, or fresh lemon juice
- 1 to 2 tablespoons honey, agave syrup, or granulated sugar
- ⅓ cup coarsely chopped pecans, toasted

1. Slice the oranges horizontally; halve the slices. Transfer the orange slices and any juice to a large bowl. Add the pineapple, cherries, coconut, sherry, and honey. Cover and chill 30 minutes or up to 24 hours. Before serving, gently stir in the pecans.

MINTED AMBROSIA: Prepare as directed except stir in 2 tablespoons chopped fresh mint along with the pecans.

FLUFFY AMBROSIA: Whip ½ cup heavy cream to soft peaks and gently stir in ½ cup vanilla Greek yogurt. Fold in 1 cup miniature marshmallows (assorted colors, if desired) and 1 teaspoon orange zest. Prepare the Ambrosia as directed except reduce sherry to 1 tablespoon. Stir the whipped cream mixture into the fruit mixture along with the pecans.

TAKING AMERICA TO LUNCH

From a point of practicality to signaling to schoolmates what flavor of pop culture you were into, the metal lunch box has taken its place in the pantheon of American icons.

Historically, midday meals were toted on hunting expeditions or to work or school in everything from animal skins to wicker baskets to brown paper bags. Then, in the early 20th century, the lunch box began to be more than just a means of transporting food.

First, there was an urban-rural split in terms of who needed to pack a lunch to go. In cities, the existence of neighborhood schools meant students usually went home for lunch and back to school. Rural areas had one-room schoolhouses that were often many miles from home, necessitating a portable repast.

Lunch boxes were also an indicator of status. Men who did manual labor such as construction or coal- or mineral-mining carried metal pails that would protect their food in a rough work environment. Children who wanted to emulate their fathers carried their lunches to school in an empty coffee can or loose tobacco tin. Then in 1902, the first commercial kids' metal lunch box came out, decorated to look like a wicker basket with scenes of children playing on it.

Characters arrived in 1935, when Mickey Mouse showed up on a lunch box. Children carried lunch boxes with Disney characters and others from popular entertainment through the 1930s and '40s until 1950, when television—and Aladdin Industries in Nashville, Tennessee—changed everything.

Someone at the company came up with the idea to lacquer their metal meal containers in bright-red paint and emblazon them with TV and radio cowboy Hopalong Cassidy. The company sold 600,000 units the first year. Other companies, including Thermos, which sponsored the "Taking America to Lunch" exhibit of vintage lunch boxes at the National Museum of American History, followed (see opposite).

New Year, New Lunch Box

Fixing a metal lunch box with a pop-culture character did more than just boost onetime sales. Despite the fact that they were nearly indestructible, parents could be persuaded to frequently trade them in for the most current obsession. That included Roy Rogers, Barbie, Daniel Boone, the Beatles, *Lost in Space,* the Harlem Globetrotters, Bruce Lee, *Star Wars*, *Sesame Street*, the Muppets, Johnathan Livingston Seagull, the rock band KISS, Cracker Jack, Pac-Man, and Indiana Jones, to name only a fraction of the designs over the years.

The lunch boxes weren't just colorful and functional. They also reflected kids' interests and personalities. In "The History of the Lunch Box" from an August 2012 article for *Smithsonian Magazine*, Lisa Bramen recounts the importance of choosing the perfect lunch box each back-to-school season growing up in the 1970s.

"It had to last all year, if not longer, and it was a personal billboard, much like the concert T-shirt was to older kids, that would tell my classmates what I

▼ The proliferation of television had tremendous impact on the popularity of novelty lunch boxes. One featuring TV and radio cowboy Hopalong Cassidy sold 600,000 units when it debuted in 1950.

was into," she writes. "The message I hoped to get across was: 'Hey, I dig Snoopy. Wanna be friends?'"

Pressed-tin lunch boxes began to fade in the 1980s as plastic lunch boxes—lighter, cheaper, but less durable—began squeezing them out. Some companies also made them out of vinyl, essentially cardboard wrapped in shower curtain–like material. By the '80s, backpacks were fully integrated into the school-supply checklist, and metal lunch boxes were not well suited to them. Smaller, softer lunch boxes fit more readily and have since for the most part supplanted them.

More recently, compartmentalized Bento boxes from Japan and tiered tiffin containers from India have become wildly popular for both their practicality and aesthetically pleasing designs.

And while the metal lunch box is largely out of use, collecting vintage versions has long been popular. As with any collectible, the condition of the lunch box matters. But personal touches—such as some wear and tear or a child's name scribbled or inscribed on it—increases the value for some.

When curators from the NMAH got in contact with Allen Woodall, founder of The Lunchbox Museum in Columbus, Georgia, and author of *The Illustrated Encyclopedia of Metal Lunch Boxes,* in the process of building its lunch box exhibit, "They wanted them as they were used," Woodall told the *Washington Post* in 2011, "not new."

THE LUNCHBOX MUSEUM

The Lunchbox Museum in Columbus, Georgia, is home to what's called the largest lunch box collection in the world. Founder Allen Woodall began collecting vintage lunch boxes in the 1990s after he inherited a small collection from a friend who had died. In less than four years, he amassed more than 1,000 lunch boxes. Today, that number is about 3,500—and in some cases, their matching Thermoses—and spans a period of about 35 years.

When the Smithsonian's National Museum of American History began creating the "Taking America to Lunch" exhibit, curators acquired several lunch boxes from The Lunchbox Museum. The selection from various sources in the small display ranges from the 1890s to the 1980s.

"No meal," reads an introduction to the exhibit, "has received more cultural attention to its transport than our lunch."

EATING BETTER

Food was central to the counterculture of the 1960s. The nut loaves and barbecued soybeans embraced by followers of the movement may no longer be mainstays, but many foods are—and the revolution they started continues to impact how we eat today.

Two decades after the end of World War II, industrial innovations had dramatically changed the American diet. All manner of processed foods—canned and powdered soups and juices, dehydrated coffee, cake mixes, processed cheese, and Wonder Bread—flooded the American food scene.

"The food Americans were eating in the mid-1960s resembled nothing that any civilization on Earth had ever eaten before," writes Jonathan Kauffman in his 2018 book, *Hippie Food: How Back-to-the-Landers, Longhairs, and Revolutionaries Changed the Way We Eat.*

For peaceniks and revolutionaries, rejecting the foods of their parents was one piece of the puzzle in rejecting their values and The Man in general—the economic system, racial violence and inequality, sexual mores, and war.

"Hippie food was a rejection of industrialized food as much as it was an embrace of new ingredients and new flavors," writes Kauffman. "Eating brown rice was a political act, just as wearing your hair long or refusing to shave your armpits could subject you to ridicule and harassment."

The food counterculture first took hold in Southern California and the Bay area. It had its roots in a practice touted by George Ohsawa, who had adopted a diet that consisted almost entirely of brown rice, tamari, tofu, and vegetables in his native Japan in the early 20th century and had seen his tuberculosis disappear. Ohsawa—who had no medical training—wrote several books on the relationship between Eastern spirituality, diet, and health, including the 1960 *Zen Macrobiotics: The Art of Rejuvenation and Longevity.* Enlightened eaters believed that eating whole foods could be restorative and re-establish the yin-yang balance in mind and body.

Drugs—another aspect of rejecting the establishment—played a role too. Hippies taking a break from pot would go on a miso soup and brown rice diet to cleanse body and mind. It wasn't uncommon to go vegetarian after using LSD and feeling a sense of connection with the universe that made the idea of eating animals repulsive.

The environmental movement, which would lead to the establishment of the Environmental Protection Agency in the 1970s, was also gaining ground in the late 1960s. Rachel Carson's *Silent Spring* came out in 1964 and woke the nation up to the perils of pesticides.

The back-to-the-land movement was bolstered by this. Young people, most of them white and middle class, began moving from cities to rural areas in huge numbers—some to communes, others to single-family farmsteads. In fact, America's rural population grew by 10 percent during the 1970s. These nascent farmers grew food for themselves—and some grew organic produce for local restaurants, the beginnings of what would come to be called the farm-to-table movement.

Alice Waters opened what could be called the first farm-to-table restaurant in the country, Chez Panisse, in 1971 in Berkeley, California. In 1973, the California Certified Organic Farmers was formed. Americans from all walks of life started demanding to know more about where their food came from.

Fast Food to Slow Food

This desire continues to impact other food movements that followed. The slow food and

▲ Tofu gained popularity in the U.S. during the counterculture movement and is now widely available.

▼ At the time it was published in 1965, George Ohsawa's book was considered the primer of the macrobiotic philosophy. The preface suggests that the volume "be considered as the guidebook whose aim is happiness through health through nutrition."

zen macro- biotics

the philosophy of oriental medicine volume one

georges ohsawa

good food movements were an outgrowth of this. Followers of countercultures believed food should be local, prepared with respect, and appreciated—a far cry from gobbling down french fries from a drive-through in your car.

Americans have in many ways embraced this philosophy. In 2010, the Healthy Hunger-Free Kids Act established the USDA Farm to School Program to encourage school districts to use locally produced food for meals served through the National School Lunch and School Breakfast Programs. Increasingly, Americans source their food through farmers markets—between 1994 and 2014, the number of farmers markets grew from 1,700 to 8,250—CSAs (community-supported agriculture), and community gardens.

The legacy of the food counterculture remains—foods such as organic chard, granola, yogurt, tofu, tempeh, hummus, whole wheat bread, and brown rice have become mainstream members of the American diet.

GROWING IN DETROIT

In the early 2000s, the city of Detroit was an example of food apartheid, where systemic disinvestment in access to nutrient-dense, affordable, and culturally appropriate foods had devasating consequences. Convenience stores and fast-food restaurants did not offer the fresh fruits and vegetables needed by its citizens, 80 percent of whom are Black, resulting in serious health problems including diabetes, obesity, and high cholesterol. In 2006, activist Malik Yakini established the Detroit Black Community Food Security Network as a way to work for food justice. One outgrowth was the D-Town Farm, a community farm that started on a ¼ acre, and has now grown to 7 acres.

Today, the city has a vibrant agriculture scene. In 2020, Keep Growing Detroit helped 26,935 residents grow almost a half-million pounds of produce.

"My meals are not the same [since starting a garden]," one gardener told Michigan State University researchers in a report on the impact of gardening on their well-being.

▼ Volunteers plant tomatoes at D-Town Farm, a 7-acre farm in Detroit's Rouge Park.

HOMEMADE GRANOLA

While granola's true roots harken back to the cereal created in the 1800s by Sylvester Graham and John Harvey Kellogg, its defining era was the late 1960s and '70s. In 1969, Hugh Romney of the Hog Farm Collective helped feed the hordes of concert-goers at Woodstock by distributing cups of organic cereal that could easily be passed through the crowd. The popularity of this all-natural, easy-to-replicate cereal eventually spread across the nation as a snack and breakfast food, but it was also embraced as a symbol of rebellious counterculture. Seen as the opposite of the industrial food products of the 1950s, "granola" even became an adjective for environmental activists, such as Euell Gibbons, who espoused liberal political views and advocated for healthier foods.

**MAKES ABOUT 7 CUPS
(TWELVE, ½-CUP SERVINGS)**

- ⅓ cup packed brown sugar or honey
- ¼ cup maple syrup or honey
- ¼ cup butter or coconut oil
- 1 teaspoon salt
- 1 teaspoon ground cinnamon
- ½ teaspoon ground ginger
- 4 cups old-fashioned rolled oats
- 1 cup coarsely chopped pecans, almonds, walnuts, and/or hazelnuts
- 1 tablespoon orange zest (optional)
- ¼ cup raw pumpkin seeds (pepitas)
- ½ cup flaked unsweetened shredded coconut (optional)
- 1 cup dried fruit, such as raisins, dried cherries, dried cranberries, and/or chopped dried apricots or apples
- ¼ cup raw sunflower seeds and/or 1 tablespoon ground flaxseed or chia seeds

1. Preheat the oven to 300°F. Line a 15×10×1-inch baking pan with parchment paper or foil.

2. In a large saucepan, combine the brown sugar, maple syrup, butter, salt, cinnamon, and ginger. Bring to boiling, stirring frequently. Remove from heat. Stir in the oats, nuts, and if using, the orange zest. Spread the mixture on the prepared pan.

3. Bake 15 minutes. Remove from oven and stir in the pumpkin seeds and, if using, the coconut. Bake 10 minutes more. Stir in the dried fruit and sunflower seeds. Bake 5 to 8 minutes more or until the oats are golden brown. Carefully transfer the parchment with the granola to a cooling rack and cool completely.

THE RISE OF AMERICAN WINE

From the time the first Europeans arrived in North America, there was a desire to produce wines that would rival those of Europe. It took more than 300 years, but that dream is now a solid reality.

In 1976, a young Brit named Steven Spurrier, who owned the only English-speaking wine shop in Paris at the time, invited nine of the most respected French wine experts of the day to a blind tasting. American wine had long been considered inferior to French wine and not infrequently without justification. But Spurrier was impressed with the wines coming out of California and included several of its Cabernet Sauvignons and Chardonnays in the tasting.

In a head-snapping outcome, the winning wines were both American—a 1973 Cabernet from Stag's Leap Wine Cellars and a 1973 Château Montelena Chardonnay, both from the Napa Valley. The Judgment of Paris, as it came to be called, was a seminal moment in the story of the American wine industry. American wine had at last won long-sought approbation.

The history of wine in the United States did not begin in 1976, however. Chemical residue on pottery shards recently found at an archaelogical site in central Texas suggest Indigenous people were making grape wine more than 500 years ago. According to the Florida Department of Agriculture, Spanish colonizers arrived there in the early 16th century and made wine from a local variety of the Muscadine grape. Spanish friars made it at missions in modern-day California, with the first vineyards planted in San Diego in the mid-18th century. Their first plantings were Mission grapes brought from Spain, which soon took to the sandy soil and bore fruit. Winemaking eventually flourished wherever soils and climate made it possible to reliably grow wine grapes.

The Seeds of an Industry Are Planted

Nicholas Longworth started America's first commercially successful winery in Ohio in 1830, using the native Catawba grape to make the first American sparkling wine. Brotherhood Winery in New York lays claim to America's oldest continually operating winery, dating to 1839.

Throughout the 19th century, wineries continued to proliferate throughout the country, but so did a growing temperance movement. Prohibition stopped most commercial wineries cold—and they wouldn't recover for decades after it ended.

After Prohibition was repealed in 1933, the viticulture and enology programs at the University of California that had been running since 1875 were reinstated in a new wine research program at UC-Davis, now considered to be one of the top facilities on the subject in the world.

In 1938, the California Wine Advisory Board was formed to promote the consumption of wine by Americans, who were much more inclined toward beer, spirits, or cocktails, or who still recalled the highly alcoholic and sweet wines produced illegally or at home during Prohibition. A 1950s-era ad from the board touting the "California Way of Entertaining!" depicts a small gathering of smartly dressed people gathered around a potluck meal, with glasses of Sauternes on the side. "At a dinner like this you have as much fun as your guests!" the ad reads. "... So easily, too. Because all you do is cool a bottle of wine and pour good, bright glassfuls for everyone."

The campaign worked. Between 1965 and 1975, Americans increased their wine consumption by

▲ A 1973 Cabernet Sauvignon wine produced by Warren Winiarski of Stag's Leap Wine Cellars, in Napa, California, outranked some of France's best Bordeaux at a blind tasting held in Paris in 1976. It was a seminal moment in the story of the American wine industry.

▼ Robert Mondavi established his namesake winery in 1966 with a vision to create Napa Valley wines that would bring worldwide recognition to the wines of California's Napa Valley.

nearly 150 percent. The health-food movement had an impact on wine consumption. Young

people on college campuses, in particular, drank it in part because it was natural and of the earth.

The growth of the industry would not have been possible without the contributions of migrant families from Mexico, who since the 1950s planted, tended, and harvested the grapes and worked in the cellars. By the 1990s, many had moved from laborers to winemakers or vineyard owners, such as the Robledo family of Sonoma County.

It was during this period, the second half of the 20th century, that American wine came of age. Idealists and dreamers from all over the country moved to California and wound up sparking a revolution in the world of wine.

One of them was Warren Winiarski, who in 1964 left a job teaching political philosophy at the University of Chicago and settled in the Napa Valley. He learned the winemaking business from Robert Mondavi and took courses through UC-Davis. In 1969, he bought 35 acres of land and planted Cabernet Sauvignon grapes. The wine he made from his second crop—harvested in 1973—was the one that won the Judgment of Paris.

Over the years, the justifiable pride in the quality and diversity of American wines led Americans to make the drink a little more democratic and a little less elitist. Even the names of some of them—Seven Deadly Zins, Fog Monster, Marilyn Merlot, Skuttlebutt—make wine more approachable.

In his 1870 book, *The Cultivation of the Native Grape, and Manufacture of American Wines*, George Husmann, considered to be the "Father of the Missouri Grape Industry," wrote: "I firmly believe that this continent is destined to be the greatest wine-producing country in the world; and that the time is not far distant when wine, the most wholesome and purest of all stimulating drinks, will be within the reach of the common laborer."

◀ This poster produced in 1965 was one in a series based on original artwork by Amado Gonzalez, a Mexican-born artist who taught at San Francisco's City College.

"DUSTY MUSHROOM" AND "WET DOG"

The aroma, flavor, and mouthfeel (texture) of wine is impacted by the variety of the grape, the climate and soil in which it is grown—known as *terroir*—when it is harvested, the yeast used, and the method and duration of fermentation and aging. In 1984, sensory scientist Ann C. Noble created a "wine wheel" of terminology used to describe the flavor and aroma notes in a particular wine. They include "tar," "butterscotch," "cut green grass," "cooked cabbage," and yes, "wet dog/wet wool." Originally intended for her colleagues at the University of California-Davis, it is now used by wine enthusiasts all over the world.

AMERICA LOVES SUSHI

Propelled by an economic boom in Japan and bolstered by American hipster culture, what started as a street snack almost 200 years ago is now as easy to get as a hamburger or hot dog.

▼ Sometime between 1964 and 1966, a Japanese importer named Noritoshi Kanai opened Kawafuku, considered to be the country's first real sushi bar, in Los Angeles' Little Tokyo.

Strictly speaking, "sushi" refers not to the raw fish, but rather to the rice seasoned with vinegar, salt, and a bit of sugar. The concept of sushi came from China, where a 4th-century cookbook mentions salted fish being placed in cooked rice to undergo a fermentation process that helped preserve the fish. It likely made its way to Japan in the 9th century. By the 15th century, Japanese cooks had discovered that the fish didn't need to be fully fermented to taste good. A new form of sushi—*mama-nare zushi*, or raw sushi—was created. It wasn't fully raw, though, until the early 19th century, when Hanaya Yohei set up a sushi stall along the Sumida River in the city of Edo, now Tokyo. From it, he served what is essentially modern sushi—freshly cooked rice seasoned with vinegar and salt and hand-pressed with a thin slice of fresh fish from the bay. The fish was so fresh, it didn't need to be fermented. By the early 20th century, there were hundreds of sushi carts around Tokyo. By the 1950s, sushi was almost always served indoors.

It is a sign of how enthusiastically America has embraced sushi that this Japanese specialty can now be found at the grab-and-go refrigerated sections of pharmacies and at grocery stores next to containers of potato salad.

It got to be ubiquitous in a relatively short window of time. Although sushi was trendy among the monied class in the early 20th century, it didn't really start to proliferate until the mid-1960s. Around that time, Japan began a period of economic growth that lasted through the 1980s, necessitating travel—often globally, to places such as the United States—by Japanese businessmen.

In "The History of Sushi in America," the Michelin Guide pins the creation of the modern American sushi bar to a single man. Sometime in the years between 1964 and 1966, a Japanese importer named Noritoshi Kanai opened Kawafuku in the Little Tokyo section of Los Angeles. He hired master sushi chef Shigeo Saito to work the knife and Saito's wife to serve. The menu was primarily local seafood such as sea urchin, abalone, mackerel, and tuna, and everything was made fresh as it was ordered by customers sitting at a counter. "It was a real sushi bar," the Michelin writer notes, "—a phrase Kanai claimed to have coined."

From California to Everywhere

At first, Kawafuku catered to Japanese and American businessmen on expense accounts, but it quickly became a sensation. More sushi restaurants opened in the neighborhood, including Tokyo Kaikan, which had an entirely different feel from the mom-and-pop-style Kawafuku. It could seat about 300 people in its main dining room, and in addition to sushi had sections of the restaurant dedicated to tempura and teppanyaki. It even had an upstairs disco, Tokyo a-Go-Go.

Other sushi spots began popping up outside the neighborhood—one right next to the 20th Century Fox studio. Los Angeles was a perfect place for sushi's debut in America. The food was new, hip, and thought to be reasonably healthy. Celebrities flocked for sushi and made restaurants buzzworthy.

Once sushi was relatively established, innovation followed. One of the first—and still one of the most popular—twists on traditional Japanese sushi was the California roll, which Tokyo Kaikan claims as having created. The story goes that chef Ichiro Mashita could not get fatty tuna belly—which was then a seasonal fish—and so substituted rich, fatty avocado, and crab for the tuna to give it the flavor of the sea. The roll later evolved to include the nori tucked inside, presumably to hide the seaweed—which could be a challenging ingredient to some less-adventuresome diners. The California roll—absent of raw fish—is often the first type of sushi many Americans try.

The most traditional Japanese sushi chefs may have been horrified to see sushi amended with ingredients like mayonnaise and sesame seeds, but in recent years American sushi has embraced a more neotraditional approach, emphasizing quality ingredients over fancy presentation. Chefs say educating diners is key—the virtues of wild versus farmed fish, types of rice, the difference between warm-water and cold-water fish. Some of those American innovations have even made their way across the Pacific to the sushi houses of Japan.

Barely more than 20 years after the end of World War II, sushi—which had been a strictly defined cuisine for a thousand years or more in the Japanese archipelago—came to America and was quickly adopted, adapted, and embraced.

A LEXICON OF SUSHI

Although there are many more regional and seasonal sushi styles available in Japan and at the highest-end sushi houses here, these are the most common types you will find in the United States:

Norimaki: Often shortened to "maki," this is the rolled sushi filled with rice, fish, and/or vegetables that is cut into bite-size pieces. "Nori" is the toasted seaweed sheet used to wrap in the ingredients and "maki" means "to roll."

Gunkan maki: Also a rolled or wrapped style of sushi, this is more oval in shape—its name translates to "battleship" or "warship," for its resemblance to a tiny ship. Space is left on the top of each piece for toppings such as roe, uni (sea urchin), and tuna belly with green onion.

Nigiri: This is sushi at its simplest—at least in shape—and likely its original form. A hand-pressed cylinder of rice topped with a piece of raw fish, vegetables, omelet, or tofu. A simple brush of marinade or a garnish such as spring onions or chives is added.

Temaki: A cone-shape sushi filled with rice, fish, and/or vegetables and greens.

FOOD FADS IN AMERICA

In the world of food—as in other arenas of American culture—we're always chasing after the hot new thing. Some food fads come and go in a flash, others arrive and stay for good—but they're almost always everywhere.

Long before the phrase "going viral" meant what it means in the age of the internet, there were food fads. In the view of journalist Michael Pollan, Americans are particularly apt to respond to them because of our history as a nation of immigrants—exposure to an array of culinary traditions creates an openness to new things. "As a relatively new nation drawn from many different immigrant populations, each with its own culture of food, we Americans find ourselves without a strong, stable culinary tradition to guide us," he wrote in an October 2004 article in the *New York Times*.

Most food fads are linked to one of three things (or a combination)—migrations of people, new technologies, and corporate marketing strategies.

Consider one of the country's longest-running food fads: gelatin salads. While jellied dishes date back to medieval Europe, it was around the turn of the 20th century when a cough-syrup maker patented the brand name "Jell-O" when Americans began to fall hard for the jiggly stuff. In 1905, a Mrs. John Cooke of New Castle, Pennsylvania, won a cooking contest sponsored by Knox with her "Perfection Salad," an aspic flecked with finely chopped cabbage, celery, and red pepper.

In 1913, inventor Fred W. Wolf Jr. of Fort Wayne, Indiana, introduced the first refrigerator for home use—an insulated unit mounted on top of an icebox. The following year, Nathaniel B. Wales of Detroit introduced a unit that ran on electrical power. Alfred Messor added a compressor in 1916, and in 1918, the Guardian Frigerator Company of Fort Wayne (later Frigidaire) bought the idea and began mass producing refrigerators for domestic use.

With the proliferation of home refrigeration, gelatin salads hit a zenith in the 1930s that lasted for decades. A recipe for Molded Mayonnaise Salad from "Correct Salads for All Occasions," published in 1931 by the General Foods Corporation, included lemon Jell-O, vinegar, American cheese, cayenne pepper, and salt. By the 1980s, gelatin salads had fallen out of favor, but they can still be found at potlucks, church suppers, and meals at home in communities across the country.

In the 2010s, photographer Victoria Belanger—tapping into the whimsical nature of gelatin—started a blog called The Jell-O Mold Mistress of Brooklyn, on which she featured modern, multicolor, and multilayered renderings in gelatin.

From Fondue to Pumpkin Spice Pringles

By the 1970s, Julia Child had been showing viewers how to make French classics on television for nearly a decade, and over that period Americans took an interest in what was then called "continental cuisine," a kind of catchall phrase referring to foods whose origins were in Europe. That decade saw the popularity of fondue first, followed by quiche—the rich French egg-and-cheese tart.

At the 1939 and 1964 World's Fairs in New York, the Swiss Pavilion featured fondue, the communally enjoyed dish consisting of bread dipped in melted cheese and meat cooked in hot oil over an open flame. By the late 1960s and into the 1970s, fondue pots were flying off store shelves. And while fondue was eventually edged out by quiche as the decade's top food trend, the fondue fad returned in the 1990s and again in the 2010s.

Child made quiche Lorraine in an episode of *The French Chef* that aired in 1963, the first year of the program. By the 1970s, writes Candy Sagon in

Food fads in America have different types of origins. While some, such as the Cronut, above, are a mash-up of food items, others—such as fondue, below—reflect a particular cultural tradition that became trendy.

▲ With the proliferation of home refrigeration in the 1930s, gelatin salads hit a zenith that lasted for decades. By the 1980s, they'd fallen out of favor, but can still be found at potlucks in pockets of the country.

a November 1995 article in the *Los Angeles Times*, "quiche was the white three-piece suit of the food world. It was every home cook's solution for what to serve for brunch and every cafe's solution for what to pair with a salad for the daily lunch special. It was omnipresent."

Ubiquity—temporary or long-term—tends to be an identifying quality of the food fad. In the 1980s, it was blackened anything—popularized by New Orleans chef Paul Prudhomme—and ranch dressing. In the 1990s, it was pesto, sun-dried tomatoes, and hot sauce; pumpkin spice (Twinkies, Peeps, Pringles, and even hummus) and bacon flavor (vodka, coffee, olive oil, soda, and coffee syrup) in the early 2000s; and kale and avocado toast in the 2010s.

Some fads are dishes, others ingredients, and still others, such as molecular gastronomy—the fusing of science and food to create completely new iterations of an ingredient or dish, such as carrot air—are methods. Some are serious, others silly, some are ridiculous, others sublime—but in the United States, the land of immigrants and migrants, they are likely to always be part of our culinary history.

THE MASH-UP CRAZE

It didn't start with the Cronut, but the creation of a cross between a croissant and a donut by New York City pastry chef Dominique Ansel in 2013 certainly set off a trend of food mash-ups on all points of the culinary spectrum. This was especially true within the fast-food industry, which is ever-evolving to chase the eyeballs, appetites, and wallets of millions of Americans. *Time* magazine declared the Cronut one of the best inventions of the year in 2013—the same year Keizo Shimamoto debuted his ramen burger, a shoyu-glazed beef patty between two crispy-on-the-outside, chewy-on-the-inside ramen buns at an outdoor food market in Brooklyn, New York. You can still buy those two items—and the sushi burritos offered up by San Francisco's Sushirrito—but there is a long list of shock-and-awe fast-food mash-ups that came and went in fairly rapid succession, including Dunkin's Glazed Donut Breakfast Sandwich (2013), Taco Bell's Taco Waffles (2014), Pizza Hut's pizza with a hot dog-stuffed crust (2015), and KFC's Double Down Dog—a hot dog with a fried chicken breast patty bun (2015).

FAD DIETS

Each year, 45 million Americans go on a diet, and while the end goal of any given diet may be the same, the path to get there can look vastly different depending on the latest conventional wisdom.

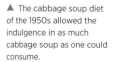

▲ The cabbage soup diet of the 1950s allowed the indulgence in as much cabbage soup as one could consume.

▼ Model Pat Ogden endures the rigors of the Wooden Barrel Massager, reputed to reduce fat in the buttocks and thighs, at a New York "slenderizing salon" in November 1940.

America seems to undergo dietary whiplash every decade or so, and it has been that way since the inception of dieting in the 19th century.

"What's striking is just how little it takes to set off one of these applecart-toppling nutritional swings in America," writes Michael Pollan in "Our National Eating Disorder," in a 2004 issue of *The New York Times Magazine.* "A scientific study, a new government guideline, a lone crackpot with a medical degree can alter this nation's diet overnight."

Dieting in America began in earnest in the 1830s, with the emergence of Sylvester Graham, a Presbyterian minister who was strident about the hazards of eating processed flours and who developed one made from the entire wheat germ, not just the endosperm.

Over the decades—and centuries that followed—all manner of food and fitness regimens and pills, potions, and pastes have been touted as the magic bullet to beauty, fitness, and svelteness. Adherents to various diets have engaged in floor rolling—literally rolling on the floor— taken baths with thinning salts, subsisted on little else but bananas and skim milk, and voluntarily underwent yogurt enemas.

In 1863, English undertaker William Banting went on a low-carb diet to lose weight and wrote about it in his booklet, "Letter on Corpulence." It became so popular in both the U.K. and America that his name became a verb, as in the response to, "Would you like a piece of cake?" was, "No, thank you, I'm Banting."

The early 20th century saw the advent of the "reducing salon," at which clients would be enveloped between two sets of rollers that would—through the power of electricity—squeeze up and down the body up to 80 times per minute.

Yogurt, Anyone?

In the 1920s, John Harvey Kellogg—at what Pollan calls his "legendarily nutty sanitarium" in Battle Creek, Michigan—prescribed an all-grape diet and "a two-fronted assault on his patients' alimentary canals, introducing quantities of Bulgarian yogurt at both ends."

The following decades saw the rise of the grapefruit diet (1930s), which promised weight loss if a grapefruit was eaten at each meal; the cabbage soup diet (1950s), which allowed the indulgence in as much cabbage soup as one could consume; and the macrobiotic diet (1960s), based on a Japanese diet of soy, brown rice, and vegetables.

Weight Watchers, which came along in 1961, encouraged Americans to eschew "dieting" and embrace "eating management," but the faddists did not disappear entirely. By the end of the decade, the 3-Way Diet Program claimed to "LITERALLY MELT THE FAT OFF YOUR BODY LIKE A BLOWTORCH WOULD MELT BUTTER."

In 1972, Robert Atkins, a cardiologist, published *Dr. Atkins' Diet Revolution* and in 2002, a revised version. The various editions have sold more than 15 million copies. By keeping carb intake at an absolute minimum, dieters send the body into ketosis, a state in which it uses up fat as a fuel source. Apples are a no, but bacon is a go.

The 1980s saw the rise of the Beverly Hills Diet, based on the idea that certain foods should be combined and others shouldn't. Fruit should only be eaten by itself, and pineapple in particular helps weight loss. Champagne is neutral and can be sipped with everything. In the era from the 1980s to the turn of the 21st century, the public whipsawed from thinking all fats were bad and carbs were good to fleeing carbs and embracing fat. In the 1990s, everyone was talking about the Mediterranean diet, based on healthy fats such as olive oil, whole grains, lean meats and fish, and lots of fresh vegetables. It is an ancient way of eating that nutritionists endorse to this day.

The remainder of the 20th century and beginning of the 21st saw the Zone Diet, Sugar Busters Diet, raw foods, the South Beach diet, Paleo diet, and Primal diet.

While Americans are not likely to return to bathing in thinning salts or having their bodies squeezed between electric rollers again any time soon, there are themes that come around again and again. The Atkins diet, Banting diet, Inuit diet of the 1920s, the keto diet, and the 1960s' Drinking Man's Diet—which held that you could freely indulge in steak slathered in Bearnaise, Roquefort-topped salads, and dry martinis as long as you didn't accompany them with a baked potato—are variations on a theme.

And while on the surface, fad diets appear to be about "health" or a desire to achieve physical perfection—or at least get as close to it as we can—Adrienne Rose Bitar, author of *Diet and the Disease of Civilization*, thinks there might be more to it than that.

"Diets," she writes, "stand in for the bigger debate about history, salvation, money, power, . . . and all the other ideas that make the world worth thinking about."

▶ On the Atkins diet—and all of those low-carb diets like it, such as keto, Paleo, and Primal diets—apples are a no, but bacon is a go.

THE GREAT MASTICATOR

At the turn of the 20th century, Horace Fletcher—an artist, writer, importer, and opera house manager who had no medical background—promoted the chewing of each bite of food at least 100 times until liquefied, then spitting out any remaining solids. The theory was that the bowel was key to good health and weight control, and that infrequent defecation led to both. He was pleased to say he only eliminated once every two weeks or so and that the output was just 2 to 4 ounces. He also declared it to be not in the least bit offensive—no more than "moist clay" and that it had "no more odour than a hot biscuit." He reportedly carried a sample at all times to prove it.

"Fletcherism," as it came to be known, became a fashionable pastime, and Fletcher, who came to be called The Great Masticator, had success in managing his own weight and health using the method. At age 40, he weighed 217 pounds and had been refused life insurance. By his mid-50s, he was reportedly doing exercises with the strength and agility of a man half his age. "Nature," he said, "will castigate those who don't masticate."

SNACKING IN AMERICA

Salt, sugar, fat, carbs. The cravings for these have, along with innovations in manufacturing, created a nation of snackers amid ever-growing concerns about the impacts of snack foods on health.

▲ Cracker Jack—a snack of molasses-flavored, caramel-coated peanuts and popcorn—was introduced at the 1893 Columbian Exposition in Chicago.

▼ The "Oreo Biscuit" was created by the National Biscuit Company (now Nabisco) in 1912. It is now the country's best-selling cookie.

Step into any supermarket, hardware store, gas station, or pharmacy and you will be presented with a staggering array of sweet and salty snacks—whole aisles devoted to them.

One of the country's favorite snacks was also one of its first. By the mid-19th century, popcorn was a popular snack in America, but it didn't become iconic until late in the century, when Charles Cretors, a Chicago candy-store owner, tinkered with an industrial peanut roaster and turned it into a steam-powered machine that could both roast nuts and pop corn—in large quantities and right in the seasonings. Cretors patented his commercial corn-popping machine, and by the turn of the 20th century, he was selling his popcorn from a large horse-drawn wagon. The national obsession with popcorn was set into motion.

Popcorn is at the center of one of the most long-lived commercially produced snacks in America—Cracker Jack, which was introduced at the 1893 Columbian Exposition in Chicago and was a huge hit.

The 1904 St. Louis World's Fair—like the Chicago exposition that preceded it—popularized what have become some of America's favorite and most enduring snacks. Attendees enjoyed hamburgers, hot dogs, Dr Pepper, cotton candy, and ice cream served in crispy waffle cones.

The "Oreo Biscuit" was created by the National Biscuit Company (now Nabisco) in 1912. Initially sold in jars for 25 cents per pound, Oreos are now the country's best-selling cookie. Two years later, in 1914, Philadelphia's Tasty Baking Company introduced individually wrapped single-serving cakes.

The company's Tastykakes proved U.S. customers enjoyed ready-to-eat sweet treats that included baked goods, yes, but also came to include candy bars. A candy bar boom in the 1920s saw the debut of Reese's Peanut Butter Cups, Butterfinger, Mounds, Baby Ruth, Mr. Goodbar, and many others. The deepening economic depression of the 1930s didn't slow the country's desire for novel snacks. Twinkies, Snickers, and Three Musketeers were all introduced that decade, as were Lay's potato chips and Fritos corn chips, which launched a snack empire.

The Birth of a Snack Empire

In 1912, José Bartolomé Martínez—known as the Corn King of San Antonio, Texas—started selling commercially produced corn tortilla chips. Competitors followed, including C. Elmer Doolin, who in 1932 bought a recipe and developed a device for extruding masa into strips and the process for frying them. He used a factory line to make his Fritos, named after a Mexican street food called fritas. Eventually the company became Frito-Lay and started producing "authentic" corn tortilla chips under the name Tostitos. In 1948, Doolin invented Cheetos and fingers all over America began turning orange with the dusty stuff.

America's involvement in World War II introduced what is now, according to a 2018 survey by YouGov, the most popular candy in the country—M&Ms. In 1941, Mars began manufacturing them to fill the need for heat-resistant chocolate to send to soldiers overseas.

By the 1950s, the rise of the suburbs and the postwar economic boom hastened the rapid growth of the industry, fueled by innovations in manufacturing. In 1952, Kraft Foods debuted Cheez Whiz, marketed as a time-saver that didn't require slicing or grating. One ad of the era touted the many "quick cheese tricks" that could be performed with it. Another proclaimed that "America's wonderful crackers are extra good when you Cheez Whiz 'em!"

In the 1960s, both Pop-Tarts and Pringles came on line—the latter thanks to researchers working for Procter & Gamble who mixed dehydrated potatoes with flour and water to create a crunchy snack with a long shelf life that was also uniform in size, texture, and shape—which meant that they could be stacked in cans, allowing them to be shipped with minimal breakage.

By the 1980s, food manufacturers were making nodding concessions to the health-food movement that took hold in the 1960s. The low-fat craze that began in that decade spawned the introduction from Kraft Foods in 1992 of SnackWells, a line of fat-free crackers and cookies that was marketed as a healthy alternative to other snacks. They may have been fat-free, but they were loaded with carbohydrates. As has been noted by many observers over the years, eating any fat-free, sugar-free, or low-carb snack isn't all that healthy if you give yourself permission to eat the whole box.

The story of snacking in America continues to evolve, reflecting the concerns of consumers and the climate and mood of the country. While there are snacking standbys that have stood the test of time, there are trends that come and go.

In the 2010s, snacks made with ingredients such as cassava and chickpeas were quickly gaining popularity with the promise of premium quality and enhanced health. Then the Covid-19 pandemic hit in early 2020, and consumers wanted comfort and familiarity. Crackers—the country's number one salty snack—began flying off shelves as readily as toilet paper. Kellogg, maker of Club Crackers and Cheez-Its, among other snacks, saw a 40 percent increase in cracker sales in March of that year over the prior year.

THE TASTYKAKE BOYCOTT

When you want to appeal to a person's appetite, you make good food. When you want social change, you put pressure on the powerful by appealing to their bottom line. The story of the Rev. Dr. Leon Sullivan and the 400 members of the clergy who joined forces with him in 1959 in Philadelphia in a campaign referred to as "selective patronage" is a story of both.

The Tasty Baking Company hired large numbers of Black workers, but always in certain production departments and in segregated facilities. Sullivan wanted to see Black workers in positions such as "driver-salesmen," which would give them the opportunity to earn commissions on top of their salaries. He and his group tried negotiating with the company's leaders, but they balked. So in June 1959, they called for a boycott of the company's products by Black consumers and grocery-store owners, who refused to sell Tastykake products. Two months later, Tastykake agreed to negotiate and the boycott was lifted.

Black men gained fixed sales routes while Black women were given jobs previously held only by white women, and the facilities were desegregated.

► A billboard advertises Laura Scudder's potato chips. Scudder—a trailblazing California attorney—started the company in 1926.

FERMENTATION NATION

Fermentation may have started trending in the early 2000s, but it's far from new. For thousands of years, humans have been joining forces with "good" bacteria to create foods and beverages.

▲ Although it's most familiarly made with cabbage, kimchi—which means "soaked vegetables" in Korean—can be made from all kinds of vegetables.

▼ Among the things a vintage label for Krasdale Sauerkraut suggests it goes well with is "pig's feet tid-bits."

It's difficult to track down exactly when human-controlled fermentation began, but historians have been able to trace signs of humans using fermentation as far back as 7000 BCE. It's thought that fermentation began spontaneously, perhaps by an airborne microorganism landing into a food or drink that happened to be at the right temperature for the right amount of time, creating the perfect environment for it to flourish. As the "culture" or colony of microorganisms consumed the sugars present in the food or beverage, it produced alcohol and/or acid—spontaneous fermentation.

Fermentation is the process of encouraging good microbes, such as *lactobacilli* or yeast, to thrive while also preventing the growth of bad microorganisms. Scientifically, it's the chemical conversion of carbohydrates into alcohols or acids.

Since ancient times, humans have learned that fermentation not only preserves food, but it also makes food more digestible and palatable. As far back as 7000 BCE, in what is now Iraq, dairy farmers found that by fermenting milk they could store it for much longer, marking the beginning of cheese making. Evidence of mead, a fermented alcoholic drink made with honey, and other wines made with fruit date back to 7000 to 6600 BCE. And ancient Chinese dynasties were making rice wine around 4000 BCE. Fermentation was also used for medical purposes in some cultures. Sometime between 1000 and 500 BCE, Chinese cultures used fermented soybean curd (aka tofu!) to treat bacterial skin infections. Later in 220 BCE, they used fermented tea to treat a variety of illnesses.

Fermentation Formation

There are several major types of fermentation. Alcoholic fermentation turns sugar into alcohol. Acetic acid fermentation takes alcoholic fermentation one step further by allowing acetic bacteria to turn the alcohol into acetic acid, creating vinegar. Lactic acid fermentation utilizes acid produced by lactobacilli to preserve everything from dairy to veggies, and even meat.

In 1856, Louis Pasteur, a French chemist and physicist, connected yeast to the process of fermentation, describing it as "respiration without air," meaning it occurs in an airless environment.

In the early 20th century, research that linked fermentation to better health created the first fermented food fad. The use of probiotic cultures and beneficial bacteria in mainstream foods took off in the 1970s. Its popularity has fluctuated during the last 50 years, but the fermented food craze has returned with marked enthusiasm in the past 15 years.

One of the most visible commercially available fermented products is the organic sauerkraut being produced by California-based Farmhouse Culture. The kraut is never pasteurized or cooked so that it loses nutrition and flavor—it's just lacto-fermented in barrels, then packed in BPA-free pouches with vents that allow the living organisms to breathe.

Kombucha, an effervescent sweet-sour beverage made from fermented tea and sugar, experienced an explosion in the mid-1990s—both commercially and with home-fermenting enthusiasts.

Sandor Ellix Katz is one of the biggest names among fermentation DIYers. His first book on the subject, *Wild Fermentation: The Flavor, Nutrition, and Craft of Live-Culture Foods*, came out in 2003 and quickly became known as the "fermentation bible." In 2013, *The Art of Fermentation* earned him a James Beard Award.

"Just the fact that people are thinking more about food means that they're thinking more about fermentation, because fermentation is so integral to food," he told *Portland Monthly* in 2017. "The other part is that after literally a century of the idea that you want to avoid bacteria and destroy bacteria, there's greater awareness that things are more nuanced than that. Many of our physiological processes involve bacteria, and we have a lot of problems that are due to diminished biodiversity in our bodies. There's a greater interest in bacteria and strategies for restoring biodiversity in the body, so that also leads people to fermented food."

FOR YOUR HEALTH

So when did formal research into the health benefits of fermented products begin? In the early 1900s, research into the longer-than-average life span of Bulgarians by Russian bacteriologist Élie Metchnikoff suggested that their longevity was due to drinking fermented milk. His research and findings inspired a boost in the drink's popularity at the time. In the 1930s, a Yale scientist, Leo F. Rettger, first discovered the type of bacteria in fermented foods that was able to survive (and thrive!) in the human gut: *Lactobacillus acidophilus*. In the last 50 years, research into lacto-bacteria has shown they improve digestive health, boost the immune system, and make food—and the nutrients in it—easier to digest. Research has also suggested fermented foods may promote mental health, weight loss, and heart health.

Salton Yogurt Maker

▶ Electric yogurt makers reached peak sales in the 1970s. Yogurt consumption increased as Americans traveled to Europe in the 1960s and were exposed to it there, as well as the tart stuff's association with alternative food movements.

SAUERKRAUT WITH CARAWAY SEEDS

This German-style "superfood"—a product of lacto-fermentation—is a good starting point for learning the process. Salt draws the water out of the shredded cabbage, which covers the cabbage in brine and allows the anaerobic process to begin. Lacto-bacteria convert the sugar in the cabbage to lactic acid, giving the sauerkraut its signature tangy flavor. Caraway seeds are traditional in sauerkraut, but feel free to leave them out or swap in another spice, such as juniper berries or dill seeds. For a more colorful sauerkraut, use red cabbage instead of green cabbage. Be sure to reserve a few of the larger outer leaves from the cabbage before shredding it. The larger leaf pieces help hold the shredded cabbage underneath in brine, which keeps the sauerkraut from spoiling during fermentation.

MAKES 1 QUART

2 pounds green cabbage

1 tablespoon fine sea salt, plus more for brine as needed

2 to 3 teaspoons caraway seeds

1. Reserve 1 or 2 of the outer cabbage leaves; set aside. Core and shred the remaining cabbage, using a mandoline slicer for a finer texture or a large knife for a coarser texture. In a large bowl, combine the shredded cabbage, salt, and caraway. Toss the mixture until evenly combined. Use your hands to squeeze and massage the cabbage to encourage it to begin releasing liquid.

2. Transfer cabbage mixture into a 1-quart glass jar, using a muddler or wooden spoon to pack it down tightly. Arrange reserved cabbage leaves on top, tearing to fit as needed. Cover jar loosely with a cloth and let stand at room temperature about 4 hours.

3. Press the mixture down again. The liquid should start to cover the cabbage. Depending on the moisture content of the cabbage, you may need to add a brine to cover the cabbage. To make brine, dissolve 1½ teaspoons fine sea salt in 1 cup water; add enough brine to jar until cabbage is completely submerged. Cover the jar with the cloth and secure with a rubber band around the top of the jar.

4. Let stand to ferment at room temperature (between 68°F and 75°F) for 7 to 10 days, continuing to press the cabbage down every day or two to keep it fully submerged. The cooler the temperature is, the longer the cabbage will take to ferment. When it tastes pleasantly tangy, cover the jar with a plastic lid and refrigerate. The sauerkraut will continue to ferment slowly in the refrigerator and will taste delicious for up to 6 months.

ARTISAN CHEESE MAKING

From 1975 to 2020, per-capita cheese consumption in the United States rose from about 14 pounds to more than 40 pounds per year—most of it mass-market mozzarella and Monterey Jack. But also in that period, there was a renaissance in handmade, small-batch cheeses that are distinctly American.

Just four ingredients—milk, rennet, salt, and cultures—plus time are the ingredients in cheese. Despite this, by some estimates, there are more than 1,800 cheeses in the world, representing a dizzying breadth of flavors, textures, colors, and complexities.

Artisanal cheese is made by hand in small batches using traditional tools and techniques with little or no mechanization and is identified by the name of the farm or cheesemaker. An artisanal cheese is also referred to as farmstead cheese if the cheesemaker uses milk produced by his or her own animals.

Cheese making requires domesticated livestock, and it wasn't until the 1630s when European colonizers arrived in New England with their dairy cows that making cheese became a tradition in North America. In the more than two centuries that followed, it was primarily women who were tasked with cheese making, just enough for their families, as a way to preserve milk.

Then farmers began to pool their resources to create centralized cheese making facilities. The first cheese factory in the country was built in 1851 in Oneida County, New York, by Jesse Williams. He bought milk from local herds and pooled it to create a bulk cheese that was less labor intensive and therefore more affordable.

This small-scale factory production continued until the early 20th century. Then World War I and the Great Depression hit, and these factories had to be more efficient to survive. Consolidation resulted in larger factories with less skilled labor. Maximizing yield became the priority. World War II effectively wiped out any regional diversity of American cheeses. Rationing forced the streamlining of production of what had become commodity cheese.

Women Lead the Cheese Revolution

And that was pretty much the state of cheese in America until the 1970s, when several women became the driving force of a renaissance in artisan cheese that was an outgrowth of the Back to the Land movement of that era. One of the first of these was Mary Keehn, who lived with her family in a cabin in northern California in the 1960s and '70s. Self-described as a "serious" hippie, Keehn found herself needing a source of milk. Her neighbor had two unruly goats. Keehn asked if she could milk the goats and the neighbor said, "Honey, if you can catch them, you can have them."

She did, and before long she had more milk than her family could drink. She began making cheese on her tiny cabin stove top. As she honed her skills, she began acquiring more goats. In 1983, she opened Cypress Grove Chèvre. Ultimately, she created Humboldt Fog, Cypress Grove's most iconic cheese.

There were others—Laura Chenel, who actually became the country's first commercial goat-cheese producer in 1979, Judy Schad of Capriole Dairy, Allison Hooper of Vermont Creamery, Laini Fondiller of Lazy Lady Farm, Barbara Brooks of Seal Cove Farm, Jennifer Bice of Redwood Hill Farm, and Paula Lambert of the Mozzarella

▼ American artisan cheeses range from sweet and creamy to funky and stinky—and everything in between. Cheeses are soaked in bourbon or rubbed with flavorings such as crushed lavender and ground coffee.

Company. The quality was indisputable—chefs such as Alice Waters and Thomas Keller were among Laura Chenel's first customers.

In the late 1970s, there were just 48 artisan and specialty cheesemakers in the U.S. By 2018, there were nearly 1,000.

A movement that started with French-style goat cheeses has exploded into an industry that produces a vast array of cheeses, including those wrapped in chestnut leaves and soaked in bourbon, bathed with fermented pear mash and pear eau de vie, or rubbed with crushed lavender and ground coffee. As in the wine industry, artisan cheeses are often given whimsical names as a way of communicating their singularity—Womanchego, Drunken Hooligan, and Squeaky Bee among them.

"Making cheese by hand has morphed from chore to occupation to vocation," writes Heather Paxson, author of *The Life of Cheese: Crafting Food and Value in America*, in the November 2010 issue of *Gastronomica*, "from economic trade to expressive endeavor; from a craft to an art."

BUILD A CHEESE BOARD

A cheese board is a wonderful way to begin to understand the nuances of each individual cheese. First, choose the cheeses. Mix up different types. At a minimum include three, but five is optimal. Choose different styles—soft, semi-hard, aged, and blue, for instance. Also include cheeses made from a variety of milks, including cow, goat, and sheep.

You need vehicles for the cheese, such as crackers, thinly sliced baguette, or small toasts. You can include thinly sliced meats such as prosciutto or salami, but it's not a necessity. Include something salty and crunchy, such as almonds, pistachios, olives, or cornichons, and also something sweet to serve as a foil, such as in-season fruit, jams and jellies, honey, or fruit paste.

Serve cheeses at room temperature to fully appreciate their flavors. Soft cheeses only need 30 minutes at room temperature—all others need 1 hour.

◀ Laura Chenel became the country's first commercial goat cheese producer in 1979, when she introduced a chèvre made in Sonoma, California.

HOMEMADE FRESH MOZZARELLA

With just a handful of ingredients, you can craft your own cheese at home in less than an hour. The best mozzarella starts from the best milk, so use high-quality whole milk, preferably from a local dairy. Steer clear of milk that's labeled "ultra-pasteurized," which could prevent the curds from forming correctly. Rennet is what helps the milk protein form the curds. If it's not available near the gelatin at your regular supermarket, look for it in liquid or tablet form at specialty food stores or online. Citric acid, key to making the cheese smooth and stretchy, can be found in the canning section of your supermarket. Be sure to have an instant-read thermometer at the ready when you begin your cheese making—it will ensure a smooth process without any guesswork.

MAKES 1¼ POUNDS

- ¼ teaspoon liquid rennet or ¼ of a rennet tablet, crushed
- 1¼ cups bottled spring water or filtered water
- 1½ teaspoons citric acid
- 1 gallon whole milk
- 1½ teaspoons fine sea salt

1. In a small bowl, combine the rennet and ¼ cup of the water; stir to dissolve. In a large pot, stir the citric acid into the remaining 1 cup water until dissolved. Stir milk into pot and place over medium heat. Heat, stirring frequently, until just warmed to 90°F. Remove from heat and stir in the rennet mixture. Stir in a figure-eight motion about 30 seconds, then cover and let stand undisturbed 10 minutes.

2. Check the mixture. The curd should be softly set like custard with a clear separation between the curds and whey. If the curd is too soft or the whey is still milky, let stand 5 to 10 minutes more. Using a long, thin knife, cut the curd vertically into grid pattern with 1 inch between cuts. If the curds don't hold a cut edge, let the mixture stand 5 to 10 minutes more before cutting.

3. Return the pot to medium heat. Cook, stirring the curds very gently, about 5 minutes or until the mixture reaches 105°F. Remove from heat. Continue stirring gently 3 minutes more. Place a colander over a large bowl. Strain mixture through the colander.

4. Transfer to the curds to a microwave-safe bowl (reserve whey for another use, such as smoothies or baking). Microwave 1 minute and transfer the curds to the colander again. Squeeze the curds together to drain, then return them to the bowl. Sprinkle with the salt and knead 1 minute. Microwave 30 seconds more, then drain and knead again. Repeat microwaving, draining, and kneading until cheese reaches 135°F and is smooth, stretchy, and taffy-like, using rubber gloves as needed to protect hands from heat.

5. Form the cheese into a ball by tucking the edges under until the cheese is tight, smooth, and shiny (if the cheese is too firm to form, microwave 10 to 20 seconds or until softened). Place the ball in a bowl of ice water about 20 minutes to cool quickly. Serve or use immediately, or wrap in plastic wrap and refrigerate up to 5 days before serving.

CRAFT BEER REVOLUTION

American beer endured a long hangover after Prohibition. Most every brewery that thrived afterward offered near-identical light lagers. That changed with the craft beer revolution.

First, a definition: Just what is a craft brewer? According to the trade group the Brewers Association, a craft brewer is "small and independent." By their definition, that means the brewery's annual production is 6 million barrels of beer or less and that less than 25 percent of the brewery "is owned or controlled . . . by a beverage alcohol industry member that is not itself a craft brewer."

More aesthetically speaking, craft beers are associated with a depth of character and flavor not found in mass-market beer—and sometimes higher alcohol content. The stylistic variety of craft beer derives from skillful, creative approaches to brewing techniques and ingredients that may be traditional or experimental, depending on the beer, brewer, and brewery.

Grassroots: Beer Brewed at Home

One breakthrough that led to the microbrewed beer movement came in 1978, when there were fewer than 100 breweries in the country—and when the federal government legalized home brewing. Prior to that, small breweries such as Spoetzl in Texas (maker of Shiner Bock) and others struggled for market share against industry giants. In 1965, Fritz Maytag, an heir to the eponymous appliance maker, revived Anchor Brewing Co. in San Francisco, breathing new life into a longstanding brewery with traditional European recipes and an artisan approach to brewing. In 1976, Jack McAuliffe, Suzy Stern, and Jane Zimmerman

founded New Albion Brewing Company in Sonoma, California, forming the first microbrewery built from the ground up. After the legalization of home brewing, beer enthusiasts with a flair for innovation and entrepreneurial nerves launched their own microbreweries. These included Sierra Nevada Brewing Company (maker of Sierra Nevada Pale Ale); New Belgium Brewing Company (maker of Fat Tire Amber Ale); and Boston Beer (maker of Sam Adams Boston Lager), among many others.

The first microbreweries didn't care about shipping their beers far and wide; they were more interested in making beer with distinctive personality and unexpected flavors, different from mass-produced, light lagers. Truly a grassroots movement, microbreweries offered their products—steam beers, pale ales, India pale ales, stouts, porters, and the like—to Americans who were eager to expand their palates.

Soon enough, microbrewing grew from a niche to a formidable force in the market. But in the 1990s, the microbrewing movement grew a little too fast, with quantity outpacing quality. Some small breweries merged with larger competing micros or closed outright. A few partnered with industry giants in an effort to expand distribution.

Nonetheless, craft beer survived and thrived. After the era of shutdowns and mergers in the early 2000s, by the 2010s, the craft beer sector began to grow again, by almost 10 percent annually. In 2016, almost 400 counties in the country had a craft brewery that didn't have one in 2012. By 2019, with more than 8,000 breweries in the country, sales of craft beer was almost 14 percent of the U.S. beer market by volume.

And that means beer drinkers now have a mind-boggling array of options. There are beers made

▼ Jim Koch, who began selling beer he brewed at his home in Cambridge, Massachusetts, founded Boston Beer Company in 1984. Koch is considered one leader of the modern craft beer movement.

with fruit and spices, beers adapted from ancient recipes, beers aged in whiskey or wine barrels, and even—on a very small scale—beers made from barley and other grains grown in space. Adventurous beer enthusiasts can find brews made with prickly pear cactus, raisins, beets, coriander, cocoa, dried orange peel, and loads of mouth-puckering hops. But the true genius of the movement may have been restoring brewing to its artisanal roots.

What started as a small corner of the industry has lobbied legislatures across the country to make it easier to make, sell, serve, and distribute beers that are an alternative to mass-market offerings. Just a few decades after it began, the American craft beer movement is a world leader in pushing the boundaries of what beer is and what it can be.

▼ The rise of the craft beer movement has offered beer enthusiasts a mind-boggling variety of options—and one of the best ways to experience them is with a beer flight.

THROUGH THE LENS OF BEER

In 2017, with the backing of the Brewers Association, the National Museum of American History launched the American Brewing History Initiative with curator Theresa McCulla—who has become accustomed to people telling her she has the best job ever—at the helm.

"If you look at beer, you can understand stories of immigration, transportation, changes to our technology, business, as well as consumer culture and how it intertwines with advertising," she told *Washingtonian* in 2017.

The initiative collects objects, archival materials, and oral histories to tell the story of brewing and its role in American history. Among the objects in the collection is the first homebrew recipe typed by Charlie Papazian, founder of the Brewers Association and the Great American Beer Festival and author of *The Complete Joy of Homebrewing*, published in 1984.

HOW HOT SAUCE GOT HOT

Salt, pepper, and hot sauce. On the tables of most restaurants across the country, a bottle (or two) of vinegary, fiery red sauce is given equal status with the world's most indispensable seasonings.

▼ Edmund McIlhenny was an American businessman and manufacturer who founded the McIlhenny Company, which was the first to mass produce Tabasco sauce, above. McIlhenny bottled the first sauce in 1868. Today, the Tabasco Company produces a variety of sauces, including Jalapeño, Habanero, Chipotle, Buffalo Style, and Scorpion.

The long history of hot sauce began about 7,000 years ago, in Bolivia, where chile peppers grew wild.

The fruits of plants from the genus *Capsicum* evolved capsaicin—the compound that gives them heat—as a means to discourage mammals from eating them. Birds can't taste the heat, so they happily ate and digested the fruit, then deposited the seeds throughout Central America and up through Mexico as they migrated north.

Ironically, human mammals were more drawn to the fiery fruit than repelled by it and began domesticating chiles about 6,000 years ago. The first hot sauce was made of ground chiles and water and eaten with tortillas made from maize.

The Indigenous peoples of the Southwest had long used chiles, and the enslaved cooks of the South—building on the West African proclivity to season foods with heat-producing spices—adopted the use of fresh chiles in their cooking.

There is some evidence that hot sauce was being made and sold in Boston as early as 1807, but it is definitively known that in the mid-1800s, J. McCollick & Company of New York City was making hot sauce—likely from small wild chiles called chiltepins or bird peppers—and bottling it in cathedral-shape glass bottles that were nearly 11 inches tall.

Oddly, though, it was a cholera epidemic that swept through the Lower Mississippi Valley in the 1840s that changed the history of hot sauce forever.

The Birth of Commercial Hot Sauce

Maunsell White, an Irish immigrant, slave owner, and entrepreneur, operated a large plantation in Louisiana, where enslaved people seasoned their food with cayenne chiles. There was anecdotal evidence at the time that suggested that eating chiles could help prevent contracting the deadly disease. (A 2019 study listed in the U.S. National Library of Medicine at the National Institutes of Health bears this out, concluding that, "Capsaicin showed great inhibitory effect against cholera toxin . . . The results showed promising insights into antivirulence effects of capsaicin.")

Although cayenne chiles were available and easy to grow, White decided to experiment with a Mexican chile brought to the United States after the Mexican American War: the tabasco.

He was successful in growing them, but found them too oily to preserve by drying. Instead, he boiled vinegar and poured it over the chiles to create the vinegary hot sauce we know today.

It's thought that White eventually gave some of his tabasco seeds and sauce recipe to a friend, Edmund McIlhenny, who planted them on his plantation on Avery Island. He mashed up the tabasco peppers with salt, aged them in wooden barrels, and mixed them with vinegar.

In 1868, McIlhenny bottled his sauce in 350 used cologne bottles and sent them as samples to prospective wholesalers. He received orders for thousands of bottles of his Tabasco sauce priced at $1 each—the equivalent of more than $18 in 2020. And that was wholesale.

Over the ensuing decades, others followed—some of which came and went and others that are still on the market.

A New Style of Sauce Arrives on the Scene

Then, in 1983, David Tran, a refugee from Vietnam, established Huy Fong Foods in California, which made a hot sauce of red chiles, vinegar, garlic, and sugar. He called the sauce sriracha.

Tran had been making hot sauce in Vietnam based on a recipe created in 1949 by a home cook named Thanom Chakkapak, who lived in a small coastal town in Thailand called Si Racha.

In the mid-1980s, Tran focused his attention on cities that had large populations of Southeast Asians. By the mid-'90s, his sriracha had developed an almost cult following among the larger population. In 2009, *Bon Appétit* magazine named sriracha "Ingredient of the Year" for 2010.

Between 2000 and 2015, hot sauce sales went up by 150 percent. The American love affair with hot sauce is seemingly a human one. "Once we develop a taste for hot food, which provides a high, there is no going back," the noted Indian cookbook author and food writer Madhur Jaffrey told *Time* magazine in 2007. "It turns into a craving."

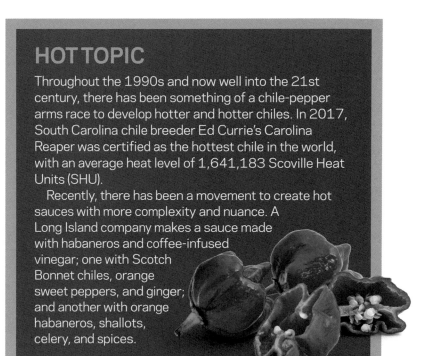

HOT TOPIC

Throughout the 1990s and now well into the 21st century, there has been something of a chile-pepper arms race to develop hotter and hotter chiles. In 2017, South Carolina chile breeder Ed Currie's Carolina Reaper was certified as the hottest chile in the world, with an average heat level of 1,641,183 Scoville Heat Units (SHU).

Recently, there has been a movement to create hot sauces with more complexity and nuance. A Long Island company makes a sauce made with habaneros and coffee-infused vinegar; one with Scotch Bonnet chiles, orange sweet peppers, and ginger; and another with orange habaneros, shallots, celery, and spices.

SRIRACHA-STYLE HOT SAUCE

David Tran, founder of Huy Fong Foods, named his iconic hot sauce for the coastal Thai town of Si Racha, where a similar sauce was invented. The popular sauce—perfect on everything from eggs to Asian noodles to french fries—is a staple on many dinner tables these days. And it's easier to make at home than you might think. With just a handful of ingredients—and a little time and patience to allow for fermentation—you can make your own version. Choose your favorite chile varieties depending on your heat tolerance. For a spicier sauce, opt for jalapeño or serrano chiles. For a milder sauce, use Fresno or Anaheim chiles. The longer you ferment it, the more flavor depth and complexity it will acquire. The fish sauce will add a little more pungence, but feel free to omit it if you prefer.

MAKES ABOUT 2 CUPS

- 2 pounds fresh red chile peppers, such as jalapeño, serrano, Fresno, or Anaheim chiles, stemmed and coarsely chopped
- ⅓ cup raw cane sugar
- 4 teaspoons fine sea salt
- 4 cloves garlic, chopped
- ⅔ cup white vinegar
- 1 to 1½ teaspoons fish sauce (optional)

1. In a food processor, combine the chiles, sugar, ⅓ cup water, the salt, and garlic. Pulse until finely chopped, then blend until smooth.

2. Transfer the mixture to a glass quart jar. Cover the jar with a clean cloth and secure around the top with a rubber band. Let stand at room temperature for 1 to 2 weeks, stirring once every day or two. After a few days, you should see bubbles appearing at the edges, which indicate fermentation is happening.

3. Return the mixture to the food processor. Add the vinegar. Puree until very smooth. Press the mixture through a fine-mesh sieve; discard the solids (skip this step for a coarser, unfiltered sauce). Transfer mixture to a saucepan. Bring to a boil. Reduce heat and simmer, uncovered, about 10 minutes or until slightly thickened. Stir in the fish sauce (if using).

4. Transfer sauce to a jar. Cover and store in the refrigerator up to 6 months.

DELIVERED TO YOUR DOOR

Pizzerias and Chinese restaurants long had a virtual lock on the meal-delivery game. Now everything can be delivered—even meals you make yourself.

Having a piping-hot pizza or pad Thai delivered to your door is a far cry from hunting, growing your own vegetables, or baking your own bread—even from provisioning at a modern supermarket and cooking for yourself. And although the ability to enjoy a fully prepared meal without leaving the comforts of your domicile might seem to be one of the most appreciated conveniences of the modern era, food delivery in America is not quite as new as you might think.

The very first food delivery is said to have been in Naples, Italy, in 1889, when Queen Margherita and King Umberto ordered a pizza from Pizzeria di Pietro e Basta Cosi be brought to the palace at Capodimonte, where they were staying on their visit to the southern Italian city. Pizza delivery—and pizza Margherita—was born. In America, Kin-Chu Cafe in Los Angeles advertised itself as "The Only Place on the West Coast Making and Delivering Real Chinese Dishes" beginning in 1922. As late as 1 a.m., just a phone call would "deliver hot dishes direct to you."

Meal delivery ramped up in the 1950s with, no surprise, pizza—which the *New York Times* introduced to its readers in 1944. The headline touted that "Pizze, a Pie Popular in Southern Italy, Is Offered Here for Home Consumption." American soldiers stationed in Italy during World War II had been introduced to the dish, and pizzerias began offering it for takeout in cardboard boxes. Delivery was something of a niche service in the restaurant business until after WWII, when many white, middle-class Americans flocked to the suburbs and gathered around the electronic hearth: the television. While fast food and drive-ins exploded, sit-down traditional restaurants saw their revenues in steady decline. Those that offered "any menu item available for takeout" saw their sales come back as much as 50 percent.

The First Online Purchase: Pizza

While a lot of restaurants covered their rent with takeout lunches for harried downtown workers, dinner takeout remained comparatively lagging. And it still took at least a phone call. That changed in the 1990s with the proliferation of mobile phones. In 1994, Pizza Hut launched PizzaNet. It was one of the first commercial sites on the World Wide Web, meaning a large pepperoni, mushroom, and extra cheese pizza was likely the first thing sold online. World Wide Waiter became the world's first food delivery service in 1995, delivering food from more than 60 restaurants throughout the San Francisco Bay Area. It still operates as waiter.com. It was a precursor to Seamless, Grubhub, Uber Eats, and other such delivery services.

The mid-2010s saw the arrival of meal delivery kits with the founding of Blue Apron in 2012. Others—such as HelloFresh, Home Chef, and Sun Basket—followed. The kits helped make menu-planning easy and helped inexperienced cooks learn about ingredients and how to cook.

They were well-funded and rapidly growing for several years until a number of factors caused stock prices to plunge, including high costs, a saturated market, complaints about excessive packaging, and the growing competence of the newbie cooks who might have originally signed on.

▲ The Chinese takeout container is uniquely American. On Nov. 13, 1894, in Chicago, the inventor Frederick Weeks Wilcox patented a version of what he called a "paper pail."

▼ In 1922, a Chinese restaurant in Los Angeles posted an ad including the text "KIN-CHU CAFE IS THE ONLY PLACE ON THE WEST COAST MAKING AND DELIVERING REAL CHINESE DISHES."

You Are Cordially Invited to Attend the
GRAND OPENING OF THE
KIN-CHU CAFE
At 137 South Brand Blvd. on Saturday, June 15
Open 9 A. M.
REAL CHINESE FOOD AND AMERICAN DISHES
C. P. LEE, MANAGER
FREE — CHINESE CANDY TO ALL
REAL CHINESE MUSIC AT 8 P. M.
Chinese and American Dishes Every Day—75c
Business Men's Lunch—45c
A LA CARTE SERVICE—We Specialize in Catering and Arranging Special Dinners for Parties
Phone and We will Deliver Hot Dishes Direct to You
We Employ Chinese Cooks Direct from Shanghai, China
KIN-CHU CAFE IS THE ONLY PLACE ON THE WEST COAST MAKING AND DELIVERING
REAL CHINESE DISHES
Special Delivery Service 11 A. M. to 1 A. M.—Phone Douglas 5276
Tomorrow will be a great day at this opening—But don't forget to give Dad a real treat by taking him out for dinner to the
NEW KIN-CHU CAFE ON SUNDAY
FATHERS' Day

Then the Covid-19 pandemic hit and meal-kit delivery was hot again as many people who could no longer eat in restaurants or easily shop for groceries signed up for delivery services. Where meal-kit services previously offered convenience and varied cuisines as incentives, they now offered safety to those who could afford them.

Another food-delivery development to come out of the pandemic was home-cooked food you don't cook yourself. Companies such as Shef—in San Francisco and New York City—and WoodSpoon in New York give opportunities to displaced restaurant chefs, immigrants, and home chefs to prepare foods of their cultures and deliver them on demand. Consumers who live in urban areas where such services thrive can enjoy Ethiopian *shiro* (chickpea stew), Indonesian *rawon* (beef soup), Ecuadorian fish tacos, and Armenian *dolma* (stuffed grape leaves) and help support food workers and their communities.

The modern food delivery industry, writes Sarwant Singh in a September 2019 article for *Forbes* magazine, "is a veritable buffet, allowing customers access to thousands of restaurants and millions of dishes."

▼ The development of the modern pizza box can be attributed to none other than Tom Monaghan, founder of Domino's Pizza®.

THE FRY THAT WOULD NOT GET COLD (AS QUICKLY)

While most foods fare fairly well upon delivery, there is one that doesn't stand a chance: french fries. The whole appeal of fries lies in their hot, salty crispiness, and a trip in a closed container in which they steam and turn soggy does them no favors.

Lamb Weston, based in Eagle, Idaho, is the largest manufacturer of french fries in the country, supplying to large chains such as McDonald's. In the mid-2010s, the company began working on a french fry that could stay crisp far longer than the 12 minutes traditional fries do once they're out of the hot oil. Researchers developed a starchy batter featuring potato starch and rice flour. After frying, the fries stayed crisp for up to 30 minutes.

The company also developed new packaging—a perforated container that allows steam to escape without the hot fries getting cold. Home delivery is "how people are eating now," says Adam Chandler, author of *Drive-Thru Dreams: A Journey Through the Heart of America's Fast-Food Kingdom*, "so the market is going to respond to that problem."

CHAPTER 4

INNOVATORS & CREATORS

The invention in the late 1940s by Earl Tupper of an airtight bowl with a lid—and the innovation of lead saleswoman Brownie Wise—led to a revolution in food storage.

There have always been those who push forward with new ways of doing and thinking about things, and who, whether intentionally or not, have changed what we eat and how we go about feeding ourselves. Their ideas and creations have improved agriculture and nutrition, expanded our culinary worlds to experience new foods, and sought equity, social justice, and empowerment.

GEORGE WASHINGTON CARVER

Agriculturist, inventor, and polymath George Washington Carver was one of the most productive innovators of his day, and the most prominent Black scientist of the early 20th century. He's most famously—and erroneously—credited with inventing peanut butter, which he did not. But he did make great strides in the study of plant disease, developed hundreds of plant-based products, and changed modern agriculture forever.

Carver was born enslaved on a farm owned by Moses Carver near Diamond, Missouri, sometime in 1864—a year before the Civil War ended. As an infant, he and his mother and sister were kidnapped by Confederate raiders. Moses Carver dispatched a neighbor who was able to locate the child and return him to the farm. The neighbor found Carver and negotiated with the Confederate raiders to exchange the child for a horse. As he grew into boyhood it became apparent Carver was not physically suited to field work. Moses Carver and his wife, Susan, taught the boy to read and write. Susan also taught him domestic skills such as cooking, sewing, doing laundry, and tending the garden.

The boy's precociousness revealed itself when he was still quite young. Fixated on plants and agriculture, he experimented with soil nutrients, herbicides, and pesticides. The elder Carvers were by then the small, quiet boy's adoptive parents—one of a series he would have in his formative years.

When he was 11, Carver moved to Neosho, Kansas, to attend the local school for Black children. While there, he lived with Andrew and Mariah Watkins, a free Black couple who had no biological children. He spent about two years there before he moved to Minneapolis to attend a private high school. He worked in a hotel kitchen to pay for his tuition.

After graduating in 1880, Carver was accepted at Highland College in Kansas—until the administration revoked his acceptance after it was discovered he was Black. He worked as a journeyman laborer in the Midwest for several years, saving money—often employing the domestic skills he had learned from his foster mothers—and trying to find a college that would accept him. By the late 1880s, he had moved to Winterset, Iowa, where he was befriended by a white couple, John and Helen Milholland, who encouraged him to look at Simpson College—a small private Methodist school in Indianola, Iowa. Simpson accepted all qualified applicants, including Carver.

He intended to study art and music—two subjects for which he also showed proclivity—in order to teach. An art teacher noticed his unusually detailed paintings of plants, and fearing a Black man would have difficulty earning a living in the arts at the time, encouraged him to study botany at Iowa Agricultural College in Ames. In 1894, he became the first African American to earn a bachelor's degree at what is now Iowa State University. There, his professors were so impressed with his work on soybean fungal infections that they encouraged him to earn his master's degree and later to join the faculty. Carver was an early student of crop rotation, a practice that replenishes soil nutrients, and was soon regarded as one of the nation's more prominent agricultural scientists and experts on the subject.

A Legacy of Giving: Tuskegee and Beyond

Carver joined the faculty of Tuskegee Institute, founded by Booker T. Washington in 1881 in Alabama to provide education and training to Black teachers. Carver saw his tenure as an opportunity to help relieve Black farmers' and sharecroppers' poverty and privation. He wanted to improve the lot of "the man farthest down." His facilities and resources were meager, but he stayed at Tuskegee for the rest of his life.

The notion of crop rotation was largely new to the South. Endless seasons of cotton plantings left fields depleted, but peanuts put nitrogen back in the soil and kept it there. On alternating years, farmers were overjoyed with the resulting bumper crops of cotton. Similarly bountiful peanut harvests were more than the market could bear, however, and they spoiled, unsold, in silos and storehouses.

Carver knew he had to find other uses for the surplus peanuts. He developed hundreds of new products using the legume: laxatives, antiseptics and other medical treatments, skin lotion, shaving cream, wood stains, flour, Worcestershire sauce, soap, paper, and countless others—eventually more than 300 in all.

During World War I, Carver answered Henry Ford's call to produce a replacement for rubber using peanuts. He also used Alabama soil to develop dyes for use in textile mills when European dyes couldn't be easily imported during the war. After the war's end, Carver continued his work with sweet potatoes, another crop that locked nitrogen into the soil. He used them to develop still more dyes, molasses, rope, breakfast cereal, and even shoe polish—more than 150 in all.

By the 1920s, he was renowned around the world as a champion of sustainable agriculture who worked to ease poverty and malnutrition. He met with Mahatma Gandhi in India to talk about nutrition in the developing world, and wrote pamphlets, with recipes, on the nutritional values of peanuts, sweet potatoes, and other plants.

Carver also revealed himself to be something of a trade protectionist. His testimony before Congress in 1921 helped lead to the passage of a tariff on imported

▶ George Washington Carver, an agricultural scientist and former enslaved person, works at the Tuskegee Institute, circa 1905.

crops. By the late 1930s, if not before, peanuts were firmly established as a cash crop in the American South to the tune of $200 million every year. Had Carver not pioneered crop rotation and found myriad new uses for surplus peanuts, that might never have happened. And he did it virtually on his own.

Upon his death in 1943, Carver left his life savings of $60,000 to Tuskegee. That same year, Franklin D. Roosevelt directed federal money to erect a monument in

his honor in Diamond, Missouri—a first for an African American.

Carver largely eschewed the money he might have made from patenting his hundreds of inventions. He only applied for and was granted three. Material gain had never driven him.

"It is not the style of clothes one wears, neither the kind of automobile one drives, nor the amount of money one has in the bank that counts," he said. "It is simply service that measures success."

SPICED SWEET POTATO PEANUT SOUP

Everyone knows peanuts and sweet potatoes are mainstream crops these days, but before George Washington Carver's agricultural innovations, few Americans knew what to do—much less how to cook—with them. Rotating peanut and sweet potato crops in the cotton fields resulted in huge surpluses of both, which drove Carver to invent hundreds of uses for them—food and nonfood products alike. He even created recipe booklets for farmers and housewives to make use of the extra harvest. This warmly spiced soup, inspired by Carver's deep interest in the two Southern crops, combines the subtle sweetness of sweet potatoes with the rich, nutty flavor of roasted peanuts. For extra heat, leave the seeds in the jalapeño (or add two).

SERVES 6 TO 8

- 2 tablespoons peanut oil
- 1 medium onion, chopped
- 1 red bell pepper, chopped
- 1 jalapeño pepper, seeded (if desired) and finely chopped
- 2 cloves garlic, minced
- 2 teaspoons grated ginger
- 2 tablespoons tomato paste
- 2 teaspoons ground cumin
- 1 teaspoon ground coriander
- ½ teaspoon ground cinnamon
- ¼ teaspoon ground cloves
- 3 medium sweet potatoes, chopped
- ½ cup chopped dry-roasted peanuts
- 1 teaspoon salt
- 1 lime
- ½ cup chopped fresh cilantro
- ¼ cup chopped green onions
- ¼ cup peanut butter

1. In a Dutch oven or large pot, heat the oil over medium heat. Add the onion and bell pepper. Cook, stirring occasionally, about 8 minutes or until the onion and pepper are tender. Add the jalapeño, garlic, and ginger. Cook and stir 1 minute. Stir in the tomato paste, cumin, coriander, cinnamon, and cloves. Cook and stir 2 minutes.

2. Stir in 5 cups water, the sweet potatoes, ¼ cup of the peanuts, and the salt. Bring to a boil, then reduce heat and simmer about 30 minutes or until sweet potatoes are very tender.

3. Meanwhile, zest and juice the lime. In a small bowl, combine the cilantro, green onions, the remaining ¼ cup peanuts, and the lime zest.

4. Using an immersion blender, blend the soup until smooth. (Or cool soup slightly. Working in batches, transfer to a blender and blend until smooth; return to pot.) Whisk the peanut butter and lime juice into the soup. Top each serving with the cilantro mixture.

THE HARVEY GIRLS

One day in 1890, 16-year-old Mary G. Wright of Joliet, Illinois, left an interview at the Chicago office of the Fred Harvey Co. with a job and an eye to the future. Although she had misrepresented herself as 18 years old—the minimum age required to work at a Harvey House rail-station restaurant in the American West—sacrificing a bit of the "high moral character" expected of employees was worth it to gain some independence, seek adventure, and bask in the appreciative glow of serving "Meals by Fred Harvey."

One such menu offered choices of bluepoints on the half shell, English peas au gratin, mashed potatoes, potatoes *Française*, boiled sweet potatoes, Elgin sugar corn, filet of whitefish with Madeira sauce, young capon, roast sirloin of beef au jus, pork with applesauce, stuffed turkey, *salmis* of duck, English-style baked veal pie, prairie chicken with currant jelly, sugar-cured ham, lamb, seven vegetables, four salads, and desserts that included charlotte of peaches with cognac, mince pie, cold custard *a la chantilly*, cakes, and cheeses and fruit—all for 75 cents.

Spreads like this could be had in Coolidge, Kansas, or Rincon, New Mexico, thanks to an ambitious young Englishman with epicurean tastes whose name became linked with fine food and dining.

Fred Henry Harvey arrived in New York from England in 1850 at the age of 15. He worked in restaurants in New York and New Orleans and owned a small one in St. Louis before winding up as a postal clerk on the Chicago, Burlington, and Quincy railroad line.

His frequent rail travel exposed him to the sorry state of rail-station dining options.

A "chicken stew" of prairie dogs found its way onto the plates of travelers, as did leathery antelope steak, rancid bacon, eggs preserved in lime, and worm-eaten biscuits called "sinkers." Topping it all off was a piece of "Railroad Pie," described by one traveler as upper and lower crusts held together by thick glue. Coffee was made once a week.

"Western dining technique consisted of hunching over assorted dishes and stabbing items with unnerving skill," wrote James David Henderson in *Meals by Fred Harvey: A Phenomenon of the American West*, "all the while chewing steadily and searching for the next mouthful."

"There wasn't a square meal or decent lodging west of St. Louis," wrote Harvey. He proposed to the Atchison, Topeka & Santa Fe a system of restaurants linked by the railroad.

A Revolution in Rail Fare

In 1876, Harvey was granted the lunchroom on the second floor of Santa Fe's Topeka, Kansas, depot. Harvey gave the place a new face and menu, and within a short time hungry throngs were clogging the restaurant—and the Santa Fe (common usage for the railway at the time).

A breakfast of thick steaks with eggs on top, hashed brown potatoes, a six-high stack of wheat cakes with maple syrup, and apple pie—cut into five pieces, not the traditional six—cost 50 cents. Bread was baked on-site and always sliced ⅜ inch thick. Fresh orange juice was squeezed only after it was ordered, and water—tested for alkali levels to ensure the best brewed coffee—was brought in by tank car.

By 1883, Harvey had 17 restaurants on the main line of the Santa Fe, and the chain continued to grow. In 1889, he signed a contract with the Santa Fe that granted him exclusive rights to the eating houses along the route.

The same year that Harvey opened his 17th dining room, he made a business decision that created, perhaps inadvertently, the first national corps of independent working women in the country.

Known for his adherence to perfection, Harvey would pop in on his crews for inspections of his establishments. On an unannounced visit at Raton, New Mexico, Harvey found his all-male crew disheveled from the previous night's bacchanal, which had included a rowdy brawl. He fired everyone and began hiring young women.

The experiment proved so successful that Harvey began advertising in newspapers in the East and Midwest for "Young women of good character, attractive and intelligent, 18 to 30, to work in Harvey Eating Houses in the West."

The job offered $17.50 a month plus room and board. The women—who had to be white and unmarried—lived in dormitories overseen by a house mother. There was a 10 p.m. curfew, and the house mother monitored visits from male guests.

Four Courses in 30 Minutes

The women completed a 30-day boot camp to learn how to serve a four-course meal in 30 minutes—the amount of time the train would stop at a station. They did so in black ankle-length dresses with crisp pointed collars, white bib aprons, and large, stiff hair bows. Makeup and jewelry was prohibited, and so was conversing with customers.

The service was defined by efficiency, innovation, and hard work. Harvey Girls worked 12-hour shifts 6 to 7 days a week. When the train was still miles from the station, the conductor requested each passenger's meal preference. He then whistled the order ahead to the Harvey House manager.

When the customer sat down at the table, their drink choice was immediately poured. The server knew what to pour

▶ Though the uniform the Harvey Girls wore evolved over the years, black and white was the enduring color scheme.

by the code of the cup. Right-side-up meant coffee; upside down meant hot tea, and upside down and off the saucer meant milk.

"Meals by Fred Harvey" became the slogan of the Santa Fe, but it was also a guarantee of the best food in the West. The Harvey House chain spread along the railroad during the 1880s and 1890s to places such as Newton and Hutchison, Kansas; La Junta, Colorado; Las Vegas, Nevada; Albuquerque, New Mexico; Winslow and Williams, Arizona; and Needles and Barstow, California.

By the time of Fred Harvey's death in 1901, the empire encompassed 15 hotels, 47 restaurants, and 30 railroad dining cars strung along 12,000 miles of the

Santa Fe. His son, Ford Harvey, took over the company.

A Legacy of Empowerment

By the end of the 1940s, as steam engines eliminated many of the stops and the airplane reduced rail travel, the Harvey chain faded away. The 100,000 Harvey Girls who contributed to its success advanced women in the workplace.

"Harvey Girls were among the most upwardly mobile women of the American West," writes Lesley Poling-Kempes in *The Harvey Girls: Women Who Opened the West*, "crossing social boundaries in their daily routines, playing the role of mother and sister to travelers rich and poor, famous and infamous."

GUACAMOLE MONTEREY

The food served at Fred Harvey establishments was always high quality, but it varied in style depending on the location of the restaurant. It was a mix of European—or "continental," as it was described then—American, and Southwestern cuisines. The Harlequin Room in Chicago served Poached Eggs a la Reine, the restaurant at the St. Louis station served Cream of Wisconsin Cheese Soup, and the El Tovar Hotel at Grand Canyon National Park served this avocado dip, among other regional dishes. It comes from an undated booklet called "Super Chief Cook Book of Famous Fred Harvey Recipes" given away to passengers on that luxury train. It was described as "One of the recipes most asked for by guests as an appetizer in the big, rustic dining room over looking a spectacular view of the Grand Canyon," and included a pronunciation guide for the uninitiated: "(pronounced Gwah-ka-mo-leh)."

SERVES 6

1 avocado, mashed

1 tomato, chopped fine

½ cup cottage or cream cheese

2 tablespoons chopped green onions

1 tablespoon lemon juice

½ teaspoon chopped chives

½ teaspoon salt

Dash black pepper

Dash Worcestershire sauce

1. Combine all ingredients thoroughly. Chill.

2. Serve on lettuce with a peeled, chilled tomato wedge or use as a dunk mixture.

LOUISAN MAMER AND THE REA ELECTRIC CIRCUS

In 1935, about 90 percent of rural homes in America did not have electricity. The Rural Electrification Act of 1936, created as part of Franklin Roosevelt's New Deal, changed life forever for millions. With REA funding and loans, Rural Electric Cooperatives—organized by farmers who were familiar with the co-op system for buying farm equipment and grain crops—transformed rural America. Those who lived there needed encouragement and education to transition to electricity, and one woman helped lead the way.

Life in rural America before electrification was tough. Night light came from candles, lanterns, or oil lamps. Fire was an ever-present danger. Farm women—who did all of the household work according to norms of the time—cleaned entirely by hand and cooked and baked with wood- and coal-fired stoves and ovens. Families were large, and laundry day was every day. While their husbands were out busting sod or tending to the livestock, women hauled wood and water, heated it, washed the clothes in hand-cranked washing machines and hung them up to dry, and later heated up irons on the stove to iron the clean clothes. It was a pre-dawn to late-evening proposition. Power companies couldn't afford to run lines throughout the countryside, and rural families found the expense of electrification very difficult to justify with a depression on. Many struggled to earn enough to eat.

The key to changing all of that was electrification. In order to organize an electric co-op, though, people who had grown up without running water and electricity needed to see how dramatically it could change their lives. To this end, a group of REA workers traveled rural roads across the country staging events in oversize tents at which they demonstrated electric stoves, refrigerators, washers, and even dryers. Prominent among these electrical evangelists was Louisan Mamer.

Relatability: A Key to Success

Mamer, who had grown up on a farm in southern Illinois without electricity or running water, had graduated from the University of Illinois, College of Agriculture, in 1931 with a BA in Home Economics. Her rigorous coursework included chemistry classes and lab experiments that showed her the changes food undergoes during cooking. She had originally looked into a career as a writer, but, she said, she needed "something to write about," so she studied home economics. Experience writing for the *Daily Illini* and the *Illinois Agriculturist* helped her land a job with the REA in 1935. She had the background to understand the lives of the farm women who came to REA demonstrations, the education to be an expert on the subject matter of her profession, and the communication skills to put the two together. In addition to planning and putting on the demonstrations, Mamer conducted research and wrote and edited REA publications.

"Never before have turkeys been so easy to cook or tasted so delicious. Why? Nowadays they are cooked the electric way," reads the introduction to "Turkey Festival Recipes," a 1939 booklet from the REA. "Modern electric ranges and roasters assure the success of any turkey dinner. For electricity is a controlled heat. You can cook with the exactitude made possible by modern science. Electricity is safe, clean, and economical, too . . . Good cooks and good turkeys deserve the best equipment—and the best equipment is electric!"

From 1937 to 1941, Mamer traveled the country participating in these "electric circuses" at which local women enjoyed cooking demonstrations and explanations of how electrical appliances worked. The circuses typically lasted for 3 to 4 days in each community and drew crowds to rival religious revivals. They also staged cooking competitions between locals—men and women alike—to determine who could best harness all this newfangled technology. The men learned about how electrical farm equipment—such as milking machines—could transform their lives as well. The circuses were enormously successful in generating enthusiasm and establishing cooperatives. Rural families banded together to electrify their communities.

▶ Louisan Mamer grew up on a farm in Illinois without electricity or running water, which gave her an understanding of the women and men she was teaching.

Added Benefits: Electrification Sparks Productivity

Although one of the goals of the program had been to show how electricity could and would make life better in the kitchen, sitting room, and barn, the other was to improve the rural economy—and therefore that of the entire country. Things did improve, and quickly. By 1939 there were more than 400 rural co-ops and one-quarter of farms were using electricity. As a result, gross agricultural production per farm hand increased by about 30 percent in the 1940s.

The government paused the program just two months before the U.S. entered the Second World War to save gasoline. Mamer resumed her work after the war, giving demonstrations, writing training manuals for other REA staff, and adapting recipes for electric appliances.

Soon after the war ended, REA programs resumed. By 1950, nearly 80 percent of rural homes had electricity, and the REA's focus changed from creating enthusiasm for adopting electricity to training rural residents how to use their new electric appliances. As a Home Electrification Specialist, Mamer helped the women learn how to transition from cooking with coal or wood to cooking with electricity.

Once they had adjusted to these new developments, rural Americans couldn't believe they'd lived so long without them. "I just couldn't believe it," one North Carolina farm woman said in an oral history. "The lights were so bright, so much brighter than what we'd ever had in there before." Another said succinctly: "To think of setting over here in the dark for years and trying to read by an oil lamp."

Mamer and her colleagues had achieved their goal of making life better for those who made their living off the land. After 46 years with the REA, she retired. Her colleagues sent her off with a nickname: "First Lady of the REA."

In *Chasing Dirt: The American Pursuit of Cleanliness*, Suellen Hoy writes that farm women would tell Mamer that electricity "saves my food, my time, my energy, my money, and most of all, my disposition."

MILITARY R&D AND THE FOODS WE EAT

Since the advent of the canning process that provided food for Napoleon's troops in 1809 to shelf-stable pepperoni pizza, technologies developed to supply soldiers in the field have revolutionized the American diet.

▲ The development of dehydrated cheese during World War II led to the invention of Cheetos in 1948.

▼ High-pressure processing makes sauces shelf-stable.

The phrase "An army marches on its stomach"—attributed to both Napoleon and Frederick the Great—alludes to the fact that military campaigns are won not with troops and weapons but with logistics and supply chains that keep trucks fueled and running, generators powering outposts in the field, and mess tents that keep troops fed. Feeding far-flung troops in distant theaters means preserving food, whether it's making jerky, canning or dehydrating food, or applying new processing technologies to create foods that can be safely transported, stored, and eaten on or near the battlefield.

This critical need has driven militaries around the world to work with food scientists and inventors to make sure a reliable source of transportable food reaches the troops, starting with the advent of the canning process in 1809 by confectioner Nicholas François Appert at the behest of Napoleon. In 1810, English merchant Peter Durand was granted a patent for a tin can, and in 1812, Robert Ayars opened the first American canning factory in New York City.

Most anything could be put in a tin—fruit, vegetables, meat, even cheese—and for more than a century, canning was the primary process by which food was preserved. It was the run-up to World War II—when the predecessor of the current Department of Defense made huge investments with food manufacturers across the country—that great leaps were made in food technology.

"There was a tremendous need for the military to develop modern rations, and it ended up not only inventing a bunch of new food-processing techniques but putting in place a food science research system that exists to this day," Anastacia Marx de Salcedo, author of *Combat-Ready Kitchen: How the U.S. Military Shapes the Way You Eat*, told *Voice of America* in a 2015 interview. "Out of that came a lot of new techniques and food, and after the war, those were incorporated into snack and convenience foods."

Cheetos, Anyone?

Goldfish crackers, granola bars, and juice boxes are in a sense an echo of portable battlefield rations. The dusty Cheeto came to life in part after the development of dehydrated cheese during World War II. Dehydrating the cheese

gave it a longer shelf life and made it lighter for transporting overseas. M&Ms were introduced by Forrest Mars in 1941 after he saw soldiers eating small candy-coated pellets of chocolate (which didn't melt) during the Spanish Civil War. Military research to develop "fabricated modules of meat" led to chicken nuggets and the McRib. Freeze dehydration was developed to preserve blood products so medics could treat wounded soldiers in the field, but it wasn't long before freeze-dried food products—including coffee, creamer, tea, and soups—showed up on grocery-store shelves.

Military scientists at the Natick Soldier Systems Center in Massachusetts were inspired in the mid-1960s by Gaines-Burgers dog food patties—created with a process that limited their moisture content enough to prohibit bacteria and fungi from growing but allowed them to remain soft and tender—to produce foods that were moist and chewy but could be stored at room temperature in low-tech packaging. The technology found its way into energy bars and commercially produced cookies, muffins, pastries, and shelf-stable bread. In the 1990s, Natick scientists in concert with industry contractors created high-pressure processing, which is used in the production of guacamole, hummus, salsa, sauces, preservative-free deli meats, fruit juices, and shelf-stable sauces.

But perhaps the crowning achievement to date came in 2018, when—using a combination of technologies around water activity, pH levels, and innovative packaging—the first shelf-stable pepperoni pizza was assembled into MREs (see right). The pizza lasts for up to 3 years and can withstand temperatures of up to 80 degrees Fahrenheit.

Whether or not Americans will someday find themselves unwrapping a slice of pizza on a backpacking trip through the remotest wilderness or stacking slices away alongside the dried beans in their disaster provisions remains to be seen, but it would not be surprising.

WHAT'S AN MRE?

Although the MRE (Meal, Ready to Eat) made its official field debut in 1983, combat rations had long been issued to military personnel, beginning in 1907 with the Iron Ration, which included three 3-ounce cakes made from beef bouillon powder and wheat, three 1-ounce chocolate bars, and salt and pepper. MREs (also referred to as "Meals Rejected by Everyone" or "Meals Rarely Edible") have made great strides since then. In 1990, the Flameless Ration Heater (FRH) was introduced, which allowed service members to enjoy a hot meal anywhere—and the food has gotten a lot better too. There are options for vegetarians and vegans, as well as kosher and halal MREs. As of March 2021, the top-ranked MRE among military personnel was the Chili and Macaroni menu, which comes with pound cake, jalapeño cheese spread and crackers, candy, beverage powder, and an accessory packet that includes both coffee and matches.

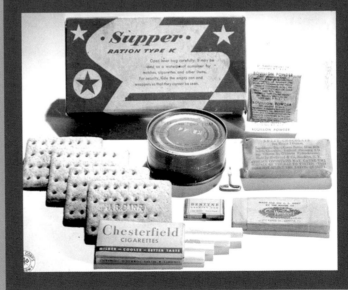

PERCY LOY

In modern America, almost anyone can, with the press of a button on a microwave, enjoy a hot lunch or dinner after a long day at work, choosing from a world of cuisines—Chinese pork and shrimp dumplings, Kung Pao chicken, Thai red curry, chicken tikka masala and spinach paneer, enchiladas and tamales, Korean-style beef short ribs—without lifting a finger or washing a single dish. It wasn't always like that. Developments in refrigeration made in the 1920s began to have a real bearing on how Americans cooked at home in the postwar 1940s. An enterprising entrepreneur combined these new technologies with a desire to expand Americans' openness to foods that were outside of the meat-and-potatoes mainstream to help change what and how Americans eat.

Beginnings: An Immigrant Story

Percy Wallace Loy was born in Vancouver, Washington, in 1920. His father, Kong Loy, immigrated to the United States from China around 1880 and found work carrying water to other immigrants who were building the transcontinental railroad. He was compensated with an apple a day and small amounts of other food. After starting a vegetable gardening enterprise that supplied Portland, Oregon, restaurants with produce, he eventually became a successful dairy farmer. His wife, Rose—a native of Portland—worked as the bookkeeper.

When Loy reached school age, he was sent to Providence Academy—a private Catholic school in Vancouver—where his tuition was paid in milk from his father's dairy. At age 12—as was the custom then— he was sent to China for higher education. When the Japanese bombed Nanjing in 1937, he returned home. When World War II broke out, he enlisted in the U.S. Army Air Force, serving as a pilot, bombardier, and flight instructor—and eventually a lieutenant colonel.

Despite his service, discrimination against nonwhite pilots kept Loy from finding work as a pilot on a commercial airline. He sold insurance for a while and toyed with the idea of opening a restaurant. Ultimately, though, his true impact would be on how Americans ate at home—not out—with a line of Chinese frozen entrees that could be bought at supermarkets throughout the western United States.

Building on Innovation: New Ideas, New Flavors

A confluence of factors made Loy's achievements possible, starting with inventor Clarence Birdseye, who patented a method for flash-freezing in 1927. While humans have been freezing foods as a means of preservation for thousands of years, up until recently, it was a decidedly imperfect process. Freezing was a slow process that resulted in the loss of proteins and nutrients. Ice crystals formed on the food and ruptured its cell membranes. When thawed, the food was mushy and flavorless.

Using Birdseye's method, the food froze so quickly that only the tiniest ice crystals formed, leaving its taste and texture largely intact.

In 1944, the W.L. Maxson Co. of New York City created the

▼ Percy Loy was a pioneer in the production of frozen dinners and one of the first to offer Chinese food in the United States.

first frozen dinner, initially sold to the navy for overseas flights and then to commercial airlines. A 1945 article appearing in the army's weekly magazine, *Yank*, crowed about this new phenomenon. "Right now, if you fly the right places, you can get a partially precooked, quick-frozen meal of steak, French-fried potatoes and carrots all ready to eat in 15 minutes. And after you're finished you don't have to wash the dishes. You just toss them away."At the time, the Maxson Sky Plate was available in six menus—steak, meat loaf, beef stew, corned-beef hash, ham steak, and breaded veal cutlets, all served with one or two vegetables and hot bread. While they had to be prepared in a special oven that was not yet in production for retail, it would soon be available to "sell to housewives for from $15 to $25."

"Some bright new dreams for the postwar world are in operation even now," the writer goes on to say.

When C.A. Swanson & Sons introduced its first "TV Brand Frozen Dinner"—turkey with cornbread dressing and gravy, peas, and mashed sweet potatoes—in 1953, it didn't require a special oven. Although Swanson was the most visible maker of frozen meals—selling more than 10 million of them the following year—Loy was a pioneer in his own way.

Kubla Khan: A Business Is Born
In 1950, Loy and his brother-in-law, Robert Wong, started Kubla Khan, making frozen Chinese entrees in the basement of a Portland restaurant. When the business started, there were other companies in the U.S. that offered Chinese food—Breyers Ice Cream had the Golden Pagoda brand that included frozen chow mein and chop

suey—but Loy focused on the quality of his product, believing that a better eating experience of what might be a new type of food to many Americans would encourage consumers to become repeat customers. Kubla Khan made much of its food using traditional methods such as wok-cooking or steaming, as opposed to the large-batch vat cooking other manufacturers employed. The products were eventually even exported to Asia.

Because commercial-scale freezers and equipment were not always readily available in the Northwestern states at the time, Loy built some of the equipment himself, then worked tirelessly to encourage supermarkets to buy freezers.

Kubla Khan manufactured frozen entrees until 2000, when that division of the company was sold. Loy died in 2006. In the intervening decades between the production of the first Kubla Khan frozen

meal to the last, Loy became a leader in education—serving as a board member and trustee of several colleges and universities—and commerce. In 1979, he led a 17-member Oregon Business Development Mission to China—the first after China reopened to the West. Committed to supporting others in their efforts to start businesses, he served as the chairman of the U.S. Small Business Administration in Portland and as the director of the Oregon Council on Economic Education, supporting several of his own employees along the way.

Loy had two goals when he established Kubla Khan: to popularize frozen foods and to make Chinese food accessible. Given that frozen entrees have been heartily embraced and Americans have grown an enduring love of Chinese food, he clearly accomplished both.

▲ Kubla Khan packaging from the 1960s.

ILHAN NEW

The supermarket shelves and restaurant menus of the 1960s looked very different than they do today. Products that were once considered new or novel—kimchi, fish sauce, coconut milk, mangoes, a dizzying array of hot sauces—have now been fully incorporated into the American diet. The process of integrating new ingredients and cuisines into the mainstream requires two things: the passion of an individual and public demand. In the 1920s, the American public was in the midst of a "chop suey craze." A Korean-born entrepreneur co-founded a company that would become synonymous with Chinese ingredients, introducing and demystifying Chinese American food for generations of American cooks.

Escaping Unrest: An American Education

Born Ilhyeong New in 1895 in Pyongyang, now the capital of North Korea, Ilhan New was the first of nine children of Gi-Yeon New, a successful aquaculture farmer, and Gi-Bok Kim, the daughter of an affluent Christian family.

In the early 20th century, the political climate in Korea was highly unstable. After years of war and intimidation, it was becoming apparent that Japan intended to colonize the country. In 1910, it did, remaining there until after World War II, when the country was divided into its current political systems. Seeing a closing in of opportunities, Korean families who could afford it sent their sons to America to be educated. In 1904, at the age of 9, New immigrated to Kearney, Nebraska, where he was placed with a Christian family.

After graduating from Hastings High School in 1915, he enrolled in the University of Michigan, earning a bachelor's degree in business administration in 1919. It was at Michigan that he would make a close friend with whom a collaboration would eventually create the oldest and largest manufacturer of Asian food products in the country.

It Started with Sprouts: Growing a Business

Wally Smith, a fellow student, owned a grocery store in Detroit. The country was in the middle of a "chop suey craze," and he wanted to sell freshly grown bean sprouts to his customers. He got in touch with his friend, New, to see if he knew anything about growing them. In fact, he did, and New began supplying Smith with fresh bean sprouts that Smith sold in paper cartons. The sprouts were highly perishable, though, and soon it became apparent that they would need to be preserved in some way.

With the financial backing of some connected Detroiters, New began canning bean sprouts in glass jars. It wasn't long before glass was abandoned for metal cans. In January 1922, New and Smith filed articles of incorporation for their new business, La

▼ Bean sprouts were the first product sold by the La Choy Food Products Company.

Choy Food Products Company. In addition to selling to grocery stores, the sprouts were also marketed to Detroit restaurants.

Throughout the 1920s and '30s, La Choy expanded its product line to include other ingredients frequently used in Chinese cooking—soy sauce, bamboo shoots, water chestnuts, a blend of Asian vegetables, brown sauce. The company regularly produced and gave away cookbooks to explain these "exotic" new foods. A 1931 version included "The Chinese Version of Chop Suey" that called for four different La Choy ingredients. (Incidentally, most historians agree that chop suey was created and popularized on American soil by Chinese cooks. It's likely that chop suey—which translates in Cantonese to something like "odds and ends"—originated in the camp kitchens of Chinese workers building the Pacific railroad line in the mid-19th century.)

"Mmmmm . . . mmmmm . . . what flavor! What aroma! are usual expressions of delight when family or guests, young and old alike, are served Chop Suey, Chow Mein, Egg Foo Yong and the many other delicacies illustrated and described in the pages to follow," reads the introduction to "The Art and Secrets of Chinese Cookery," published in 1949.

By this time, though, New had already left the company. After marrying Mi-ri Ho, a Cornell-educated Chinese physician, in 1925, he returned to Korea in 1926 to reunite with his family. He became distressed at the state of his country, where Koreans lacked education, health care, and economic opportunities.

It compelled him to withdraw from La Choy and stay in Korea to do something to improve the conditions for the Korean people. In 1926, he established Yuhan Corporation—what would become one of Korea's largest pharmaceutical companies—on the core belief that "Only healthy people can reclaim their sovereignty."

The growing success of Yuhan gave New the financial resources to establish schools, scholarships, and—most notably—the Korean Social and Educational Assistance Trust Fund (now the Yuhan Foundation) in 1970, an organization dedicated to promote the welfare of the nation and to provide educational support.

A Lasting Legacy: Rebuilding Korea

By the time New died in 1971, he had donated 40 percent of all Yuhan stock ($700 million in U.S. dollars) as well as most of his personal estate to the foundation.

Unarguably, New contributed to the resilience and success of modern South Korea. While his philanthropy through the Yuhan Foundation may have been his most meaningful contribution to

▲ In 1926, Ilhan New returned to Korea, where he established Yuhan Corporation, which is now one of Korea's largest pharmaceutical companies.

the world, those first cans of bean sprouts, and the La Choy product line in general, had a very different kind of positive impact—the broadening of the American culinary mind.

"La Choy and Chun King," says Laresh Jayasanker, writing of La Choy and its primary competitor in *Sameness in Diversity: Food and Globalization in Modern America*, "bridged the introduction of ethnic foods to the wider public in American supermarkets during the late twentieth century."

BEEF 'N' BROCCOLI

This recipe appeared in a 1984 recipe booklet put out by Beatrice Foods, the owner of La Choy at the time. The introductory copy in the booklet references the growth in and popularity of Asian foods that Ilhan New helped promote. "The best foods of the Far East have become favorites in the American kitchen. Chow meins, [Asian] style vegetables and sweet and sour dishes are popular fare in millions of homes," it read. In truth, these dishes were actually adaptations, not authentically Chinese. A 1949 La Choy recipe booklet, "The Art and Secrets of Chinese Cookery," put it this way: "Chinese foods as we know them (actually they're Chinese and domestic ingredients artfully blended to satisfy the American appetite) offer welcome departures from dull, everyday dishes, though they cost no more to prepare."

SERVES 6 TO 8

- 3 tablespoons La Choy Soy Sauce
- 1 tablespoon cornstarch
- 1 pound lean top sirloin steak, sliced across the grain in 2-inch sections
- ½ cup Wesson Oil
- 1 tablespoon minced fresh gingerroot
- 1 tablespoon minced garlic
- 4 cups broccoli florets, approximately 2 inches long
- 3 tablespoons oyster sauce
- 1 tablespoon dry white sherry
- ⅛ teaspoon crushed red pepper
- ⅛ teaspoon sesame oil
- 1 (8-ounce) can La Choy Sliced Water Chestnuts, drained

1. In a large bowl, mix together the soy sauce and cornstarch. Add the meat and toss to coat. Let marinate 30 minutes.

2. In a large Dutch oven, brown the meat quickly in ¼ cup oil until it just loses color. Remove from pan, set aside, and discard the extra oil. Add the remaining ¼ cup oil to pan, and sauté the ginger and garlic over medium-high heat.

3. Add the broccoli to pan (stirring constantly) and cook until just tender. Blend in the oyster sauce, sherry, red pepper, and sesame oil and cook 1 to 2 minutes longer. Add the water chestnuts and reserved meat; mix so that everything is blended.

4. Serve immediately.

BROWNIE WISE

In the late 1940s, Brownie Wise—a divorced single mother—spotted a new product called "Poly-T" in a department store. It was a line of sleek, modern plastic food-storage containers that came in a rainbow of colors, including orange, raspberry, "sapphire," and "frosted crystal." The containers had air- and watertight "burpable" lids to keep the contents fresh. While innovative, the product line wasn't selling well. Home cooks, used to storing food in glass or ceramic containers, were wary of plastic and perplexed by the strange lid. Wise's chance enounter with Poly-T would eventually have a tremendous impact on food storage as well as product marketing and American business history.

Humble Beginnings: A Born Saleswoman

Brownie Wise was born Brownie Mae Humphrey in 1913 in Buford, Georgia. Her parents divorced when she was very young, and her mother took a job as an organizer for a hatmakers' union. The job required frequent travel, resulting in Brownie being left in the care of her Aunt Pearl, a dressmaker near Atlanta. There Brownie was raised with a large group of cousins. She left school after the eighth grade and joined her mother in giving speeches at union meetings.

Brownie aspired to be a writer and illustrator, and in 1936, she won an art contest for which the prize was the opportunity to paint a mural at the Texas Centennial in Dallas. There, she met Robert W. Wise, who was in charge of the Ford Motor Company's exhibit. In December of that same year, they married.

They moved to Detroit, where Robert Wise worked as a machinist. Two years later, in 1938, their only child, Jerry, was born. With a young child at home, Wise became a regular contributor to the "Experience" column in the *Detroit News*, a forum in which readers wrote about their lives. Wise chose the nom de pen "Hibiscus" and waxed poetic about her home, "Lovehaven," and her wonderful husband, "Yankee."

The truth was that Robert Wise turned out to be a violent alcoholic. They divorced in 1942, and Brownie Wise had a child to support. Although she worked in a clothing shop and as an executive secretary for Bendix, she needed additional income. She began selling Stanley Home Products, a Massachusetts-based company that sold cleaning supplies and kitchen necessities. Stanley was an early adopter of direct selling, and Wise demonstrated that she had a knack for it, quickly becoming one of the company's top salespeople.

In 1949, when Jerry became ill, on his doctor's advice, Wise moved her son—along with her mother—to Miami. She continued selling Stanley

Home Products as well as West Bend and other home-related items—but added Poly-T to the offerings available through her new business, Patio Parties.

It Takes Two: The Inventor and the Innovator

At about same time, Earl Tupper was sitting in his office in Leominster, Massachusetts, trying to figure out how to increase sales of a new product he had invented. During World War II, DuPont mass-produced

▼ The Wonder Bowl, featuring a two-step seal (press the lid down, then "burp" it), debuted in 1946.

polyethylene for war purposes. After the war, the company—hoping to find new uses for it—began distributing it to plastics companies. Tupper reached out to DuPont and asked if they would send him some polyethylene before it had stiffening agents added to it. With it, he created a new kind of pliable plastic he called "Poly-T: Material of the Future." He molded it into lightweight food storage containers with a revolutionary double-sealed lid he debuted in 1946.

Tupper began to notice that there was one location in the country where the Wonder Bowl was selling head-spinningly fast: South Florida. Wise had adopted the home selling model of Stanley Home Products, which featured parties at which products were demonstrated, but there was also food, drink, socializing, and some lively games—such as tossing a sealed bowl filled with grape juice around the living room to demonstrate the strength of the seal—as well. The hostess would receive free product for hosting. Wise encouraged satisfied customers to become sellers themselves. And they did. One woman sold more than 56 bowls in a week in 1949.

Tupper—who had unsuccessfully tried to create a home party program for his product line—reached out to Wise, and in 1951 he hired her as his vice president of marketing for what was by then called Tupperware. That year, Wise had about 200 women selling the product. The company used marketing tactics such as the "carrot experiment." Sellers would go door-to-door asking homemakers to place a few carrots in a Tupperware container and some in the container they would normally use. After several days, they'd return to compare freshness.

Wise incentivized her sales force with an annual event she called Tupperware's Jubilee, a four-day sales meeting packed with motivational speeches, entertainment, new product introductions, and gifts such as appliances, vacations—even a speedboat. For many women, whose primary job was housekeeping and child care, being rewarded for their intelligence, sales skills, and ambition was life-changing. "You build the people and they'll build the business," she liked to say.

By 1954, the Tupperware sales team had grown to more than 9,000. Sales hit $25 million that year (more than $240 million in 2021 dollars). Wise became the first woman featured on the cover of *BusinessWeek*.

The Split: A Struggle for Power
Despite her success, by the late 1950s, a rift had widened between Wise and Tupper, and they argued increasingly over

company strategy and management. He was looking to sell the company and didn't want to do it with Wise, whom he considered too outspoken, at the helm. In the ensuing power struggle, Wise was pushed out by the board in 1958. She filed a $1.6 million lawsuit against the company for conspiracy and breach of contract, but wound up settling out of court for $30,000—about one year's salary.

Wise went on to found three direct-sales cosmetics companies, but none of them really took off. She tried working in Florida real estate and as an artist of textiles and raku pottery, but never matched the level of success she had at Tupperware. She died in December 1992.

Still, to this day, if you look in your cupboards and cabinets, you're likely to find at least one piece of Tupperware—maybe even a Wonder Bowl.

▲ To demonstrate Tupperware's patented seal, Wise would toss bowls filled with liquid around the room.

SPACE FOOD

Eating in zero gravity presents a whole host of challenges, from floating crumbs to the dulling impact it has on the ability to smell and taste. Over the course of the American space program, astronaut grub has gotten better and better.

On a 15½-day flight on the Space Shuttle *Endeavour* in 1995, pilot Bill Gregory ate 48 straight meals that started with rehydrated shrimp cocktail, including breakfast. He may have set a record at the time for consumption of shrimp cocktail in space, but he is not alone in his fervor for it. In fact, shrimp cocktail has consistently been a favorite food of astronauts since NASA introduced it in the mid-1960s.

The reason lies more in the sauce than the shrimp itself. In space, with no gravity to pull blood toward the feet, astronauts' nasal passages become congested—as they do when you have a cold—reducing the ability to smell and taste by about 30 percent. The zing of the horseradish-heavy sauce breaks through that and, in fact, wakes up the taste buds for the food to follow—whether that's beef stew, chicken tetrazzini, or Swedish meatballs and mashed potatoes, all of which are positively gourmet compared to the sustenance supplied to astronauts during the earliest days of the space race.

Designing food for astronaut consumption is a challenge. Food has to be nutritious, easy to digest, and palatable. It has to be something that can be eaten in zero gravity. (Fine particles such as bread crumbs and dry salt and pepper can float around and interfere with equipment, so on modern space flights, salt is dissolved in water and pepper is stirred into oil.) Space food also has to store well, open easily, and create little waste.

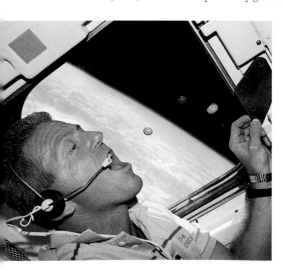

▼ Loren J. Shriver, commander of the STS-46 NASA Space Shuttle mission in 1992, pursues a few floating candies on the flight deck of the Shuttle *Atlantis* as it makes one of 127 orbits on the eight-day mission.

From Bacon Cubes to Breakfast Burritos

Because of the special circumstances of dining in space, early on NASA developed a "tubes and cubes" regimen for astronauts. John Glenn, the first American to orbit the Earth on the Friendship 7 Mercury mission in 1962, dined on applesauce and pureed beef and vegetables squeezed directly into his mouth from tubes. The first food eaten on the moon was a bacon cube.

With each succeeding mission, astronaut food improved. During the Gemini missions (1965–1966), freeze-dried foods could be rehydrated with cold water injected into the packaging with a water gun. By the time of the Apollo missions (1968–1972), hot water could be injected into a new invention, the spoon bowl, which allowed the astronaut to open a zipper and eat the food with a spoon. "Wet packs"—regular unrehydrated food that is thermostabilized, or heat-processed, to kill pathogens and wrapped in plastic or aluminum foil pouches so they can be stored at room temperature—were introduced during Apollo 8. The crew famously enjoyed turkey, gravy, and cranberry sauce on Christmas Eve of 1968.

Big strides were made with Skylab (1973–1974)—the precursor to the International Space Station (ISS). It had a full galley equipped with a refrigerator, a freezer, and a convection oven. At a table fitted with footholds, astronauts could sit in a stationary position and enjoy lobster Newburg and ice cream. Flatware was affixed to a metal tray with magnets to keep it from floating away.

These days, astronauts aboard the ISS—as well those participating in other programs—eat a mix of space-specific and regular foods. Drinks are usually freeze-dried or come in pouches. They enjoy fresh fruits and vegetables—and tortillas, which don't create crumbs—thanks to regular resupply missions. Latter-day developments in space food reflect the increasingly international nature of otherworldly exploration. Chinese astronauts have herbal tea, an Italian astronaut became the first person to brew fresh coffee and espresso in space, and Japanese astronauts enjoy ramen and sushi—with chopsticks.

Ryan Dowdy, former ISS Food System Manager, told *Magazine Singapore* in 2019 that he was working on the menus for the first space tourists scheduled to fly on a round-the-moon mission in 2023 with SpaceX. At the time, he hadn't figured them all out yet, but he was certain of one thing.

"For sure," he said, "they're going to ask for shrimp cocktail."

▼ A tube of pureed food, left, provided John Glenn with sustenance on the Friendship 7 flight in February 1962. A packet of instant noodles and one containing shrimp cocktail, right, float freely in the International Space Station.

SUGAR CRAVINGS IN SPACE

Fans of all things outer space have likely seen video of astronauts gobbling up M&Ms seemingly floating in midair. Because microgravity occurs when a spacecraft orbits Earth, the craft and all of its contents are in a state of free-fall. When the candy is released, it doesn't drop to the floor because the floor is falling too. And there are a couple of reasons—one pragmatic and the other mood-boosting—that when astronauts crave something sweet, they often reach for the candy-coated chocolates. Biting into a chocolate bar may create pieces that could break off, fly away, and damage equipment. And, says Jennifer Levasseur, space history curator at the Smithsonian National Air and Space Museum, "Chocolate is a universal thing and has psychological effects here on Earth. It serves the same purpose as a comfort food in space."

PERCY SPENCER

As unlikely as it may sound, it was the penchant of an engineer for feeding his furry friends on his lunch break while working for a defense contractor during World War II that led to the development of the microwave oven.

In 1945, Percy Spencer was working for Massachusetts-based Raytheon doing research using magnetrons—vacuum tubes that produce microwave radiation, a type of electromagnetic radiation that has a wavelength of between 1 mm and 30 cm—to see how these microwaves might improve radar.

Spencer, a self-taught engineer who never got beyond grade school, grew up in rural Maine surrounded by wildlife and, according to his grandson, he enjoyed giving snacks to some of the creatures running around the Raytheon campus. "He loved nature . . . especially his little friends the squirrels and chipmunks," Rod Spencer told *Popular Science*, "so he would always carry a peanut cluster bar in his pocket to break up and feed them during lunch."

One day, after working with the magnetrons, he realized the peanut cluster had melted into a gooey mess. He connected it to the microwaves coming out of the tubes and the next day, he experimented with popcorn, which popped. He placed an egg under the tube. It began to shake, then exploded, shooting hot yolk everywhere.

He surmised that if microwaves could make an egg cook that quickly, certainly it would work with other foods. He built a metal box and fed microwaves into it. When food was placed in the box, its temperature rose very quickly. He had discovered that when microwaves bombard molecules of water and other substances in the food, the molecules begin to collide rapidly, which creates heat.

By the end of 1945, Raytheon filed for a patent proposing microwaves be used to cook food, and in 1946, the company released the first commercial microwave, aimed at restaurant use. The "Radarange" was a monster that stood more than 5 feet tall, weighed more than 750 pounds, and cost between $3,000 and $5,000.

In 1955, Tappan introduced the first microwave oven for home use. It was priced at $1,295—still prohibitively expensive for all but a fraction of Americans—and was still the size of a conventional oven.

Then, in 1965, Raytheon acquired Amana Refrigeration. Just two years later, in 1967, the Amana Radarange—a countertop, 100-volt microwave oven—was introduced to the market for $500.

Over the next few years, other companies entered the market and made improvements, but microwave ovens were still too expensive for most households, and the public wasn't yet completely sold on its safety. As fears faded, more Americans bought microwaves. Today, more than 90 percent of households own a microwave.

Swept Away by the Magic of the Microwave

When manufacturers imagined the future, they saw microwave ovens replacing gas and electric ranges. They encouraged consumers to try making meals in record time by producing illustrated cookbooks featuring tantalizing roast turkey, bread, casseroles, and pies, all made in the microwave. A 1978 cookbook, *The New Magic of Microwave*

▼ The 1974 model of the Amana Radarange. The company first sold compact microwave ovens for home use in 1967.

Cooking, featured recipes for Bouillabaisse, Escargot, Cornish Hens and Rice, an entire standing rib roast, and Pheasant in Wine Cream Sauce.

▲ When the microwave first proliferated in the late 1970s, a flurry of microwave cookbooks appeared. Now it's mostly used to heat leftovers and prepared foods such as Hot Pockets®, opposite.

There was even a section on how to "Stir-Fry the Microwave Way." Although "browning dishes" were marketed for the microwave, over time it became apparent what the best uses of the microwave were and weren't. Home cooks weren't convinced of its universal use, but soon embraced the frozen prepared meals made especially for the microwave.

Spencer stayed at Raytheon as a senior consultant until his death in 1970 at the age of 76. He accumulated 150 patents over his lifetime and was inducted into the National Inventors Hall of Fame in 1999.

As much impact as he had on the world of high-tech, there was no invention of his that had more impact on the lives of everyday Americans than the microwave oven.

A "SPEEDY WEENY"

Although George Devol, the "Father of Robotics," had more impactful inventions—most notably a digitally operated robotic arm that revolutionized the workflow of factories and assembly lines all over the world—he had a hand in the early adoption of microwaves as a method of cooking food as well. In the 1940s, he adapted microwave technology in what he called the "Speedy Weeny," a coin-operated vending machine that debuted in 1947 at New York's Grand Central Station that could cook and serve up a "sizzling delicious" hot dog in mere seconds to astonished commuters. The Speedy Weeny was short-lived, but it was a small step in demonstrating to the public that microwaves could be useful in making food prep faster and more efficient.

IRVING NAXON

The next time you walk through the door at the end of a long day, hungry and tired, and the aroma of beef stew, lamb curry, or Thai coconut soup greets you—and a hot home-cooked dinner is ready to eat—you can thank this prolific inventor.

▼ This avocado-green Crock-Pot® was donated to the Smithsonian's National Museum of American History by Robert and Shirley Hunter of Pennsylvania. Shirley's mother Martha gave it to her as a Christmas present around 1974.

When Irving Naxon applied for a patent in 1936, he could never have predicted the profound impact his invention would have on the way Americans cook. Out of the nearly 123 million households in the United States, about 100 million of them have at least one slow cooker.

The story of the Crock-Pot® goes back to a city in Lithuania called Vilnius, specifically in the Jewish neighborhood of Vilna, where Naxon's mother grew up. When Naxon was a child, she would tell him about how Jewish families would prepare for the Sabbath—when observant Jews are prohibited from doing any kind of work, including cooking. His grandmother would fill a crock with dried beans, root vegetables, and a little meat, and then take it to the local bakery after hours and put the crock in the oven. The oven was turned off at the end of the day, but the residual heat cooked the stew, called cholent, slowly overnight. By the next day, it was cooked and ready to eat.

"Dad asked himself, 'How can I emulate this kind of slow, even cooking in a crock-lined pot?'" Naxon's daughter, Lenore, told *Tablet* magazine in 2017.

A Busy Mind Begets Progress

Naxon (née Nachumsohn—the family changed its name during World War II, when German surnames were suspect) was born in 1902 in Jersey City, the youngest of three children. His father died when he was 2 and his mother moved the family from relative to relative, first to Fargo, North Dakota, and then to Winnipeg, Manitoba, so that his older brother would avoid being drafted in World War I. While living there, Naxon got a degree in electrical engineering. The family eventually moved to Chicago, where Naxon become the first Jewish engineer for Western Electric.

When he wasn't at work, he was inventing things and applying for patents. Eventually, he formed his own company, Naxon Utilities Corp. Because he couldn't afford a patent attorney, he took the patent bar exam, which allowed him to represent himself. Naxon was no mere tinkerer. He held more than 200 patents, including an electric frying pan, an early version of the lava lamp, and a portable washing machine that attached with a hose to the kitchen faucet. His "telesign" was the

precursor of the electronic news scroller—the most famous example is Times Square's "Zipper."

And then there was the Naxon Beanery, an electric crockery cooker with an integrated heating element. He received the patent in 1940 and brought the appliance to market in the 1950s, selling it primarily to coffee shops and luncheonettes for commerical use.

In 1970, Naxon retired and sold his business to Rival Manufacturing. Rival gave Naxon's device a makeover and debuted its "Crock-Pot®" at the 1971 National Housewares Show in Chicago. The following year, Rival sold 80,000 units. With increasing numbers of women entering the workforce during the 1970s, demand grew exponentially. "Cooks all day while the cook's away," touted ads of the era. Rival sold about 3.7 million units in 1975, which netted the company an astounding $93 million.

The slow cooker (all Crock-Pots are slow cookers but not vice-versa; Crock-Pot is a brand name) has become an indispensable appliance for millions of Americans.

"The idea of being able to produce something delicious, without a lot of prep or cleanup, was and is still liberating for home cooks," says Paula Johnson, curator for the Division of Work & Industry at Smithsonian's Museum of American History.

▼ Slow cookers are popular among tailgaters at football games. In 2015, Rival introduced Crock-Pots emblazoned with all 32 NFL team logos.

THE "MAGIC POT"

Not since the proliferation of the slow cooker in the 1970s and the microwave in the 1980s has there been a nationwide craze over an appliance quite like the one over the Instant Pot®. In 2008, engineer Robert Wang and two colleagues, all of whom worked in the high-tech industry in Canada, were brainstorming ways to get a quick, healthy, delicious meal on the table after long days at work. Their solution was the Instant Pot electric multicooker, the first of which was released in 2010. Instant Pot fever hit the country hard in the late 2010s. In 2018, it sold out on Amazon's Prime Day. There are 3 million members of Facebook's Instant Pot Community—and that's just one group devoted to the appliance. "Can I just say I've cooked more things in this Instant Pot in two weeks than I have in my life? Made things I've never attempted pre-Pot," wrote one user. "I can't imagine life without my magic pot!"

SLOW-COOKER CHICKEN PAPRIKASH

Lenore Naxon, daughter of Irving Naxon, inventor of the slow cooker, told *Tablet* magazine in a 2017 interview that her mother Fern's signature slow-cooker dish was Chicken Paprikash, with "paprika, celery, peppers, onions, a can of tomato soup, and a tub of sour cream." This isn't Fern's recipe, but it celebrates both Fern and the brilliance of Irving's invention.

SERVES 4 TO 6

- 1 (4- to 5-pound) chicken, cut into 8 pieces, trimmed of excess skin and fat*
- Kosher salt and freshly ground black pepper
- 2 tablespoons butter
- 2 tablespoons canola oil
- 2 medium yellow onions, finely chopped
- 1 red bell pepper, seeded and finely chopped
- 1 clove garlic, finely chopped
- ½ cup chicken broth
- ½ cup dry white wine
- 2 tablespoons sweet paprika
- 1 teaspoon hot paprika (optional)
- 2 tomatoes, seeded and chopped
- 2 tablespoons cornstarch
- ¾ cup sour cream
- Cooked buttered egg noodles
- Chopped fresh dill and/or parsley

1. Season the chicken with salt and black pepper.

2. In a large skillet, heat the butter and oil over medium-high until butter is melted. Working in batches to avoid overcrowding, brown the chicken pieces, turning as needed, about 10 minutes. Set aside.

3. Pour off all but 2 tablespoons of the fat from the skillet and return to medium-high heat. Add the onions and bell pepper. Cook, stirring occasionally, until slightly softened, 2 to 3 minutes. Add the garlic and cook and stir an additional 2 to 3 minutes. Stir in the broth, wine, paprika(s), tomatoes, and ½ teaspoon salt. Deglaze the pan, stirring and scraping any browned bits from the bottom of the skillet with a wooden spoon.

4. Transfer to the slow cooker. Add the chicken pieces, turning to coat with the tomato mixture, and any accumulated juices. Cover and cook on low for 6 hours.

5. Transfer the chicken to a serving platter. Tent with foil to keep warm. In a small bowl, whisk together the cornstarch and 2 tablespoons water. Stir into the cooking liquid in the slow cooker. Cover and turn heat setting to high. Cook about 15 minutes or until sauce is thickened. Whisk in the sour cream. Cover and heat for 5 minutes or until hot.

6. Serve the chicken and sauce over egg noodles. Garnish with fresh dill or parsley.

*****NOTE:** Cut the breasts in half crosswise into two pieces to get the 8 pieces.

FRANCES MOORE LAPPÉ

While the phrase "plant-based diet" may be the latest definition of eating a plant-centric diet, the adherence to (primarily or completely) vegetarian and vegan diets has been practiced for thousands of years. Famous devotees include the ancient philosopher Pythagoras, Leonardo da Vinci, Mahatma Gandhi, doctor and nutritionist John Harvey Kellogg, writer Mary Shelley, and playwright George Bernard Shaw. Reasons cited for eschewing all or most animal products were—and still are—a desire to avoid animal cruelty or improve physical health. But it was a young woman distraught by human hunger on a planet of plenty that brought to the world's attention how the enduring tragedy of starvation could be solved by changing the way we eat.

Mother of a Movement: A Plan for the Planet

In 1968, Frances Moore Lappé was a graduate student in the School of Social Welfare at the University of California at Berkeley. She had graduated from Earlham College, a small Quaker school in Richmond, Indiana, in 1966. In addition to academics, the school emphasizes integrity, community decision-making, and a commitment to peace and social justice. Lappé has described herself as "a classic child of the 1960s."

After graduating from Earlham, she worked in Philadelphia as a community organizer for two years with the National Welfare Rights Organization to help ensure that welfare recipients received everything they were entitled to by law. During this time, she says, she began to understand the root causes of poverty and grew desperate to do more to help people in need.

Lappé entered graduate school to study community organizing, and part of her training involved working on fair housing policies in Oakland. The work only made her more frustrated and miserable, so in 1969, she dropped out and began doing her own research, delving into books on politics and economics. Eventually, she focused on food, influenced by the growing ecology movement reflected in the first Earth Day, in 1970, and books such as William and Paul Paddock's *Famine 1975!* and Paul Ehrlich's *The Population Bomb.* Both books described a global future where millions would die unless major changes were made to unsustainable food production and consumption patterns in wealthy countries.

She began hiding out in the agricultural library at Berkeley. She learned that (at the time) more than half of farmland was devoted to growing grain to feed livestock, and for raising livestock—and that only a tiny fraction wound up on dinner plates in the form of meat. (Today, 77 percent of global farmland is devoted to livestock, while it produces just 18 percent of the world's calories and 37 percent of its protein.) Lappé also learned that Americans were consuming twice the protein they needed. Research at the time suggested that combining certain plant foods—most notably rice and beans—created a high-quality protein equal to that provided by animals. Although that notion is now

▼ The first edition of *Diet for a Small Planet* was published in 1971.

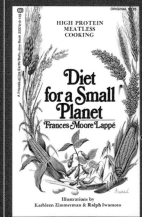

disputed—adequate protein can be taken in over a day of eating rather than a single meal—focusing on plant foods instead of animal proteins reaped benefits for the earth, for the world's population, and one's personal health.

It was a revelation. Lappé began to realize that the answer to alleviating hunger was not simply increased production, but an entire shift in the way we eat. "You could," she says, "have more food and still more hunger."

She changed her own diet, focusing on foods she had seen fellow Berkeleyans eating—tofu, soy grits, bulgur, mung beans, brown rice, and buckwheat groats. And she wrote up a one-page explanatory handout that she planned to give to friends and to post in places where "sympathetic souls" might read it. The one-page handout turned into a 5-page handout, and then into a 70-page booklet. She decided to publish it herself. Then a friend told her he was going to New York to meet with several publishers, including Ballantine Books, and that he wanted to share her booklet with them.

Ballantine bought it, and encouraged her to turn her manifesto into a cookbook that would demonstrate the ease of preparing delicious meatless meals. She enlisted her friend Ellen Buchman Ewald to help assemble recipes.

Tofu and Tempeh: "Hippie" Food Goes Mainstream

In 1971—the same year her first child was born—Lappé's groundbreaking book, *Diet for a Small Planet*, was published. It laid out Lappé's argument for eating a plant-based diet and recipes for doing just that. There was Betty the Peacenik Gingerbread, Spaghetti for Peanuts—a layered casserole that included spaghetti, black olives, cheddar cheese, and peanuts, all baked in a buttermilk sauce until bubbly—a garbanzo bean loaf, and tofu burgers. The collection included recipes from cultures around the world that were probably new to most Americans at the time, such as Sabji (Lentil Curry) from India, Gado Gado (Indonesian Peanut Sauce), and Lebanese Tabouli.

Overnight, the book became a sensation. All of a sudden, Lappé was everywhere in the media, stirring together pots of rice and beans on television talk shows. To date, *Diet for a Small Planet* has sold more than 3 million copies and has been translated into 15 languages.

The National Museum of American History at the Smithsonian calls *Diet for a Small Planet* "one of the most influential political tracts of the times." Lappé went on to author or co-author 19 more books and to establish with Joseph Collins the Institute for Food and Development Policy, now Food First. In 2001, she formed the Small Planet Institute with her daughter, Anna Lappé.

In 2020, Lappé and the institute published *It's Not Too Late! Crisis, Opportunity, and the Power of Hope*, in which the authors address the economy, a broken democracy, and the climate crisis. In the fall of 2021, an updated 50th anniversary edition of *Diet for a Small Planet* was published.

The idea of eating a plant-based diet, and the common ingredients found in it—tofu, tempeh, plant-based milks—has gone mainstream. For Lappé, adopting a plant-based diet isn't just about feeding people and saving the planet—it's also about creating equality.

"No society has fulfilled its democratic promise if people go hungry," she has said. "If some go without food, they have surely been deprived of all power. The existence of hunger belies the existence of democracy."

ITALIAN RICE & BEANS

After *Diet for a Small Planet* was published in September 1971 and became a sensation, Frances Moore Lappé hit the TV talk show scene. "Overnight I became the Julia Child of the soybean circuit," she writes in *Diet*. The producers always wanted her to "bring my own beans and rice! I was asked to stir them on camera, explaining how to combine protein." This recipe, inspired by Lappé's Roman Beans and Rice, is an Italian-style vegetarian main that combines the complementary proteins of beans and brown rice to create a complete meal in one pot. Lappé recommends serving it alongside a green salad and Italian bread, but also notes it makes a wonderful dish for large gatherings.

SERVES 6 TO 8

- 2 tablespoons extra-virgin olive oil
- 1 onion, chopped
- 1 carrot, chopped
- 1 stalk celery, chopped
- 1 small red or green bell pepper, chopped
- 3 cloves garlic, minced
- ½ cup chopped fresh parsley
- 2 teaspoons dried Italian seasoning, crushed
- 4 cups reduced-sodium vegetable broth or water
- 2 (15-ounce) cans kidney beans or cannellini beans, rinsed and drained
- 2¼ cups brown rice, rinsed
- 2 cups chopped fresh tomatoes or one 14.5-ounce can whole tomatoes, undrained and chopped
- 1½ teaspoons salt
- ½ teaspoon black pepper
- ½ cup grated Parmesan and/or Pecorino Romano cheese
- ½ cup chopped fresh basil

1. In an extra-large deep skillet or Dutch oven, heat the oil over medium heat. Add the onion, carrot, celery, and bell pepper. Cook, stirring occasionally, about 8 minutes or until the vegetables are softened. Add the garlic, parsley, and Italian seasoning; cook and stir 1 minute more.

2. Add the broth, beans, rice, tomatoes, salt, and black pepper. Bring to a boil, stirring occasionally. Reduce heat to low and simmer, covered, about 45 minutes or until the rice is tender and most of the liquid is absorbed. Remove from heat. Stir in cheese. Cover and let stand 5 to 10 minutes. Season to taste with additional salt and black pepper. Sprinkle with the basil just before serving.

MERA KITCHEN COLLECTIVE

A group of women in Baltimore made up of refugees, immigrants, and native-born alike have created a community that empowers its members through shared support and effort while preparing dishes from their homelands for eager consumers in and around the city.

▼ Although there is an evolving roster of Collective members, past and present chefs have come from Syria, Afghanistan, Nigeria, Sudan, Cameroon, Honduras, El Salvador, and Burkina Faso.

In 2016, Iman Alshehab's second full day in Maryland as a refugee fleeing violence in Syria happened to be Thanksgiving. She decided to make her neighbors dinner. She went door to door, knocking and using Google Translate to invite them. More than 20 people, including several refugee women from other countries and her caseworker, came. Alshehab—a former chef at the Four Seasons Hotel Damascus whose husband was killed by police and 6-month-old granddaughter died when a bomb leveled her son's house—made hummus, rice, chicken, and tabbouleh pasta salad.

"Food has always been the source of bringing people around me," Alshehab told *Baltimore Magazine* in 2018.

The dinner was the seed of something that would provide empowerment, community, and income to a diverse group of refugee women, and to celebrate and share their cultural and culinary traditions with the Baltimore community at large: the Mera Kitchen Collective.

Just two years after Alshehab's arrival in the United States, she helped cook for more than 500 people at an arts festival, and sold out every last morsel.

The Collective was founded in 2016 by five women. In addition to Alshehab, there was Liliane Makole, who ran a café in her native Cameroon; Aishah AlFadalah, who came from Kuwait to attend college in the U.S. and who mentors refugee families for the International

Rescue Committee; Brittany DeNovellis of Baltimore City Community College's Refugee Youth Project; and Emily Lerman, who had worked with Doctors Without Borders.

"It was born out of a few people coming together wanting to do something around food as a vehicle for building community," Lerman says. "There was all of this great food, and obviously recognizing that if you're an immigrant, if you're a single mom, if language is a barrier . . . we could come together and make it work."

From Private Pop-Ups to Public Dinners

The first thing the Collective did was host a couple of pop-up dinners for family and friends—one was Cameroonian and the other Syrian. Then a local restaurant, Hersh's, let them take over its kitchen.

Next, they began cooking for the Baltimore farmers market, arts festivals and other community events, and a wedding. They prepared a Syrian brunch at the Lord Baltimore Hotel. In 2019, they catered 100 events. When Covid-19 hit in 2020, they moved to a new kitchen space at Alma Cocina Latina, another restaurant in Baltimore—and sold takeout only. With funding from José Andrés' World Central Kitchen, they provided free meals to health-care workers, out-of-work restaurant workers, and anyone else in need.

Mera's menus reflect the diversity of its chefs. At any given moment, they may feature chicken shawarma sandwiches, pupusas, hummus, tabbouleh, black-eyed pea fritters, sorrel chicken stew, maize dumplings, stuffed grape leaves, charcoal-smoked saffron rice, a special mezze platter of roasted eggplant dip, tomato jam, cauliflower skordalia with a side of za'atar chips, or chicken musakahn rolls—paper-thin pita stuffed with roasted chicken seasoned with lemony sumac and spices, then toasted until crispy.

Though ongoing support comes from their nonprofit foundation, the Collective itself is a for-profit cooperative. The workers are the owners, all profits are shared equally, and all decisions are made democratically. Their ultimate goal is to open up their own restaurant.

The Collective took its name from the Greek word *meraki*, which means to do something with so much care and devotion that you leave a piece of yourself in it.

"So many times people are like, 'Oh refugees, they come to this country—or immigrants—and they're just using all the resources,'" DeNovellis told *The Baltimore Sun*. "And we're trying to say, 'They are the resources in this case.' We've all gotten so much out of this."

▼ Iman Alshehab, a former chef at the Four Seasons Hotel in Damascus, lays out the spread at a Mera Kitchen Collective event.

BUILDING NEW LIVES

When Chef Iman Alshehab landed at JFK Airport from Syria in 2016, she came alone, and there was no one she knew who could greet her there. A caseworker from the International Rescue Committee picked her up and drove her four-and-a-half hours to drop her off at her temporary home in Dundalk, Maryland. The IRC has a long history of providing assistance to refugees fleeing poverty and war all over the world. Founded in 1933 at the request of Albert Einstein to help Jews suffering under Hitler, the organization was first known as the International Relief Association. In 1942, it joined forces with the Emergency Rescue Committee to form the International Relief and Rescue Committee, later shortened to the International Rescue Committee. The IRC is now in 40 countries and in addition to resettlement, it aids people around the world by supporting education, health care, safety, economic well-being, and the empowerment of women and girls.

VEGETARIAN DIRECTEUR GENERAL WITH SAFFRON SMOKED CHARCOAL RICE

This dish is a fusion of two recipes created by two of the chefs of Baltimore's Mera Kitchen Collective. The Vegetarian Directeur General, created by Liliane Makole, is a take on Poulet Directeur General ("chicken for the Director General"), a Cameroonian dish often served on special occasions. The Saffron Smoked Charcoal Rice, created by Iman Alshehab, is a version of a smoked chicken and rice dish (minus the chicken) popular in the Arabic Peninsula. Although the rice is traditionally cooked in a pot that's suspended over smoking wood charcoal in a tandoor, Chef Iman came up with a method to infuse the rice with smoke flavor without using a clay oven. After the two chefs had been cooking together for some time, it became apparent that their recipes worked very well together—a metaphor for the Collective as a whole.

SERVES 6 TO 8

Canola oil

3 ripe plantains, cut into 1-inch slices

3 tomatoes, seeded and chopped

2 yellow onions, chopped

2 carrots, trimmed, peeled, and cut into ½-inch slices

½ green bell pepper, sliced

½ yellow bell pepper, sliced

1 stalk celery, chopped

1 leek, trimmed, rinsed, and chopped (white and light green parts)

1 teaspoon curry powder

6 cloves garlic, minced

2 vegetable seasoning or bouillon cubes (such as Maggi)

½ teaspoon herbes de Provence

1 habanero chile pepper, thinly sliced, or ½ to 1 teaspoon red chile flakes

¼ teaspoon salt

¼ teaspoon ground white pepper

¼ teaspoon ground black pepper

Sliced fresh chile, for garnish (optional)

Chopped fresh parsley, for garnish

1. In a large deep pot, heat about 2 inches of oil to 350°F. Fry the plantains in batches (6 to 8 pieces at a time), turning occasionally, until dark golden brown, about 4 to 5 minutes. With a slotted spoon, transfer to a paper towel–lined pan to drain. Set aside.

2. In a small pot, cook the tomatoes over medium heat, stirring frequently, until broken down and slightly reduced, about 10 minutes. Set aside.

3. In a large pan, heat 1 tablespoon oil over medium-high heat. Add the onions, carrots, bell peppers, celery, leek, and curry powder. Stir to combine. Reduce heat to low. Cover and let steam for about 10 minutes. (If vegetables start to get dry, add another tablespoon or so of oil.)

4. Add the garlic, seasoning cubes, fried plantains, cooked tomatoes, herbes de Provence, chile, salt, white pepper, and black pepper. Stir until well combined. Bring to a simmer and cook for about 5 minutes. Taste and adjust seasonings, if necessary.

5. Garnish with sliced chile, if using, and parsley. Serve with Saffron Smoked Charcoal Rice (p. 233).

This recipe is for the exclusive use for *American Table: The Foods, People, and Innovations that Feed Us* to be published by HarperCollins (or its successors and assigns) with the Licensed Publishing group of Smithsonian Enterprises. Recipe by Iman Alshehab and Liliane Makole of Mera Kitchen Collective.

▲ Saffron is the most expensive spice in the world. These stamens of a type of crocus flower must be laboriously harvested by hand.

SAFFRON SMOKED CHARCOAL RICE

The confetti-like white and yellow color of this rice is created by tossing half of the cooked, smoked rice with a mixture of saffron threads soaked in orange blossom syrup. Look for the orange blossom syrup at international or Middle Eastern food markets—and be sure not to skip the soaking step for the rice. Soaking, then draining and rinsing and draining again, washes away a lot of the starch so that the cooked rice kernels have nice separation and do not stick together.

SERVES 6 TO 8

1 tablespoon orange blossom syrup

½ teaspoon saffron threads

2 cups extra-long grain basmati rice

½ teaspoon salt

2 tablespoons extra-virgin olive oil, plus more for greasing foil

1 charcoal tablet*

1. In a small bowl, combine the orange blossom syrup and saffron threads; set aside.

2. Place the rice in a medium bowl and cover with cold water. Let soak for 30 minutes. Drain in a fine-mesh colander. Rinse and drain again.

3. In a large pot, bring 4 cups water and the salt to boiling. Add the rice and the 2 tablespoons olive oil. Cover and cook on low for 15 to 20 minutes, or until all of the liquid is absorbed.

4. While the rice is cooking, lightly oil a square of aluminum foil. Place the charcoal tablet on it and light. When lit, wrap the bottom and sides of the tablet with the foil (be sure to leave the top uncovered). When the rice is done cooking, turn off the heat. Set the smoking charcoal on top of the rice. Cover and let stand for 5 minutes.

5. Remove half of the smoked rice to a large bowl. Add the orange blossom syrup mixture and stir until all of the rice is colored. Add the remaining rice and stir gently to combine.

6. Serve with Vegetarian Directeur General (p. 230).

*NOTE: Charcoal tablets, or small coal briquettes, are available online. Be sure that any you buy are food-safe.

This recipe is for the exclusive use for *American Table: The Foods, People, and Innovations that Feed Us* to be published by HarperCollins (or its successors and assigns) with the Licensed Publishing group of Smithsonian Enterprises. Recipe by Iman Alshehab and Liliane Makole of Mera Kitchen Collective.

NICO ALBERT

Food has always been the language Nico Albert has spoken, and now she, as a chef and citizen of the Cherokee Nation, is using her voice and cooking skills to help reintroduce her community—and the wider world as well—to the foods eaten by her ancestors. "There are certain foods that were introduced to Indigenous people after colonization that have been very detrimental in general to health, both physical and spiritual," she says. "We're talking about commodity foods like white flour and sugar and dairy and things like that. Those foods—processed foods in general—things that all modern people are eating right now that aren't good for any of us, Native or otherwise."

Albert, whose father is Acadian and mother is Cherokee, was born and raised in California. Her mother and grandmother both had large gardens, and her mother made everything from scratch. "She was a health nut—all about local, sustainable, homemade before it was a thing," Albert says.

She says her mother was always in the kitchen and that her method of provisioning for her family had an effect on Albert's future. "It was kind of like culinary school—all the skills you needed as a chef," she says. "Like looking at the price per ounce of the product you're buying. My mom would shop like a chef. She would have a budget and she would come up with a meal plan for a month. It was insane how meticulous she was about that stuff, and it never occurred to me that was out of the ordinary. That was really kind of my foundation, I guess."

That foundation was built upon when her father's job was transferred to northeastern Oklahoma when Albert was 19. It happened to be where her mother's extended family lived, and the move had

a profound impact on Albert. Up until that time, "our Cherokee heritage was always known to us and important to us, but there weren't specific traditions tied to that," she says.

A Journey of Self-Discovery

That all changed when Albert attended her first wild onion dinner—an event put on by women's groups, churches, community centers, and tribal organizations. Every spring, the Cherokee community gathers to dig up wild onions. The pungent onions are sautéed with scrambled eggs and served with salt pork, hominy, fry bread, and grape dumplings, which used to be made from wild possum grapes but are now made with grape juice.

The dinner was the start of a journey in immersing herself in her heritage. "Being introduced to all of those foods, being able to connect with the whole community by being invited to that—to make an emotional and cultural connection to others—made me feel right at home in the culture I wasn't raised in but do have ties to."

Albert's education in Cherokee culture continued with exposure to friends who had been raised with traditional ways. One friend's mother taught her how to make fry bread. Another friend's grandmother shared her recipe for *kanuchi*, a kind of hickory nut soup.

Albert is a self-taught chef and "research and history nerd." She began reading other Indigenous chefs, gathering knowledge of traditional ingredients and techniques. She wanted to know what they grew up eating, what they were eating now, about their food memories.

She started working in a restaurant kitchen at age 23 and eventually went on to be the founding Executive Chef of Duet Restaurant + Jazz, a new American restaurant in the Tulsa Arts District. She left there to found Burning Cedar Indigenous Foods, which offers catering, consulting, and educational events.

For Albert—and many across all tribal Nations—there is an urgent need to decolonize diets.

Commodity foods, she says, are "produced in mass quantities and with genetic modification and factory farming. All of it ties together. We've come to rely on foods that don't take care of the earth and are also bad for our bodies. They're harmful all around. They're causing serious stress to our planet, and a lot of that has to do with modern agriculture, which is basically stripping the nutrients from the soil. Our traditional ways of farming are on a smaller scale and on a local level and give back to the earth. The way Indigenous people farmed, they helped put nutrients back into the soil. There was a very keen knowledge of how to work the earth in a way that had a positive effect on the earth and on the water and the plants."

"Reindigenizing" Native Diets

Reclaiming food sovereignty—the power to feed oneself and community—is all about what Albert calls "reindigenizing" the diets of Native people and "reintroducing traditional foods so we can once again be stewards of the land and have our practices of producing food strengthen the environment and restore the health of our people."

In order to do that, those foods have to be readily available. This process is relatively new, she says, and tribes are working at getting back to producing enough food to feed their communities. She encourages hunting, fishing, foraging, growing crops on a local scale, and buying foods from Indigenous sources.

For her part, Albert cooks and teaches at community and museum events and

▶ Nico Albert is working to "reindigenize" the diets of Native Americans, turning toward traditional foods.

through media. She has done programs with the Smithsonian's National Museum of American History, Cherokee Nation's OsiyoTV, PBS, the BBC, and Food Network, among others. Her culinary vision looks to the past but always with an eye to the future. "I look to find ways to introduce foods to my community that are delicious and modern and healthy," she says.

Connecting Through Food

Albert sees food not only as a path to physical health but also as a way to connect and open up conversation about the country's painful past. "The educational system doesn't talk about Native people in a contemporary context," she says. "I'm starting from square one." It's the reason her approach is "laid back and fun. But a lot of what we're talking about is not fun. It's genocide and hardship and I never want to gloss over that. It is still real, and it still affects our families today."

But, she says, "It's so much easier to understand and talk about tribal history when you're doing it over a plate of comforting food. Maybe you're having blue corn mush with someone from a white Southern background who grew up eating grits, and they can see themselves in that."

BISON & WILD RICE LETTUCE WRAPS

Chef Nico Albert of Tulsa, Oklahoma, a citizen of the Cherokee Nation, likes to combine Indigenous foods with modern preparations. "I try to come up with recipes that make it fun and delicious to eat Indigenous foods," she says. "Our ancestors were not eating lettuce wraps, but these were all ingredients our ancestors would have used. The contemporary way we're making food now has so many global influences, and it would be a shame to ignore those to keep it authentic with all of the knowledge we have." Albert says these wraps make a light lunch or dinner but can also be served as a shared appetizer. If you can't find ground bison, ground turkey makes a great subsitute—or add extra mushrooms to make it vegan. "Feel free to play with adding whatever herbs you may have available in addition to or in place of the parsley," she says. "Fresh foraged spring herbs or herbs from the garden like cilantro, mint, or thyme would all be at home in this dish."

SERVES 4 TO 6

- 1 tablespoon cooking oil (sunflower, safflower, or extra-virgin olive oil, or any oil suited to high-temperature cooking)
- 1 pound ground bison
- 8 ounces mushrooms, chopped (baby portobello, shiitake, oyster, maitake, or any sturdier type of wild mushroom)
- ¼ cup dried cranberries
- 2 teaspoons kosher salt
- 1 teaspoon ground black pepper
- 2 teaspoons ground sumac
- 2 cups cooked wild rice (about ⅔ cup uncooked rice, cooked according to package directions)
- ½ cup small-diced jicama
- ½ cup small-diced celery
- ½ cup chopped fresh parsley
- ½ cup chopped green onion or finely chopped wild onion (if available)

  Little gem, butter, green leaf, or romaine lettuce

1. Heat the oil in a large skillet over high heat. Add the bison and sauté, breaking meat into crumbles, until the bison is cooked through and some browned bits stick to the pan. Add the mushrooms, cranberries, salt, pepper, and sumac. Continue to cook, stirring frequently.

2. When the mushrooms have softened, add 1 cup water and stir, scraping the bottom of the pan to loosen up all the flavorful browned bits. Cook until almost all of the moisture has evaporated.

3. Add the wild rice, jicama, and celery, and stir to combine. When the mixture has heated through, remove the pan from the heat and stir in parsley and green onion.

4. To serve, spoon the mixture into lettuce leaves and eat taco-style.

JESSICA B. HARRIS

Although she is one of many Black culinary historians who have helped bring to the world's attention the impact Black Americans have had on American food, Jessica B. Harris is perhaps the most influential. She has spent a career researching, writing, and publishing books that delve into how the African diaspora transformed foodways all over the world, but most significantly in a country to which Africans were involuntarily brought, "molded in the crucible of enslavement, forged in the fire of disenfranchisement, and tempered by migration . . . ," she writes in the introduction to *High on the Hog: A Culinary Journey from Africa to America*. "Despite all this, we have created a culinary tradition that has marked the food of this country more than any other."

Opportunity and Achievement

Jessica B. Harris' road to Lifetime Achievement Awards from both the James Beard Foundation and the Southern Foodways Alliance—among many other honors—began in 1948 in Queens, New York.

She was the only child of Jesse Brown Harris and Rhoda Alease Jones Harris, and her parents were determined to provide her with opportunities. Although they were comfortable but by no means wealthy, the family had a second home on Martha's Vineyard. They traveled to Europe. Harris attended the United Nations International School in New York—an experience she described in a 2004 interview with *The History Makers*—the country's largest collection of African American digital oral histories—that attending the U.N. School was probably "one of the seminal experiences of my life." She was the first non-U.N.-connected student there.

She graduated at age 16 from the High School of Performing Arts, then went on to earn an A.B. degree in French from Bryn Mawr College in Pennsylvania—studying for two years in France—then a master's degree from Queens College in New York, and a Ph.D. from New York University.

From the Beginning, an Interest in Food

A confluence of formative experiences in Harris' life spurred her to write about food. Early on, her mother—a trained dietician—schooled her in the pleasures and intricacies of food. Then, in the 1970s, she was teaching French at Queens College and working as the book review editor at *Essence* magazine. Her editors decided they needed a fill-in article—maybe a travel piece. They sent her on a Caribbean cruise to write about it. After that, they decided she should do some travel writing. She became assistant travel editor, then travel editor. Her column began being a travel column that featured a lot of food content.

At the same time, Harris fell into a relationship with Samuel Clemens Floyd III, an English professor, writer, and accomplished cook 15 years her senior. His circle included members of the Black intelligentsia such as James Baldwin, Maya Angelou, Nina Simone, and Toni Morrison—among others—and he entertained them

▼ Jessica B. Harris' book *High on the Hog* was turned into a documentary series that first aired on Netflix in 2021.

often and well. Harris literally had a seat at the table with these luminaries and regularly attended dinner parties that ranged from the West Village to Harlem, from Sonoma, California, to the Caribbean and to the Left Bank in Paris. The illustrious company made an impression—and so did the food.

Eventually, all of this led to her first book, *Hot Stuff: A Cookbook in Praise of the Piquant*, published in 1985. It became the first of 12 books to date, all written while she taught in the English department at Queens College—a job she held for 50 years until her retirement in 2018.

And while most of those were cookbooks, all of which placed the recipes in context, she turned to narrative history with *High on the Hog*, published in 2011. The book has a smattering of recipes in the back, including her favorite recipe, for chicken *yassa*—a Senegalese dish of marinated, grilled, then stewed chicken flavored with onions, habanero chile, and lemon she first tasted in West Africa in 1972 when she was researching her Ph.D. dissertation.

Connecting Through History

Harris was drawn to writing narrative history about food because it creates connections between people and their understanding of both themselves and others.

"You don't have to be a scholar, you don't have to have a high school degree, a college degree, or even a grade school degree to know dinner," she told *The History Makers*. "But if somebody comes to you and says, 'What you got on your plate for dinner?' And you say, 'I got some chitterlings and some black-eyed peas and rice and some collard greens with some hot sauce, and maybe some cornbread or some corn pone,' that person can get back to you and say, 'Well, you know your history's on that plate.'"

Harris has described the role of food in the lives of African Americans as being much of what it is for anyone else of any other cultural background—Europeans, Asians, Africans, and Latinx people. "It is nourishment. It is sustenance. It is history. It is culture," she told the *Washington Post* in 2011. But it is more than that, too, because of their history of enslavement. "And with that mark of enslavement, we've got that denser history with food," she went on to say. "Let's start at the beginning. We have planted it. Harvested it. Processed it. Cooked it. Served it. Cleared the table. Washed the dishes and emptied the chamber pot. Which pretty much gives us the full food chain there. With all of that, we have another, deeper attachment."

It is that particular connection to food—particularly, but by no means exclusively, in the South—that led African American cooks to have the powerful impact they have had on what all Americans eat today.

"I think part of the history of food in the South is undeniably connected to race . . . " Harris said in an oral history interview with the Southern Foodways Alliance—which she helped found—in 2005. "[I]t's a part of the food of the South, and it's a part of the SFA, and it's a part of who we all are. And I think part of the wonderful thing, if you will, of the organization is [that] it's an elephant under a rug, but everyone knows there's an elephant under the rug. We just put a table on top of his back and eat."

▲ Jessica B. Harris, who has by turns been a college professor, journalist, and book author, has written extensively about the foods of the African diaspora.

CHAPTER 5

TASTE MAKERS

In 2001, Julia Child donated her Cambridge, Massachusetts, kitchen to the Smithsonian's National Museum of American History, where it is on display.

What we're eating at any given time depends on the foods that are available to us, our own personal backgrounds and histories, personal preferences, and our exposure to those who seek to share their food knowledge and culture with the wider world. These are the teachers, cookbook authors, food writers, chefs, bakers, and home cooks— many of whom are groundbreakers—who have shaped, and continue to shape, the appetites and tastes of people throughout the country.

FANNIE FARMER

In addition to the antiquated language, there's a reason modern cookbooks don't call for "a goodly amount of sriracha," a "handful" of lentils, a "dessert-spoonful" of salt—or for simmering sauces to the "proper" thickness—as they did until the late 19th century. While there were some ingredient measurements provided, nothing was standardized—it was assumed that women knew how to cook. That changed with the Industrial Revolution, when food-related domestic skills such as bread baking and cheese making ebbed. Young people, single women, and immigrant families began arriving in cities looking for jobs, homes, and ways to feed themselves. In the late 19th century, a skilled and highly trained "domestic scientist" published a cookbook that would change how Americans cook.

The "Mother of Level Measurements"

Fannie Merritt Farmer—often referred to as the "mother of level measurements"—was born in Boston in 1857 to John Franklin Farmer, a master printer and editor, and Mary Watson Merritt. The family was educated and progressive but struggled financially. Fannie was the eldest of four girls. A great-niece referred to the family as "Unitarian and bookish." Farmer's parents believed in the education of women, and her intention was to go to college until a paralytic stroke at the age of 16—likely from polio—left her unable to walk, derailing her plans.

Eventually, she regained her mobility. To help support her family, Farmer took up cooking and housekeeping. She turned her parents' home into a boarding house known for its excellent meals. She took a job as a "mother's helper" to the influential Shaw family. Farmer's interest in and talent for cooking became apparent to the Shaws, and they and her parents encouraged her to enroll in the Boston Cooking School, which at the time was focused on teaching professional cooks. Its mission was "to lift this great social incubus of bad cooking and its incident evils from households of the country at large."

The Art and Science of Food

The field of food science—studying cooking using the scientific method of observation, measurement, experimentation, and testing—was growing rapidly at the time, and the school embraced it. Farmer finished the two-year program in 1889, graduating as its star student. She was immediately hired as the school's assistant director, and in 1891 became director. She spent the next five years writing what would become one of the most influential cookbooks in American culinary history.

The Boston Cooking-School Cook Book was published in 1896. It contained tips on housekeeping, food preservation, and nutritional information as well as 1,800 recipes—all of which included precise measurements and employed the scientific method of cooking. "Correct measurements are absolutely necessary to ensure the best results," Farmer wrote.

The publisher— Little Brown & Company—

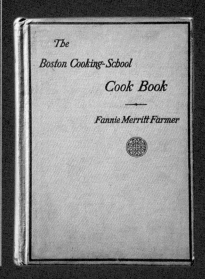

▼ *The Boston Cooking-School Cook Book*, published in 1896, was the first American cookbook to provide precise measurements.

The
Boston Cooking-School
Cook Book
———
Fannie Merritt Farmer

predicted poor sales. The first print run was just 3,000 copies, and the company insisted Farmer put up the funds for printing. She retained the copyright, and that turned out to be a very good thing. It was an instant hit.

"I'm sure the fact that her cake and pie recipes actually worked was a huge part of her success," food writer and author Laura Shapiro told the *New York Times* in 2018.

Revised for a New Generation

Over her lifetime, the book sold more than 4 million copies—more than 7 million copies to date. Farmer left the Boston Cooking School in 1902 and started Miss Farmer's School of Cookery. She was able to buy land, build a house, and support her parents, sisters, and other family members. She would go on to become a frequent figure on the lecture circuit, speaking mostly on nutrition, diet, and health. She gave regular lectures to Harvard Medical School—one of the first women to do so.

Farmer's approach to cooking was both revolutionary and timeless. In 1979, Knopf published an updated and revised edition of the book—now called *The Fannie Farmer Cookbook*. At the urging of James Beard, the publisher hired California homemaker Marion Cunningham to edit the new volume. Cunningham had taken Beard's cooking classes and impressed him with her passionate but practical approach to food.

Cunningham worked diligently for more than four years on the book. Recipes

► Fannie Farmer instructs a student in the ways of proper cooking. "Correct measurements are absolutely necessary for the best results," she wrote.

were added, recipes were thrown out, and the whole work was modernized without losing the spirit of the original. It vaulted Cunningham to the upper echelons in the food world and introduced Fannie Farmer to a whole new generation.

The Backbone of Good Cooking

The Boston Cooking-School Cook Book had contemporaries but no equals.

"[W]hy did Fannie Farmer survive and not the others? There was something about the book, about her personality, that came right off the page," Beard wrote in the introduction to the 1979 edition. "The book was not just *The Boston Cooking-School Cook Book*, it was Fannie, and she was the authority at all times, the final reference.

Her book was so prized that it was something one could put confidently in the hands of a bride. The early editions reflect her love of all the good family foods of the time and she had pictures of them. Who else had sweetbreads under glass, for instance? She belonged to an era."

The new edition, Beard wrote, "represents a rebirth of the principles of good cooking that Miss Farmer established at the turn of the century. And now it stands still blessed by generations of appreciation—a book that respects the past and yet embraces progress and all the good new methods in the field of cookery. So it is not only a new Fannie Farmer, it is a monument to the great past as well."

COCKTAIL PARTY STUFFED EGGS

Filled Things, described as "foods that can be eaten with the fingers and on the run", take up a whole chapter in the 1979 edition of *The Fannie Farmer Cookbook*. Even prior to that, stuffed eggs were popular cocktail party fare for post-World War II entertaining, and fancy deviled egg plates were manufactured to display the eggs in small divets that kept them from rolling. Hard-cooked, filled eggs—the ultimate economic picnic, party, and snacking food—offer opportunity for variation. Start with the familiar yolk-mayonnaise filling and embellish it as you like with the stir-in additions. Piping the filling into the egg white halves saves time and gives them extra flair. Use a piping bag and large star tip or a plastic storage bag with the corner snipped. You can fill the eggs up to 24 hours ahead and refrigerate so they're ready to travel or serve.

MAKES 12 EGG HALVES

6   large eggs

¼   cup mayonnaise or a mix of 2 tablespoons each mayonnaise and plain Greek yogurt

1   teaspoon Dijon-style mustard

⅛   teaspoon sweet paprika, plus more for garnish

Pinch salt and black or white pepper

1   tablespoon finely chopped fresh parsley or basil

1. To help keep the shells from cracking during cooking, pierce the large end of each egg with a needle. Place eggs in a pan and cover with water at least 1 inch above eggs. Bring water to boiling; reduce heat and simmer 12 minutes. Immediately transfer eggs to a bowl of ice water.

2. When the eggs are cool enough to handle, peel them and cut in half. Carefully scoop out the yolk halves into a medium bowl. Arrange the white halves on a deviled egg dish or other serving platter.

3. Use a fork to finely mash the egg yolks. Add the mayonnaise, mustard, paprika, salt, pepper, and fresh parsley. Stir until very smooth.

4. Scoop or pipe the filling into the egg white halves. Sprinkle with additional paprika.

SMOKED PAPRIKA AND CHIVE STUFFED EGGS: Prepare as directed except substitute smoked paprika for the sweet paprika, and stir 1 teaspoon finely chopped fresh chives into the yolk filling. Omit the parsley. Sprinkle filled eggs with additional smoked paprika.

BACON STUFFED EGGS WITH TOASTY TOPPER: Prepare as directed except stir 1 tablespoon finely chopped cooked bacon and 1 teaspoon chopped basil into the yolk filling. Omit the parsley. In a small skillet melt 2 teaspoons butter. Add 2 tablespoons fresh bread crumbs; cook and stir until toasted. Top filled eggs with bread crumbs.

SPICY-CURRY STUFFED EGGS: Prepare as directed except stir ½ teaspoon curry powder and a dash bottled hot pepper sauce into yolk filling. Substitute 1 tablespoon chopped fresh cilantro for the parsley.

ZA'ATAR STUFFED EGGS WITH MICROGREENS: Prepare as directed except stir ½ teaspoon za'atar into the yolk filling. Substitute 2 tablespoons microgreens for the parsley.

FRENCH TARRAGON STUFFED EGGS: Prepare as directed except stir 1 teaspoon white wine vinegar and 1 teaspoon chopped fresh tarragon into yolk filling. Substitute minced green onion for the parsley, or sprinkle each egg with minced fresh lavender.

LIZZIE KANDER

Between 1883 and 1900, almost 4,000 Russian, Polish, Lithuanian, and Slovakian Jewish immigrants arrived in Milwaukee, fleeing religious persecution and poverty in their native countries. Most of them settled in the 14th Ward on the south side of the city. At the turn of the century, University of Wisconsin sociologists found the area to have the city's highest rates of infant mortality, crime, and juvenile delinquency. It was also one of the most congested residential areas in the city. These new arrivals may have been able to escape religious persecution, but the poverty persisted. An energetic and progressive activist, herself the daughter of Jewish parents, felt compelled to help.

From 1890 to 1893, Elizabeth "Lizzie" Kander worked as a truancy officer inspecting the living conditions of immigrant families. She found them to be "a deplorable situation, threatening the moral and physical health of the people," and encouraged her fellow members of the Ladies Relief Sewing Society, whose mission was to "alleviate the suffering of the poor and needy by furnishing them with clothing," to do something about it.

The results of their efforts became *The Settlement Cook Book*, considered to be the most successful fundraising cookbook of all time. More than 40 editions have been published and more than 2 million copies have been sold since its first printing in 1901. It's also raised hundreds of thousands of dollars for educational projects in Milwaukee.

With personal funds of $75, Kander founded the Keep Clean Mission in 1896, next to one of Milwaukee's many breweries. The mission tapped into the hot water the brewery used to wash bottles, and for a penny, a person could get a hot bath. When the Keep Clean Mission joined a night school to form The Settlement in 1900, the services went far beyond bathing.

The Origins of "Settlement"

The concept of "settlement" has its origin in London in the late 19th century. A group of young men and women— teachers, lawyers, and health workers— set up residence in a house (called the settlement house) in an economically distressed neighborhood. Their work was to improve the circumstances and quality of life of the people living in the neighborhood through education and medical care.

At settlement houses in this country, workers provided classes in American civics and writing and speaking English for newly arrived immigrants, encouraged and preserved their native folk arts, and gave hands-on lessons in music, sewing, cooking, and skills such as whittling and clay modeling. At its inception, a primary aim of settlement in America was assimilation.

"Kander and her contemporaries saw this second wave of Jewish immigrants as needing civilizing," Kennan Ferguson, a professor at University of Wisconsin-Milwaukee who researches the social politics of cookbooks, told *Tablet* magazine in an April 2016 article.

▼ A post-Prohibition edition of *The Settlement Cook Book* touts its "repeal recipes," meaning it contains recipes for mixed drinks and punches.

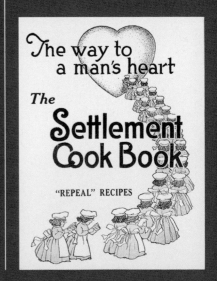

"She was working in the domestics realm but really instructing students about how to become better Americans."

Kander was tapped to teach after-school cooking lessons to girls, focusing on American foods and economical meal preparation.

Part of the lessons involved hours of laborious recipe-copying from a blackboard, which Kander soon found to be a waste of time. She knew if these recipes were printed and bound into a volume, the children would take them home to their families where they could be put to good use.

When she approached the all-male settlement board for the $18 to do such a project, they rejected her request, claiming a lack of funds. They also suggested that she could go ahead and finance the project herself and that they would gladly share in the profits.

She turned to Gussie Stark Yewdale, who convinced her husband—the owner of a local printing company—to assist her in soliciting ads for the manual from the German-Jewish community and to print it.

In 1901, a 174-page volume called *The Way to a Man's Heart: The Settlement Cook Book* was published. It contained 500 recipes gathered from throughout the Milwaukee community as well as 24 lessons on everything from rendering fat and making *kuchen* to building a fire and dusting a room.

Books not needed for the classes were sold for 50 cents, and within a year, the original 1,000 copies were gone. The $500 profit was turned over to the settlement board to be distributed to local charities, most of which served children.

After repeated demands for the book, a second printing in 1903 rapidly sold out. Several printings later, the settlement committee realized they needed a more permanent arrangement. In 1921, the Settlement Cook Book Company was created, which consisted of a board of women in charge of revising the book to suit the needs and interests of the times and directing its profits to relevant causes.

The Settlement Cook Book Today

In 1953, Simon and Schuster took over publication and expanded the book to 665 pages. The most recent edition, which came out in 1991, has 816 pages and 1,200 recipes that reflect a broader picture of the nation's immigrant history, but retains an air of its original audience in recipes for such foods as brisket, matzo balls, and rye bread.

Ferguson, the professor, believes the book achieved its blockbuster status partly because of times into which it was born.

"At the turn of the century, America had a higher percentage of immigrants than just about any other time," he told *Tablet*.

"Although it was specifically compiled for Jewish immigrants," wrote Leah Koenig, author of the article, "*The Settlement Cookbook* spoke to anyone who had recently arrived in America and felt a strong desire to belong . . . Kander dedicated her life to helping Americanize Jewish immigrants. But more than a century on, her greatest legacy is, ironically, a book that captures and celebrates the immigrant's soul."

▲ The all-male settlement board rejected Lizzie Kander's request for $18 to print the original cookbook and suggested she fund it herself.

IRMA S. ROMBAUER

Most cookbook authors are inspired to write books by a personal passion for cooking or a desire to share their cultural heritage or history through the lens of food. For Irma S. Rombauer, a St. Louis homemaker and socialite who was raising a family, hosting parties, and bettering her community through civic engagment, it was very different. An unexceptional cook by all accounts, Rombauer's cookbook was spurred by a personal tragedy and resulted in one of the best-selling and best-loved cookbooks of all time.

The Mother of Invention

In February 1930, Rombauer's husband, Edgar, committed suicide after years of suffering periodic bouts of depression and having lost nearly everything in the stock market crash of 1929. Irma found herself at age 52 with a family to support, no obvious marketable skills despite an elite education, and a sum total of $6,000 and some worthless stocks to her name.

She came up with the idea to write a cookbook—despite having the reputation among family and friends as being a quick-witted and engaging hostess but not a particularly good cook, other than baking. "'Worst idea I ever heard of,' was the consensus," writes Anne Mendelson, quoting Rombauer's brothers' family in her biography of Rombauer, *Stand Facing the Stove*—which happens to be the first instruction she gave to women in the book she would eventually create. "Irma's a TERRIBLE cook."

Undaunted, she began collecting recipes from family, friends, and fellow women's club members, testing them in her own kitchen and tweaking where necessary. She saw a space in the market for a book that would feature recipes

that were clearly written, instructive, and no-fail. Due to changing economic circumstances, many women were suddenly without domestic help and had to learn to cook to feed their families. Middle-class women had to learn to make do with less, and lower-income families had to learn to do with even less than that. Into that gap, Irma compiled a book she called *The Joy of Cooking: A Compilation of Reliable Recipes with Casual Culinary Chat.*

Joy, Not Toil

In 1931, she put up $3,000 of her remaining funds to self-publish a 396-page collection of about 300 recipes through A.C. Clayton Company, a printing company that made labels for high-end St. Louis shoe companies and Listerine but had never published a book. The initial print run was 3,000 copies. The dust jacket—designed by Irma's daughter, Marion, who would later illustrate subsequent editions—featured a silhouette of St. Martha of Bethany, the patron saint of cooking, slaying the dragon of kitchen drudgery.

Irma's position was that cooking for one's family—and especially the

communing around the table that was a result—could be a joy. "Mother's early housekeeping days . . . gave little evidence of culinary prowess," Marion wrote in a biography of her mother housed online at Harvard Square Library. She goes on to quote her mother from one of *Joy's* prefaces: "Will it encourage you to know that I was once as

▼ The first trade edition of *The Joy of Cooking,* published in 1936.

THE JOY OF COOKING 1 Irma S. Rombauer

ignorant, helpless and awkward a bride as was ever foisted upon an impecunious young lawyer? Together we placed many a burnt offering upon the altar of matrimony.'"

▶ Marion Rombauer Becker poses with her mother, Irma Rombauer, left, and the 1951 edition of *The Joy of Cooking*—the first to be more than 1,000 pages.

A Culinary Conversation

In addition to the recipes, it was Rombauer's wit and facility with words that made *Joy* so appealing. The *St. Louis Post-Dispatch* wrote a glowing article about the book, which Rombauer sold directly herself, as well as in bookstores and gift shops throughout St. Louis—and as far away as Michigan and Chicago. By 1932, two-thirds of the initial print run had sold out.

Rombauer began soliciting publishing companies to produce a second edition. After a few years and several rejections, the Bobbs-Mill Company, an Indianapolis-based publisher, released a revised and updated version of *The Joy of Cooking* in 1936 that had expanded to 640 pages, with a print run of 10,000. It introduced Rombauer's signature recipe-writing style in which the ingredients were listed in bold face and introduced as they were needed, followed by steps instructing readers what to do with them. This "action method" created the sense of a warm conversation between Rombauer and her readers. There were subsequent printings and revisions, and with each one, the book got larger and more comprehensive.

Julia's First Cookbook

By the 1940s, Rombauer was a verified culinary star. According to biographer Noël Riley Fitch, Julia Child's first cookbook was the 1943 edition, from which—along with *Gourmet* magazine—she learned to cook. By the 1950s, editions of *The Joy of Cooking* were more than 1,000 pages. (The 2019 edition, the ninth and most recent, stands at 1,200 pages and more than 4,600 recipes.)

In the 1960s, "The" was dropped from the title, to be simply *Joy of Cooking*. Irma Rombauer was involved in the revision of each edition until her death in 1962 at the age of 84. From the beginning, the Rombauer family has retained the rights to the book and continues to be involved in editing and revising each edition—first her daughter, Marion, listed as a co-author; then her son, Ethan Becker; and now her great-grandson, John Becker, and his wife, Megan Scott.

The 1975 edition was the last one to be edited by Marion and to this day remains the most popular. Out of nearly 20 million copies of *Joy of Cooking* sold since the beginning, it alone sold 6 million and is one of the most sought-after editions by avid collectors of *Joy*—which are legion.

Considered by many to be the most popular American cookbook of all time, *Joy of Cooking* has been a reliable kitchen companion to millions of cooks over its nearly 100-year history. Cooking from it is a bit like having Irma standing by your side, encouraging you and chatting you up as you slice, chop, stir, and sauté.

BAKED STUFFED MUSHROOMS

Part kitchen handbook and part cookbook, *The Joy of Cooking* has been there to help readers cook since debuting in 1931. Need to skin a squirrel, make your own cheese, or create a fruit-stuffed bird of paradise from a pineapple? See the line drawings in the 1975 edition, which was the last version Marion Rombauer Becker helped to update. Her mother Irma Rombauer's friendly and somewhat quirky lexicon included the term "Cockaigne," which was reserved for a handful of personal recipe favorites. As Marion explains in the introduction to the edition, this was considered an imaginary land of "peace and plenty" in medieval times and the name of their country home. Irma's broiled and stuffed mushrooms carried this moniker, so you know they were near to her heart. Serve this *Joy*-inspired sherry-flavored crimini mushroom variation as an appetizer, a meatless entrée, or a side dish by varying the mushroom size and number of servings.

MAKES 24 MUSHROOMS

24 large crimini or white mushroom caps (about 2½ inches across)

2 cloves garlic, minced

1 tablespoon butter or olive oil

1 tablespoon sherry, white wine, or chicken broth

½ cup dried bread crumbs

4 ounces cream cheese, softened

½ cup grated Parmesan or pecorino cheese

2 tablespoons chopped fresh Italian parsley, mixed fresh herbs, or minced green onion

2 tablespoons chopped sun-dried tomatoes packed in oil, drained, or 1 tablespoon chopped Kalamata olives

½ teaspoon salt

⅛ to ¼ teaspoon crushed red pepper or black pepper

1. Preheat the oven to 400°F. Line a shallow baking pan with parchment paper or lightly grease.

2. Slice off just the tips of the mushroom stems and discard. Gently twist remaining mushroom stems from caps and finely chop. In a medium skillet, cook the mushroom stems and garlic in hot butter 2 minutes or until tender and liquid evaporates. Add the sherry; cook 30 seconds more. Add the bread crumbs; cook and stir 1 minute more. Remove from heat and cool slightly.

3. Stir in cream cheese, half of the Parmesan cheese, the parsley, tomatoes, salt, and red pepper.* Spoon into the mushroom caps. Sprinkle with the remaining Parmesan cheese. Place the filled mushroom caps on the prepared pan. Bake about 20 minutes or until tender and lightly browned on top. Makes 24 mushrooms.

*NOTE: If filling is too dry and crumbly, stir in 1 to 2 teaspoons olive oil or melted butter until it just binds together.

LENA RICHARD

On December 18, 1948, WDSU-TV in New Orleans went live for the first time. Less than a year later, Lena Richard stepped onto a family-style kitchen set to film the first episode of *Lena Richard's New Orleans Cook Book*—a first-of-its-kind cooking show on which she demonstrated how to prepare recipes from her own cookbook. First self-published in 1939 as *Lena Richard's Cook Book* and a year later, in 1940, by Houghton Mifflin, later Houghton Mifflin Harcourt, as *New Orleans Cookbook*, this was considered the first Creole cookbook by a person of color.

Early Promise Realized: A Groundbreaker Grows

Lena Richard was a Black female chef. The fact of her appearance on this relatively new technology, in the Jim Crow–era South, showing an audience of largely white middle- and upper-class women how to prepare New Orleans classics such as Grillades a la Creole and Daube Glacéx is a testament to Richard's skill, hard work, and training. This was nearly 15 years before Julia Child first appeared on WGBH in Boston to demonstrate how to make a proper omelette and promote her new cookbook, *Mastering the Art of French Cooking*.

The show became so popular the station began airing it twice weekly, on Tuesdays and Thursdays, for almost a full year, until Richard's untimely death in November of 1950 at the age of 58.

Like many Black women of the era, Richard began her working life at the age of 14 as a domestic, assisting her mother and aunt at the home of the Vairins, a wealthy white New Orleans family. Alice Vairin, the matron of the family, noticed Richard's interest in and proclivity for cooking and set aside one day a week for her to experiment with unique dishes. After eating one of the budding chef's dinners, Vairin hired her as a full-time cook and increased her pay. She also sent her to cooking school—first in New Orleans and later to Boston's prestigious Fannie Farmer cooking school, where permission had to be sought by the school from every white woman in her class to allow Richard to study with them.

She graduated from the eight-week course in 1918, with respect and admiration from her classmates for her culinary dexterity and much-expressed enthusiasm for her Creole specialties. "I cooked a couple of my dishes like Creole gumbo and my chicken vol-au-vent, and they go crazy, almost trying to copy down what I say," Richard said. "I think maybe I'm pretty good so someday I'd write it down myself." The result was the 300-recipe collection that became *Lena Richard's Cook Book*.

The experience also propelled her to continue growing her culinary career. "When I got way up there," she recalled later in a newspaper interview, "I found out in a hurry they can't teach me much more than I know. I learned things about new desserts and salads. But when it comes to cooking meats, stews, soups, sauces, and such dishes, we Southern cooks have Northern cooks beat by a mile. That's not big talk; that's honest truth."

Paying It Forward: A School for Black Chefs

In 1937, Richard opened a cooking school specifically to train Black students in the culinary and hospitality skills that were necessary for employment in the Jim Crow South. She wanted her school, she said, "to teach men and women the art of food preparation and serving in order that they would be capable of food preparation and serving food for any occasion and also that they might be in a position to demand higher wages."

After the release of her cookbook, the Bird and Bottle Inn in Garrison, New York, persuaded her to take a position as head chef. She returned to New Orleans in 1941 and opened Lena's Eatery—"The Most Talked of Place in the South." In 1943, she headed north again to take the

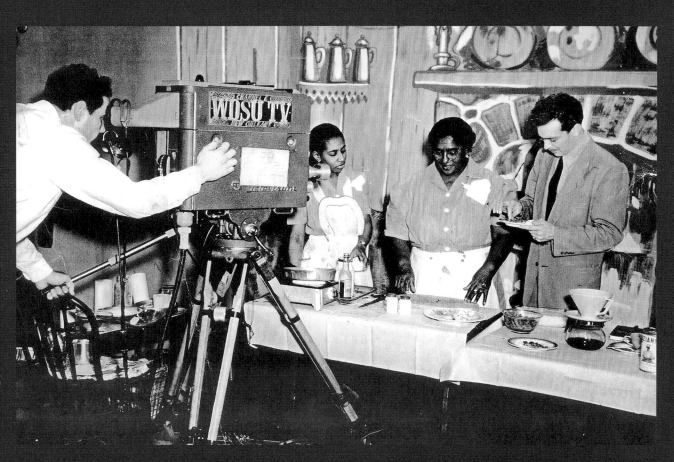

top position at Travis House at Colonial Williamsburg, where she remained for about two years before returning to New Orleans. Diners raved about her cooking in notebooks of reviews. They waxed particularly rapturously about her Scalloped Oysters. "To be scalloped by Lena—the oyster's prayer," one patron wrote. Winston Churchill's wife and daughter dined there and went to the kitchen to trade autographs with Richard.

After her time at Travis House, she returned to New Orleans and founded a frozen food company. Then in 1949, she founded Lena Richard's Gumbo House, where Black New Orleanians and white New Orleanians dined side by side, defying segregation laws.

Becoming Visible: Modeling Access, Mentoring for the Future

Richard accomplished many things in her life, among them shedding light on the truth behind New Orleans' reputation as a culinary phenomenon. As historian Ashley Rose Young wrote in a 2012 post about Richard on her blog, Lena Richard: Pioneer in Food TV, "Too often in the mid-twentieth century, the identities of the top chefs of New Orleans' world-renowned restaurants remained anonymous. They were the creative genius hidden behind the swinging doors of their kitchens. Often, those men and women were African Americans."

Lena Richard stepped out from behind the kitchen doors onto the set of a television show and beyond. She helped expand the influence of Creole cuisine and forged a path for later generations of young Black chefs with talent, skill, and singular visions.

▲ Chef and cookbook author Lena Richard was the star of a popular 30-minute cooking show that aired on New Orleans' WDSU-TV in 1949 and 1950.

CRAB A LA KING

Lena Richard—a highly regarded Black woman chef and caterer in 1930s and '40s New Orleans—had her own cooking show on a local television station based on a book she had written in the 1930s and which was published as *New Orleans Cookbook* in 1940 by Houghton Mifflin Harcourt. The book, considered to be a classic in the repertoire of Creole cookbooks, was the first Creole cookbook to be written by a person of color. It contains more than 300 recipes for New Orleans staples such as shrimp bisque, baked stuffed oysters, and *pain perdu*, but also classic American dishes—some of which Richard gave a New Orleans touch—such as this rich and elegant Crab a la King.

SERVES 4

- 6 tablespoons butter
- 4 tablespoons all-purpose flour
- 1 cup light cream or half-and-half
- 1 cup whole milk
- 8 ounces lump crabmeat
- ½ cup sliced mushrooms
- 3 tablespoons finely chopped green pepper
- 3 tablespoons chopped pimiento
- 1 teaspoon Coleman's dry mustard
- Salt and black pepper
- 2 egg yolks, beaten
- 2 tablespoons fresh lemon juice
- 2 tablespoons dry sherry (optional)
- 4 puff pastry shells, baked according to package directions

1. In a medium saucepan, melt the butter over medium-low heat. Add the flour and whisk until combined. Slowly whisk in the light cream and milk. Add the crabmeat, mushrooms, green pepper, and pimiento. Add the dry mustard and salt and black pepper to taste. Bring to a simmer and cook for 5 minutes. Turn heat to low.

2. Add the eggs and lemon juice. Turn heat to medium and cook, stirring frequently, until thickened, 3 to 5 minutes. Stir in the sherry, if desired.

3. Serve in the puff pastry shells.

Adapted from *New Orleans Cookbook*, by Lena Richard, © 1940, reprinted 1998.
Used by permission of the publisher, Pelican Publishing. www.pelicanpub.com.

JAMES BEARD

"In the beginning," Julia Child famously said, "there was Beard." Indeed, James Beard—dubbed by the *New York Times* in the 1950s as the "Dean of American Cookery"—was in large part the leader of a culinary evolution in the United States that saw the cuisines of Europe, particularly that of France, held up as the epitome of fine food, to an understanding that American food equaled or even surpassed French cuisine in its quality and variety. The James Beard Foundation sums up Beard's legacy: "He was a tireless traveler, bringing his message of good food, honestly prepared with fresh, wholesome, American ingredients, to a country just becoming aware of its own culinary heritage."

A Life Lived in Food

To understand how that evolution happened, it's instructive to understand how Beard's life experience and personal evolution informed a passion for American food that he so easily imparted to others.

James Andrews Beard was born on May 5, 1903, in Portland, Oregon, the only child of Mary Elizabeth and John Beard. His mother—an English emigré—ran a successful boardinghouse and was an excellent and passionate cook. His father worked at Portland's customs house. Mary Elizabeth hired a skilled Chinese cook, Jue-Let, to help in the kitchen. Beard grew attached to Jue-Let and attributed much of his upbringing to him. Later in life, Beard referred to Jue-Let as his "Chinese godfather."

It wasn't just at his mother's boardinghouse that Beard was exposed to good food. The family spent summers at a cabin on the beach in Gearhart, Oregon, with Mary Elizabeth's friends, the Hamblets. Beard and their daughter, Mary, became fast friends and remained

so to the end of his life. While at the beach, they fished for salmon, clams, and Dungeness crab, and gathered wild berries, making a feast out of whatever they caught or found.

The Cooking Show Is Born

After graduating from high school, Beard enrolled in Reed College in Portland but was expelled less than two semesters in after it was discovered he had several relationships with other men, both fellow students and a professor. (The school gave him an honorary degree in 1976.) Beard wrote in a revised 1981 edition of his 1961 memoir, *Delights and Prejudices*, that he had known since he was 7 that he was gay, but during most of his life, the fact remained an open secret.

The physically imposing Beard—over 6 feet tall and weighing in at more than 300 pounds for most of his life—looked to have a career in theater and opera. He traveled to London and Paris to study, then returned to the States and tried to make a go of it in New York City, but had little luck. So he turned to something

he knew very well and had an enduring passion for: food. He joined with a few friends to open what would become a highly successful catering business, Hors d'Oeuvre, Inc. In 1940, he published his first book, *Hors d'Oeuvre and Canapés*.

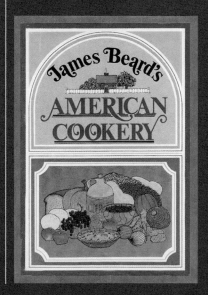

▼ *American Cookery*, first published in 1972, included more than 1,500 recipes celebrating regional American cooking.

James Beard led a conversation in the country around food that created a relationship between the East and West Coasts and everything in between, one that resulted in the formation of a culture of American food—what it was, what it is, and what it could be. Any chef whose cooking is referred to as "new American" is his culinary offspring.

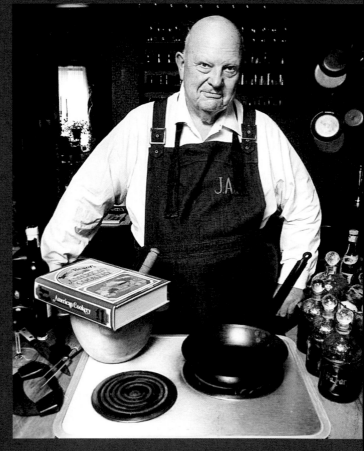

▲ James Beard led a conversation that resulted in the formation of a culture of American food.

A Legacy of Excellence

Beard died of heart failure in 1985 at the age of 81 at his home in New York City. His old friend, Mary Hamblet, received his ashes and drove to the Oregon Coast to scatter them at Tillamook Head and along the tideline at Gearhart Beach.

Another old friend, Julia Child, wanted to honor him and his place in American food history by turning his home into a place for gathering, cooking, innovation, and education. With the help of Peter Kump, a former student of Beard's, and a group of culinary luminaries, Beard's New York City brownstone was renovated and became the home of the James Beard Foundation, established in 1986. The annual James Beard Foundation Awards held around Beard's birthday each year have become synonymous with excellence and innovation in the world of food—for chefs, restaurateurs, authors, and journalists.

▲ One of Beard's chef jackets, circa 1980, is in keeping with his preference for denim aprons.

After a brief stint in the Army during World War II, Beard returned to writing cookbooks. He was invited to do a cooking spot on a New York City television show. Soon after, he hosted the country's first nationally televised cooking show, *I Love to Eat*, which ran on NBC from August 1946 to May 1947.

Defining American Food

Beard was a born teacher, and in 1955, he established the James Beard Cooking School in New York City. In 1972, he published *James Beard's American Cookery*, a compendium of more than 1,500 of his favorite recipes.

"In a time when serious cooking meant French Cooking, Beard was quintessentially American," author and food writer Mark Bittman explained, "a Westerner whose mother ran a boarding house, a man who grew up with hotcakes and salmon and meatloaf in his blood."

In the preface to his 2020 biography of Beard, *The Man Who Ate Too Much*, author John Birdsall quotes writer and restaurant critic Gael Greene. "'In the beginning, there was James Beard,'" she said, echoing Child. "'Before Julia, before barbecuing daddies, . . . before a wine closet in the life of every grape nut and the glorious coming of age of American wines, before the new American cooking, chefs as superstars, and our great irrepressible gourmania . . . there was James Beard, our Big Daddy.'"

COCKTAIL CANAPÉS

In its most basic form, a canapé—French for couch—simply refers to a small piece of toasted or firm bread topped with a savory nosh. Canapés and cocktail parties, both popular in the 1950s and '60s, went hand-in-hand. Their purpose was to give cocktailers a one-handed snack, but canapés also served as palettes for creative cooks, who would design outrageously chic and artful spreads. James Beard encouraged practical canapés that maximized flavor but were also easy to negotiate while holding a glass. He penned his first book, *Hors d'Oeuvre and Canapés* (1940), after co-launching a wildly successful catering company called Hors d'Oeuvre, Inc., where he realized the need for guiding hosts and cooks to make better party food. This recipe is not Beard's, but recalls those served at cocktail parties of the era.

MAKES ABOUT 18

8   slices firm-texture bread or ½ of a 12-ounce package party rye bread slices

1   teaspoon olive oil

1   stick butter (½ cup), softened, or ½ cup cream cheese, softened

1   teaspoon lemon zest

     Pinch cayenne pepper

½   cup chopped smoked trout, smoked salmon, or hard-cooked egg

1   tablespoon lemon juice

2   tablespoons chopped fresh dill, Italian parsley, or green onion (or a mix)

     Desired toppers such as capers, finely chopped marinated artichoke hearts, thin-sliced lemon wedges, chopped roasted red pepper, watercress, microgreens or sprouts, fresh herbs, and/or sliced green olives with pimiento

1. If using firm-texture bread slices, remove crusts. Use a 2-inch scalloped round cookie cutter to cut two rounds from each slice or use a knife to cut two 3x½-inch fingers. In a large skillet, toast the bread cutouts (or rye slices) in the oil until golden on one side; transfer to a paper towel, toasted side down (do this in batches, adding more oil if needed). Since the bread is the base for these bites, toasting gives it more structure and flavor.

2. For the flavored butter spread, in a bowl, beat the butter, lemon zest, and cayenne with an electric mixer on medium-high for 30 seconds. Beat in the smoked trout, lemon juice, and dill. If desired, season to taste with salt. Spread the untoasted side of the bread rounds or rye slices generously with the flavored butter. Decorate with desired toppers. Serve immediately or cover and refrigerate for up to 2 hours.

CANAPÉ SANDWICHES: Double the amount of bread. If using rye slices, remove crusts. Toast one side of bread cutouts or rye slices in several batches, using 2 teaspoons olive oil. Continue as directed, generously spreading flavored butter on half the bread pieces all the way to the edge. Top with the remaining pieces, toasted side up. Omit the toppers and roll sides of each sandwich in chopped parsley.

LEAH CHASE

There is a story about an encounter Chef Leah Chase had with President Barack Obama when he visited her legendary New Orleans restaurant, Dooky Chase's, in 2008. The account speaks volumes about how she viewed food not only as an art form that provides nurturance but also as a vehicle for building community and an equalizer among people. The president had ordered a bowl of her famous gumbo. When she set it down, "First thing he does is take the hot sauce," she said in a 2018 interview. That's when she "had to slap him. Mr. Obama, you don't put hot sauce in my gumbo. So I had to reprimand him."

A Love Affair with Restaurants

Food was the driving force of Chase's long life—she died in June 2019 at the age of 96 and could be found working in her restaurant seven days a week until just a few months before that—but it was not the only one. She wove the three main threads of her life—food, art, and activism—into a single tapestry that brightened the lives of all who encountered her.

Born in 1923 in Madisonville, Louisiana—a small town on the north shore of Lake Ponchartrain—Chase, who was of African, French, and Spanish descent, was the second oldest of 11 children of Charles Lange, a farmer and shipyard worker, and Hortensia (Raymond) Lange, a seamstress. Her parents encouraged their children to work hard and get a good education—which was difficult in the segregated South. The Lange children learned to read with books their father pulled from a trash heap at a school for white children. The family was poor, but they ate well. They grew greens, onions, okra, tomatoes, "you name it," Chase told the New York Times in 1990. There was fresh fish from the bayou and chickens and pigs in the barnyard. "We

like to eat," she said, "and we're still always cooking, every time we get together."

Because there were no schools beyond the 6th grade for Black girls in Madisonville, at the age of 13, Chase went to live with her aunt in New Orleans to attend a Roman Catholic high school, where one of the subjects she studied was art. She graduated at age 16 and returned to Madisonville, only to return to New Orleans two years later.

She took a job as a waitress at a restaurant in the French Quarter called The Coffee Pot, which, she told the Times, "was a double no-no." Nice girls, she said, did not go to the French Quarter at all—and especially to work in restaurants. "But I loved it," she said, "I love waiting on tables. I could do that today for a living if I had to." She later said that she saw "just how wonderful the restaurant business was, how you could sit down and enjoy a meal and have someone serve you. Oh, I thought that was the most beautiful thing I'd ever seen."

Equal-Opportunity Fine Dining

In 1946, she married Edgar "Dooky" Chase II, a jazz trumpeter and band

leader. His parents owned a street-corner stand that sold lottery tickets, drinks, and Chase's mother-in-law's po'boys stuffed with chaurice—a spicy Creole pork sausage—or fried oysters. The stand was built in a double shotgun house in the predominantly Black Tremé section of New Orleans. When all of the couple's four children were old enough, Chase began working in the kitchen.

Over time, the younger Chases took over the restaurant, and while Edgar continued to work as a musician, Leah began to transform it into a fine-dining establishment that catered to Black patrons, who were not allowed at restaurants such as Galatoire's and Antoine's.

"Even in the days when my parents were courting, Black people had Little League championship teams, college graduations, and date nights with special people," author and filmmaker Lolis Eric Elie is quoted as saying in Chase's New York Times obituary.

Initially, Chase wanted to "have a restaurant like the ones on the other side of town," she told the Times. "I wanted to do lobster thermidor and cream sauces.

But it didn't work. It wasn't what our clients wanted."

She returned to the Creole classics—jamabalaya, gumbo, and étouffée—that were embraced by the community and that define Dooky Chase's offerings to this day.

Building Bridges with Food

During the Civil Rights movement, Dooky Chase's played a pivotal role in bringing together activists—both Black and white—to strategize. Chase broke segregation laws by serving racially mixed groups. She served Martin Luther King Jr. and the Freedom Riders. "In my dining room," she would often say, "we changed the course of America over a bowl of gumbo and some fried chicken."

"Food builds big bridges," she said in a 2018 interview. "If you can eat with someone, you can learn from them, and when you learn from someone, you can make big changes . . . We can talk to each other and relate to each other when we eat together."

Chase applied this philosophy when—facing pressure from a community still reeling and angry over the federal government's response to Hurricane Katrina two years after the event—she served President George W. Bush crab soup and shrimp Clemenceau. Damage from the storm kept the restaurant closed for two years and nearly destroyed it forever, but she soldiered on. The extensive collection of paintings and sculptures created by African American artists Chase began amassing after Edgar

▶ Chef Leah Chase broke segregation laws in New Orleans by serving racially mixed groups, some of which gathered at her restaurant, Dooky Chase's, to strategize during the Civil Rights Movement.

gave her a work by the late painter Jacob Lawrence was saved by her grandson and reinstated when the restaurant reopened. "Art softens people up and warms them up to deal with each other in humane ways," she told a congressional committee in 1995 at a hearing about funding for the National Endowment for the Arts.

Chase has received nearly every honor the culinary world has to offer. She received the Lifetime Achievement Award from the James Beard Foundation in 2016 and one from the Southern Foodways Alliance in 2000. She was the inspiration for Princess Tiana—Disney's first Black princess—

the heroine of *The Princess and the Frog*, about a waitress who wanted to own a restaurant. One of her iconic red chef jackets hangs in the Smithsonian's National Museum of African American History and Culture.

But for Chase, it was never about the accolades. Cooking for and interacting with her guests was reward enough.

"It makes me feel good. It makes me feel like I have accomplished something, like I have performed a service to someone else," she once said. "When people come back and tell me they remember something I told them, that makes me so happy. I stuck with them in some way."

JULIA CHILD

At a towering 6 feet 3 inches tall—with an imposing intellect to match—a passionate but unlikely advocate for French cuisine burst onto the scene in the early 1960s with a groundbreaking cookbook and television show that would fundamentally change the way many Americans related to food. With wit, candor, humor, contagious enthusiasm, and *ragoût de beouf,* Julia Child challenged the reliance on emerging technologies and the widespread acceptance of convenience foods prevalent in the culture at the time—as well as evolving ideas about the value of time spent in the kitchen—that threatened to wipe out real cooking.

Privilege and Pranks

Julia McWilliams was born on August 15, 1912, in Pasadena, California, the eldest of three children born into a wealthy and highly educated family. Child attended the elite Katherine Branson School for Girls, where friends recalled she loved pulling pranks and could be "really, really wild." She had an appetite for adventure and an aptitude for athletics, excelling in golf, tennis, and small-game hunting.

After graduating from high school, she enrolled at Smith College in Northampton, Massachusetts—her mother's alma mater—to study history, with the intention of becoming a writer. (To this day, Smith College Dining Service celebrates Julia Child Day each November by serving some of her most famous dishes.) Upon graduation in 1934, she returned to California but moved back to Massachusetts the following year to take a secretarial course. One month in, she quit to take a secretarial job in the advertising office of W. J. Sloane, a prestigious furnishings company in New York City, where she worked until 1939, when she was fired for insubordination over the mix-up of a document.

Spy Agency to TV Chef

Back in Pasadena, Child began volunteering with the American Red Cross as the country readied for war. Wanting to become more involved with the war effort, she moved to Washington, D.C., in 1942 and began working as a senior typist for the Research Unit of the Office of War Information. She went on to work as a junior research assistant for the Secret Intelligence Branch of the Office of Strategic Services (OSS), the predecessor of the CIA. She held several positions there, including two that took her to both Ceylon (Sri Lanka) and China during the years 1944–1945. She and her OSS colleagues—including one named Paul Cushing Child—reveled in experiencing the foods of these countries. Julia and Paul developed an interest in food—and in each other.

They married in 1946, and in 1948, Paul Child's work for the U.S. Information Service took them to Paris. It would prove to be pivotal. "As soon as we got over there and I tasted that food," Child said, "I just couldn't get over it."

While living there, Paul encouraged Julia to find something to do, and suggested she enroll at Le Cordon Bleu cooking school. Because of her war service, she was eligible for U.S. government-funded training. She signed up for a professional course

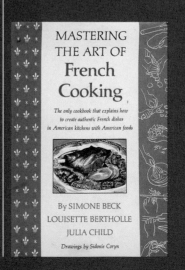

▼ *Mastering the Art of French Cooking* has sold more than 3 million copies.

MASTERING THE ART OF French Cooking

The only cookbook that explains how to create authentic French dishes in American kitchens with American foods

BY SIMONE BECK
LOUISETTE BERTHOLLE
JULIA CHILD

Drawings by Sidonie Coryn

including many former American servicemen. She was the only female student in the class. While in Paris, she met Simone Beck and Louisette Bertholle, with whom she began a decade-long project that became *Mastering the Art of French Cooking*, published in 1961.

The Childs moved back to Massachusetts, and in 1962, Julia made an appearance on public television station WGBH in Boston to promote her new cookbook. She brought along a copper bowl, balloon whisk, apron, and eggs to demonstrate how to make a proper omelette. Viewers were hungry for more.

In 1963, the station launched *The French Chef*—initially contracting with Child to create 26 episodes at $50 each. In the first episode, she demonstrated how to make *boeuf bourguignon*. The series ran for 10 years, gathering a large following.

Not everyone was enthused. She received letters criticizing her for not washing her hands and for her kitchen etiquette. "You are quite a revolting chef, the way you snap bones and play with raw meats," one viewer wrote. "I can't stand those oversanitary people," she retorted.

Others expressed concern about the voluminous amounts of cream and butter she used. "I would rather eat one tablespoon of chocolate *russe* cake than three bowls of Jell-O," Child said.

Education and Entertainment

Child's attention to the details of cooking technique was legendary, and so was her lovable goofiness—two of the qualities that made *The French Chef* so educational and entertaining. In a 1971 episode, "To

▶ Among many other honors over her lifetime, Child received three Emmy nominations, winning one, for her work in educational television.

Roast a Chicken," she opened the show with six plucked raw birds standing at attention on the counter, enthusiastically introducing them as "the Chicken Sisters!" Tapping each with a huge chef's knife, she named them "Miss Broiler! Miss Fryer! Miss Roaster! Miss Caponette! Miss Stewer! And Old Madame Hen."

Over her 40-year career, Child published 17 books—two posthumously—and hosted 11 cooking shows. When she moved from Massachusetts back to her home state of California in 2001, she donated her entire Cambridge kitchen—the cabinets, appliances, cookbooks, kitchen table, and hundreds of utensils

and gadgets—to the Smithsonian's National Museum of American History, where it was reconstructed exactly as it was on the day she left.

When the exhibit was unveiled in 2002—and ever since then—visitors have been able to savor the home kitchen where Julia cooked with family and friends and where her last three television programs were taped in the 1990s.

In 2015, the Julia Child Foundation for Gastronomy and the Culinary Arts established the Julia Child Award to recognize an individual or team that has made "a significant difference in the way America cooks, eats, and drinks."

SMOKED SALMON & DILL SOUFFLÉ

Julia Child understood how to entertain home cooks and ease their fear of failure in the kitchen, while introducing them to her beloved French cuisine. One of the most iconic "Julia" dishes is the very-French soufflé. During a soufflé segment of *The French Chef*, her wildly successful cooking show, she demonstrated how a few staples—butter, flour, milk, and eggs—become, as she calls it, a stupendous soufflé. She deconstructs a seemingly technical dish into a few simple steps and offers helpful tips at every turn: Room-temperature eggs mount higher than chilled ones and should increase sevenfold. If you overbeat the whites and they look dry and speckled, add another egg white or two and re-beat until you get back to the desired sheeny consistency. Stir a big dollop of the egg whites into the soufflé base to lighten it before folding the base into the remaining eggs. This recipe follows Child's soufflé technique, but offers a variation on her classic flavor profile.

SERVES 4

- 4 egg yolks
- 5 egg whites
- 3 tablespoons butter
- 3 tablespoons all-purpose flour
- 1 cup hot milk
- ½ teaspoon paprika
- ½ teaspoon salt
-    Pinch white pepper or cayenne pepper
- ½ of a 4-ounce package hot-smoked salmon, skin removed and flaked (about ½ cup)
- 2 teaspoons chopped fresh dill
- ½ cup shredded Swiss cheese

1. Let the egg yolks and whites stand at room temperature for 30 minutes. Butter the bottom of a 1- or 1½ -quart soufflé dish;* set aside. Set the oven rack to lower third of oven. Preheat the oven to 400°F.

2. In a medium saucepan, melt the butter. With a wooden spoon, stir in the flour to make a loose paste. Cook and stir about 2 minutes or until the mixture foams but does not turn color. Remove from heat. Add the hot milk all at once and whisk vigorously to blend. Return to heat and simmer, stirring constantly, for 3 minutes. Sauce will be thick. Remove from heat and stir in the paprika, salt, and pepper. Add the egg yolks, one at a time, to the sauce, stirring constantly. Stir in the salmon and dill.

3. In a large mixing bowl, beat the egg whites with an electric mixer on medium-high speed until stiff peaks firm (tips stand straight). Stir a cup of the egg whites into the salmon white sauce. Gently fold the remaining egg whites into the sauce, sprinkling in the cheese as you fold. Pour into the prepared dish.

4. Place in the preheated oven and immediately turn the oven to 375°F. Bake until the soufflé is puffed and golden and a knife or skewer inserted near the center comes out clean. Serve immediately.

*NOTE: Julia used a soufflé dish (1 quart) that is slightly small for the soufflé and wrapped the top of the dish with a collar. The soufflé puffs into the collar for extra drama. For the collar, butter a double layer of foil or parchment paper that is large enough to overlap around the dish and is 3 inches taller than the dish. Insert a straight pin or toothpick to hold the collar in place. Gently remove the collar from the dish as soon as you remove the soufflé from the oven and discard.

CURRIED CHICKEN BAKE

In 1960, when Peg Bracken penned her famous *The I Hate to Cook Book*, she was a full-time writer, mother, and wife who was expected to cook too—a task she didn't love. According to her daughter, Jo Bracken, her famous phrase regarding women who actually liked to cook was, "Invite us over often, please. And stay away from our husbands." Bracken's very practical book was positively freeing for other women who felt no affection for the kitchen. She embraced canned soup, tossed-together combinations, and repurposed leftovers as strategies for getting a respectable dinner on the table. The real treat was her acerbic humor, sprinkled throughout in chatty stories, household hints, and clever recipes. She eased the cooking burden and made her readers laugh. This recipe is a modern take on those inspired by those in her book. In the era of James Beard and Julia Child, Bracken's recipes represent the tremendous range of culinary expression of the time. Skid Road Stroganoff or Muffin-Tin Supper anyone?

SERVES 6

- 6 bone-in chicken thighs or 3 pounds assorted meaty chicken pieces, skinned if desired
- 1 sweet yellow onion, cut into thin wedges

  Salt and black pepper
- 1 tablespoon butter
- 1 apple, seeded and chopped (peel if you prefer)
- 2 to 3 tablespoons curry powder
- 1 10.5-ounce can condensed cream of mushroom soup
- 1 cup canned coconut milk or half-and-half
- ⅓ cup chopped dried apricots or golden raisins
- 2 to 3 tablespoons sliced almonds, toasted* (optional)

1. Preheat the oven to 375°F. Place the chicken and onion in a single layer on a 15×10×1-inch sheet pan and sprinkle with a little salt and pepper. Bake, uncovered, for 20 minutes. Meanwhile, in a medium saucepan, melt the butter. Add the apple and curry powder; cook for 2 minutes, stirring when you think of it. Stir in the mushroom soup, coconut milk, and apricots.

2. Remove the sheet pan from the oven. Spoon off the excess fat from the pan and discard. Pour the curry sauce over the chicken and onion. Bake, uncovered, for 30 minutes more or until chicken is no longer pink (170°F for thighs) and sauce is bubbly. If desired, top with the toasted sliced almonds.

*TIP: To toast the almonds, add to a corner of the sheet pan (where there's no chicken or sauce) for about the last 5 minutes of cooking time.

SERVING SUGGESTION: Microwave two 8.5-ounce precooked basmati rice pouches. Top hot rice with the chicken and sauce.

JOYCE CHEN

The next time you order food from a Chinese restaurant, choose from numbered items described in both English and Chinese, enjoy a Chinese buffet, or stir-fry dinner in a flat-bottom wok that sits neatly on your stove, you can thank Joyce Chen. These were among the innovations credited to Chen, who, in her nearly 40-year career as a chef, restaurant owner, businesswoman, inventor, patent holder, cookbook author, culinary teacher, and host of a trailblazing television show, broadened the appeal of Chinese food and helped create widespread enthusiasm for it.

A Narrow Escape

Chen came very close to not making it to the United States at all. Born Liao Jia-ai in 1917 in Beijing to a wealthy family, Chen grew up watching the family chef cook, and she was fascinated. By the time she was 18, she had organized and cooked her first professional dinner.

In 1949, as the Communist Party was taking over China, Chen and her husband, Thomas, and their children, Henry and Helen, got on the second-to-the-last boat to leave Shanghai before the port was closed. They settled in Cambridge, Massachusetts, where Thomas worked as a fine art importer and Joyce settled into her role as a homemaker—until a batch of egg rolls changed everything.

Run on Egg Rolls at the School Bake Sale

In 1957, their three children were attending the Buckingham School, the only Asian American students in a mostly white school. Each year, an event called the Buckingham Circus was held to raise funds for scholarships. Parents brought baked goods to sell at the event, and Chen decided to contribute pumpkin cookies and egg rolls.

The egg rolls, she later cautioned in the *Joyce Chen Cook Book*, were "not authentic." The filling was a combination of "good hamburger," sherry, cornstarch, black pepper, sugar, and a product called brown gravy syrup. She made them with ground beef to make them more familiar to her neighbors.

Chen dropped off the egg rolls at school and returned home. When she went back later that day, the egg rolls were gone. She was afraid there had been no takers and that perhaps someone tucked them under the table or had simply thrown them out. Far from it.

A fellow parent ran into her at the supermarket and told her that her egg rolls had sold out in less than an hour and begged Chen to make more. She did, and brought them to the school, where the students nearly inhaled them.

"Peking Ravioli" and Other Delights

By 1958, Chen had opened the first Joyce Chen Restaurant in Cambridge, where she introduced to patrons Peking duck, hot and sour soup, moo shu pork, scallion pancake, Chinese dumplings, and potstickers—which she called "Peking ravioli." It was here, and at the three additional restaurants that followed, where she tried a number of innovations that still stand in many Chinese restaurants. An all-you-can-eat buffet was set up as a draw on quiet weeknights.

▼ The *Joyce Chen Cook Book*, published in 1962, contains a glossary of common Chinese ingredients in both English and Chinese.

JOYCE CHEN COOK BOOK

家常食譜

FOREWORD BY PAUL DUDLEY WHITE, M. D.

According to her youngest son, Stephen, Chen initially stocked the buffet with authentic northern Chinese dishes—and a ham and a turkey at a carving station. "She felt she had to put a ham and turkey on it because people were familiar with ham and turkey, and they'd think, 'Well, that's a good deal,'" he says. "Within just a few weeks, people weren't eating the ham and turkey."

She insisted on a single menu with both English and Chinese language, and numbered different items to make communication between servers and guests easier. Frequent guests included Henry Kissinger, Jacqueline Onassis, James Beard, and Julia and Paul Child.

Chen also began teaching Chinese cooking at the Cambridge Center for Adult Education. There were waiting lists weeks long. In 1962, she published the *Joyce Chen Cook Book*, which employed a similar tactic to the dual-language menu. In the back of the book, a glossary of common Chinese ingredients was listed in both English and Chinese so it could be taken to a Chinese grocery and, should there be a language barrier, ingredients procured by pointing.

Ruth Lockwood, producer of Julia Child's *The French Chef* on WGBH, approached Chen about hosting a show on Chinese cooking. In 1966, the first of 26 episodes of *Joyce Chen Cooks* debuted, shot on the same stage as *The French Chef*. Chen was the first woman of color to host a nationally broadcast cooking show, demonstrating dishes such as beef and vegetables, Peking duck, egg foo yung, and a variety of Chinese soups.

Bringing Chinese Cooking Home

In 1970, Chen added "inventor" to her list of achievements. She was awarded a patent for her flat-bottom wok with a handle that sat more easily on American stovetops than traditional round-bottom models. Joyce Chen Products, founded in 1971, sold the wok in addition to a line of high-quality Chinese cooking utensils, and in 1984, Joyce Chen Foods began selling Chinese cooking sauces at supermarkets across the country.

Chen died in 1994 of heart failure after a battle with Alzheimer's. Although the last Joyce Chen Restaurant closed in 1998, and her story may not be as widely known as the other famous television chef from Cambridge, her legacy and impact on the fabric of how America eats is undeniable.

"She is the Chinese Julia Child," chef Ming Tsai told the *Chicago Tribune* in 2013. "Joyce Chen helped elevate what Chinese food was about. She didn't dumb it down. She opened people's eyes to what good Chinese could taste like."

▲ Over her lifetime, Joyce Chen was by turns a cookbook author, chef, restaurant owner, cooking teacher, and PBS television program host.

EDNA LEWIS

Edna Lewis has been gone since 2006, but when you open her classic memoir-cookbook, *The Taste of Country Cooking*, she is instantly there in the room with you—quietly unwinding stories of her childhood growing up in Freetown, Virginia, a community established by emancipated slaves, including her grandparents. Lewis' writing is rhythmic, lyrical, and so evocative of place that the reader feels that he or she is there, hearing the snowmelt gurgling in the stream, smelling freshly cut hay, feeling the heat emanating from the woodstove. Lewis' legacy is far more than the telling of beautifully wrought memories of her childhood. She opened the eyes of the country to the fineness of Southern food and how the roots of American fare lay in the Black cooks who created it.

From Farm to Table

Lewis was born in 1916, one of eight children in a family with a long line of excellent cooks. Like all of the families in Freetown, they farmed, foraged, hunted, and fished for all of their food—save staples such as coffee, sugar, and vanilla. It was an in-depth observational and participatory education in the ways of food—how it is attached to season, economy, art, and instinct.

Lewis' father died when she was 12. Lewis set out for Washington, D.C., at age 16, eventually landing in New York City in her early 30s. There, she found work in a Brooklyn laundry, where she lasted only 3 hours—she had never ironed before. She was an experienced seamstress, though, and soon found work making dresses for the likes of Dorcas Avedon, then-wife of photographer Richard Avedon, and Marilyn Monroe. She also began sewing the African dresses that would become her iconic attire.

In the evenings, she threw dinner parties for friends, one of whom was antiques dealer John Nicholson, who in 1948 was opening up a café on the Upper East Side. Having tasted Lewis' cooking at her own table, he asked her to cook at Café Nicholson. There, she prepared simple foods of the best quality—roast chicken, fish, mussels in broth, green salads, cheeses, cake, chocolate soufflé.

The restaurant was a rousing success and became a gathering place for artists, activists, and bohemians. Eleanor Roosevelt, Paul Robeson, Marlon Brando, Richard Avedon, Gloria Vanderbilt, Marlene Dietrich, Diana Vreeland, Gore Vidal, and a trio of Southern writers—Tennessee Williams, William Faulkner, and Truman Capote—were among the regulars.

In 1951, restaurant critic Clementine Paddleford deemed Lewis' soufflé to be "light as a dandelion seed in the wind." Faulkner asked Lewis if she had studied cooking in Paris. No, she told him. She had learned to make soufflés from her mother, on the farm in Freetown.

Lewis left the café after five years and for the next decade-plus worked variously as a pheasant farmer, restaurant owner, caterer, cooking teacher, and docent in the Hall of African Peoples in the American Museum of Natural History.

Then, in the late 1960s, laid up with a broken leg, with the encouragement of legendary editor Judith Jones, she collaborated with socialite Evangeline Peterson on

▼ *The Taste of Country Cooking*— Edna Lewis' most famous book—is organized around the seasons.

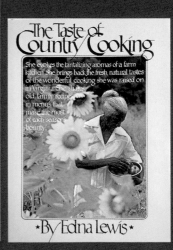

The Edna Lewis Cookbook, published in 1972. When Jones read the manuscript, she found it lacking the warmth and delight that emanated from Lewis as she sat in Jones' office recalling her childhood in Virginia.

▶ Lewis confers with chefs at a 1985 tribute dinner to James Beard, where her biscuits and baked Virginia ham were served.

The Edna Lewis Cookbook was already well on its way to publication, but Jones wanted Lewis to try again, this time in her own prose. Peterson withdrew from the project and in 1976, *The Taste of Country Cooking* was published.

"Breakfast was about the best part of the day," Lewis writes in the introduction to the chapter on Spring. "There was an almost mysterious feeling about passing through the night and awakening to a new day . . . If it was a particularly beautiful morning it was expressed in the grace. Spring would bring our first and just about only fish—shad. It would always be served for breakfast, soaked in salt water for an hour or so, rolled in seasoned cornmeal, and fried carefully in home-rendered lard with a slice of smoked shoulder for added flavor. There were crispy white potatoes, fried onions, batter bread, any food left over from supper, blackberry jelly, delicious hot coffee, and cocoa for the children. And perhaps if a neighbor dropped in, dandelion wine was added."

Selling Southern Food

Lewis would go on to publish two more cookbooks, *In Pursuit of Flavor* in 1988 and *The Gift of Southern Cooking*, a collaboration with chef Scott Peacock, who became her protégé and companion, in 2003. Along the way, she also continued to cook in restaurants,

most notably Brooklyn's Gage & Tollner. Among many other awards, honors, and accolades, Lewis received the James Beard Living Legend Award in 1999—the first given by the foundation.

Eventually, she moved to Atlanta to live with Peacock. Lewis—an older, widowed Black woman and Peacock, a young, white gay man—had an intimate, enduring friendship that earned them the sobriquet of "The Odd Couple of Southern Cooking." Peacock was her caretaker until her death in 2006.

In "My Life with Edna Lewis" for *Bon Appetit*, Peacock describes what was a turning point for him as a young chef, when he crossed paths with Lewis while working as a chef for the governor of

Georgia at age 26. At the time, he writes, he thought "the South was something to recover from. I was eager to put my Alabama childhood behind me."

"Nervous and eager to make an impression on this majestic woman," he writes, "I told her about my job." When Lewis asked Peacock where he attended cooking school, he was embarrassed to tell her he hadn't. "Great," she replied, "Let's go have a drink!"

Over mint juleps, he told her of his dream to travel to Italy and study Italian cooking. "I'd expected encouragement," he writes, "but instead she grew serious. 'I love Italian food too,' she said, 'but you should really learn about your own cooking before running off to study someone else's.'"

SOUTHERN COCONUT CAKE

In Edna Lewis' time, Southern bakers were known for (and judged by) their best cakes. While she had a bevy of beauties, her coconut cake was one of the most popular. It was a signature dessert around Christmas, when fresh coconuts were available. Lewis spread her lemon-touched layer cake with boiled frosting and decorated it with freshly grated coconut. In *The Taste of Country Cooking,* she described cracking the coconut with a "stout hatchet" before prying out the meat with a knife and grating it on a four-sided grater. This version—inspired by Lewis' classic—simplifies the process significantly if you use preshredded coconut.

SERVES 12 TO 16

2   egg yolks, beaten

3   egg whites

1   cup full-fat coconut milk or milk

1   stick butter (½ cup)

2   cups sifted all-purpose flour

2½ teaspoons baking powder

½   teaspoon baking soda

¼   teaspoon salt

1¼ cups granulated sugar

2½ teaspoons lemon juice

1½ teaspoons vanilla

1   recipe Fluffy Coconut Frosting (recipe follows)

    Freshly grated coconut or shredded coconut

1. Let the egg yolks, egg whites, coconut milk, and butter stand at room temperature for 30 minutes. Preheat the oven to 375°F. Grease and flour two 9×2-inch baking pans. Sift together the sifted flour, baking powder, baking soda, and salt; set aside.

2. In a large mixing bowl, beat the butter with an electric mixer on medium to high speed for 30 seconds. Add the sugar, ¼ cup at a time, beating on medium speed and scraping sides of the bowl after each addition. Beat for 2 minutes more. Beat in the egg yolks until well combined, scraping sides of the bowl. Beat in the lemon juice and vanilla. Starting and ending with the flour mixture, alternately add flour mixture and milk to butter mixture, beating on low speed after each addition just until combined. Set aside.

3. In a clean large mixing bowl, beat the egg whites to soft peaks (tips curl) and fold them gently into the batter. Spoon batter equally into the prepared cake pans.

4. Bake on the middle rack of the oven for 20 to 25 minutes or until the cake has shrunk away from the sides of the pan and a wooden toothpick inserted near the center comes out clean. Cool the pans on a wire rack for 10 minutes. Remove the cake layers from pans. Cool completely on racks, gently covering with a clean towel after 10 minutes (to keep the outside of the cakes from drying out).

5. Dust any crumbs from the cooled cake layers. Place a cake layer on a serving plate and frost top generously with some of the Fluffy Coconut Frosting. Top with the second layer, and frost the top and sides with remaining frosting. Sprinkle the top and sides with coconut.

FLUFFY COCONUT FROSTING: In a small saucepan, combine 1 cup plus 2 tablespoons granulated sugar, ¼ cup water, and a pinch of salt. Let stand for 15 minutes. Cook the mixture over low heat, stirring until the sugar dissolves. Cover and cook over medium heat 2 to 3 minutes to dissolve the sugar crystals from the sides of pan. Uncover and cook until 230°F to 233°F (This is the thread stage. When a teaspoon is dipped into the syrup in the pan and lifted out, the syrup falls off the spoon in long, thin threads). Remove the pan from heat. Working quickly, in a large mixing bowl, beat 3 egg whites and ½ teaspoon cream of tartar to stiff peaks (tips stand straight up). Gradually pour the hot syrup into the egg whites, beating constantly. Add 1 teaspoon lemon juice and ½ teaspoon coconut or vanilla extract, and continue beating until the frosting is spreading consistency. Immediately use to frost cooled cake.

ALICE WATERS

While James Beard may be considered the "Dean of American Cookery," there is no question who holds the title of "Mother of Modern American Cuisine." Chez Panisse, the legendary restaurant founded by Alice Waters in Berkeley, California, in 1971, served as the headwaters of a new style of American cooking that embraced fresh, organic, and locally produced ingredients. From there, this ethos flowed and expanded across the United States. Waters and the chefs who worked in the Chez Panisse kitchen, many of whom went on to establish their own restaurants, helped inspire many Americans to care about and get to know locally sourced ingredients, from arugula to goat cheese to heirloom tomatoes.

Apricot Jam on a Hot Baguette

That Waters made her life in the kitchen was something of a surprise—perhaps to no one more than herself. "When I graduated from college it was just kind of expected you would get married and have children," she has said, ". . . it never occurred to me that I would go down another path."

She did do both of those things—giving birth to daughter, Fanny, in 1983, and marrying Fanny's father, Stephen Singer, a winemaker, olive oil merchant, and painter, in 1985 (the couple divorced in the late 1990s)—but she also did far more than that.

In the early 1960s, Waters left Chatham, New Jersey, where she was born and raised— the second of four daughters of Charles Waters, a management consultant, and Margaret Waters, a homemaker—for college in California.

▶ The kitchen staff of Chez Panisse poses for a picture in 1982. Founder Alice Waters has said that the structure is not a "pyramid." Everyone does a bit of everything, and everyone tastes the dish.

Waters graduated from UC Berkeley with a degree in French cultural studies in 1967 after spending her junior year studying at the University of Paris. It was in France, she says, that she "really woke up to real food. I remember that first taste of apricot jam on a baguette that was still hot from the oven," she recalled in an interview with the online magazine *First We Feast*. "I wanted to eat that every day—and I did!"

Eat Local

After college, Waters returned to Europe to do postgraduate study at the Montessori School in London and travel. In Brittany, she ate at a restaurant at which the chef came out to the

dining room and announced what that night's menu would be—trout caught from a nearby stream, fresh raspberries, and other ingredients that were entirely locally sourced. "I tasted things I couldn't believe," she told *People* magazine. "I just absorbed everything."

When she returned to Berkeley, she was determined to re-create that experience. She borrowed $10,000 and bought an old house on Shattuck Avenue, and in 1971 opened Chez Panisse—named for a character in a triology of French films—with Victoria Wise, the first chef, and Lindsey Shere, the first pastry chef. The restaurant featured just one menu each night.

From the beginning, Chez Panisse relied solely on locally produced meats, poultry, fish, vegetables, fruits, cheeses, olive oil, and wine. They baked their own bread. They filled the rustic dining room with fresh flowers. Waters and her staff were creating French-inspired meals with American ingredients, and the world took notice.

"Where American gastronomy is concerned, there is one commodity that is rarer than locally grown black truffles or homemade foie gras. That is a chef of international repute who was born in the United States," *New York Times* food writer Craig Claiborne wrote of Waters at the 10th anniversary of Chez Panisse. "Ever rarer is such a celebrated chef a woman."

Chef and Activist

In the mid-1990s, Waters—an activist at heart—turned her attention to changing children's diets and educating them

▶ Waters in the kitchen of Chez Panisse in 2014.

on how food is produced. Starting with Berkeley's Martin Luther King Jr. Middle School, she established the Edible Schoolyard program in which students grow, harvest, and prepare their own school lunches in a kitchen classroom. Since then, the Edible Schoolyard program has grown to more than 9,500 schools around the country.

Waters has been lavished with praise, but she also has been the target of critics who call her elitist or tone deaf to those who can't afford organic ingredients.

"That's a message coming from a fast-food industry that would prefer you buy packaged meals," Waters told the

Harvard Business Review. "It suggests that you don't want the drudgery of cooking or going to a farmers market or having a garden. But when you buy direct and cook yourself, it cuts out the middleman: The money goes to somebody who is taking care of the land, and you're giving your family more-nutritious food. I understand that when people don't know how to cook, it might be hard to imagine making three meals out of one expensive chicken. But it's not difficult to learn, and it's a pleasure. If we all learn basic cooking skills, we can make extremely affordable food."

MIXED GREEN SALAD WITH BAKED GOAT CHEESE

Alice Waters, the first woman to win the James Beard Award for Outstanding Chef, has said that she would rather make salads than almost anything else. "When I was invited to New York to receive an award, out of 25 chefs, I was the only woman," she told *Time* magazine. "We each presented a dish. All of the men had fancy French dishes—ice carvings, sautéed lobster. I had brought a salad. I will never forget how self-conscious I was. I kept saying, 'I borrowed the bowl from James Beard, I made the vinaigrette, and these are the kinds of lettuces.' It was excruciating to think I had been so naive. And yet when they reviewed the dishes, all they talked about was the salad." It's no surprise, then, that she dreamed up one of the most iconic dishes of the late 1980s—baked goat cheese salad. It spurred the creation of many admiring versions, including this one.

SERVES 4

FOR THE GARLIC TOASTS

12 (¼-inch-thick) slices day-old baguette

2 tablespoons butter, melted

1 clove garlic, halved

FOR THE CHEESE

1 cup plain dry bread crumbs

½ teaspoon freshly ground black pepper

2 large eggs

1 tablespoon Dijon mustard

2 teaspoons minced fresh thyme

2 teaspoons minced fresh chives

1 (8-ounce) log goat cheese

Extra-virgin olive oil

FOR THE VINAIGRETTE AND GREENS

2 tablespoons white wine vinegar

1 tablespoon Dijon mustard

1 teaspoon minced shallot

Kosher salt and freshly ground black pepper

6 tablespoons extra-virgin olive oil

8 cups loosely packed sturdy lettuces and/or greens (such as arugula, frisée, baby Swiss chard, sorrel, mizuna, red or green leaf, and/or baby green or red oak)

1. **FOR THE GARLIC TOASTS:** Preheat the oven to 350°F. Brush both sides of the baguette slices with melted butter. Arrange in a single layer on a baking sheet. Bake until golden brown, about 15 minutes, turning once halfway through baking. Rub both sides of the toasts with the cut sides of the garlic cloves. Set aside.

2. **FOR THE CHEESE:** Turn oven to 475°F. Combine bread crumbs and pepper in a medium bowl. In another medium bowl, whisk together the eggs and mustard. Combine thyme and chives in a small bowl.

3. Using kitchen twine or dental floss, cut cheese into 8 even pieces. Roll each piece into a ball; roll each ball in the herbs to lightly coat. Place 4 of the pieces in the egg mixture, turning each piece to coat. Place in bread crumbs and turn to coat, pressing the crumbs into the cheese. Flatten each ball into a 1½-inch-wide, 1-inch-thick disk and set on a baking sheet. Repeat with remaining cheese. Freeze until firm, about 30 minutes.

4. Brush tops and sides of cheese evenly with olive oil. Bake until crumbs are golden brown and cheese is slightly soft, 7 to 9 minutes.

5. **FOR THE VINAIGRETTE AND GREENS:** Meanwhile, in a large salad bowl, combine the vinegar, mustard, shallot, and ¼ teaspoon salt. Whisking constantly, drizzle in the olive oil. Season with pepper to taste.

6. When cheese is done baking, remove from oven and let stand for 3 minutes. Add greens to the bowl, toss gently to coat with vinaigrette, and divide among four salad plates.

7. Arrange 2 pieces of warm goat cheese and 3 toasts on each plate. Serve immediately.

MOLLIE KATZEN

In 1989, shortly after her third cookbook, *Still Life with Menu*, was published, Mollie Katzen told the *New York Times* that she was 10 years old when she discovered that spaghetti didn't come from a can, and that she was into her teens before she ate fresh broccoli, cauliflower, or asparagus. "I grew up believing that vegetables were something that grew in my mother's freezer," she told the *Times* in 2013. Her first professional cooking job was flipping burgers at a department-store grill at the age of 16. This did not appear, the *Times* noted, to be the "curriculum vitae" of the author of one of the best-selling vegetarian cookbooks of all time. The road to that outcome was, of course, a journey.

"Beholding" Food

Katzen grew up in Rochester, New York, in a Conservative observant Jewish home, where *kashrut*—dietary laws— were followed. Although she's no longer observant, "Kashrut is the beginning," she told the *Jewish Telegraphic Agency* in 2011. "Keeping food is real sacred to me. Even a bowl of popcorn in front of the TV, I love to 'behold' the popcorn and not just mindlessly reach in and eat it."

When she left home for college at Cornell University in the late 1960s, Katzen generally avoided what she called the "mystery meat" at the dining hall. "I didn't trust meat out in the world. That was my Jewish upbringing," she told *JTL*. "Kashrut gave me a sense of: 'What's the origin of my meat?'"

It was a time when young people questioned many things about America. Some were turning to vegetarianism as a way to do their small part to better the world, or to protest the larger society's values.

"In my day, vegetarian was a generational statement . . . It was

very much about our own statement of who we were in the late '60s and through the '70s—defining the counterculture, differentiating ourselves from our parents' culture of the '50s and '60s," Katzen told *Epicurious* in a 2013 interview. "It was a coming-of-age identity frame for a lot of us. We wanted to express a love of nature, and a concern about the environment, and a sense of the spiritual, and a sense of our own rebellion against our parents. It was a lovely alternative, the whole lifestyle as a statement for a lot of people."

The Collective Comes Together

That search for a way of doing things led Katzen and a small group of friends to establish a vegetarian restaurant, to be run collectively, in downtown Ithaca, New York, in 1973. They called it Moosewood Restaurant after a local maple tree and began serving up vegetarian fare to a highly enthusiastic community.

After more than a year of getting recipe requests from customers,

▼ Mollie Katzen hand-lettered the recipes in *Moosewood Cookbook* and filled its pages with whimsical illustrations.

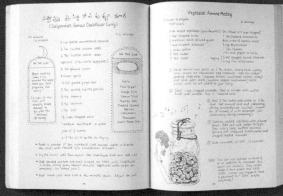

Katzen, who holds a bachelor's degree in fine art from the San Francisco Art Institute, hand-lettered, illustrated, and self-published 5,000 spiral-bound copies of recipes from the restaurant. The book was a runaway hit, selling 800 copies a week in a town of 15,620 people.

It wasn't long before the late Phil Wood, then publisher of Ten Speed Press in Berkeley, California, got hold of Katzen's book. He had an "instant instinct" for it and offered her $10,000 for the rights to republish it—five times what Doubleday had bid—and gave her complete editorial control.

His instincts were spot on. The first trade edition of *Moosewood Cookbook* was published in 1977. To date, *Moosewood*—the original and a revised version that came out in 1992—has sold more than 3 million copies. According to the *New York Times,* it's on the top-10 list of the best-selling cookbooks of all time.

Whimsy and Wheat Berries

The appeal of the book lies not only in the recipes themselves but also in the warmth and playfulness of its author.

Katzen's concept of beholding food radiates from the pages of *Moosewood*. Many of the hand-lettered recipes have whimsical titles such as Cream of Summer Green (a soup), White Rabbit Salad (a cottage cheese and apple salad with raisins, toasted nuts, and sunflower seeds), Bulgarian Pepper and Cheese Delight, and Vericheesey Casserole. A recipe for Chinese Duck Sauce is accompanied by an illustration of a duck saying "No duck in there." Its pages are covered with illustrations of vegetables,

▶ Katzen in front of Moosewood Restaurant in Ithaca, New York, in 1974.

cooking utensils, winged pears, and cherubs holding up a cheesecake.

Katzen followed up the original *Moosewood* with *The Enchanted Broccoli Forest* in 1982 and has since published a total of 15 cookbooks, more than 6 million in print, including three highly regarded cookbooks for children—*Pretend Soup and Other Real Recipes, Honest Pretzels,* and *Salad People and More Real Recipes*. She was inducted into the James Beard Cookbook Hall of Fame in 2007, and in 2017, her notebooks, correspondence, and original hand-lettered pages were collected by curators at the Smithsonian's National Museum of American History, where they are housed.

Although Katzen is among a handful of people credited with bringing about the plant-based revolution, she does not consider herself a vegetarian. For her, there has never been any dogma about avoiding meat, she says, and she was never a proponent of being vegetarian. She is, she says, simply a "vegetable lover." She eats small amounts of meat on occasion and only that which is sustainably raised and sourced.

"For me," she told *Epicurious,* "vegetarian these days refers to the food and not the person . . . It's no longer necessarily the big identity type of thing. It's not who I am, but what I'm eating."

ZARELA MARTÍNEZ

In many ways, Zarela Martínez was born to be the unofficial ambassador for Mexican food and culture in the United States. Her outlook on life reflects attitudes and traditions from both cultures. She explains, "I think like an American, but I act like a Mexican. I raised my kids as Mexican and most of my traditions are Mexican, and I honor and cherish my background. My mission in life is to promote the culture and make us understood." But, she says, "In business, I think like an American."

Martínez grew up on a large ranch in the northern state of Chihuahua, Mexico. At the start of the Mexican Revolution in the 1910s, she says, "anyone who had money moved to the United States." Martínez's maternal grandparents moved to Santa Monica, California. Martínez's parents and her siblings were born in the United States. Her parents went to Chihuahua, where Martinez was born, in order to have her name put on the property.

Although Martínez was sent at age 8 to a private boarding school in El Paso, Texas, she returned to the ranch on breaks all the way through high school and the year spent at an elite finishing school in Guadalajara. After graduating, she endeavored to discover what career she would like to pursue. Martínez spent a lot of time experimenting in the kitchen. It was this combination of cross-cultural education, living and breathing the rhythm of a working ranch, and parental modeling of fearlessness, hospitality, and cooking (her mother) and a deep interest in all things artistic (her father) that endowed her with the attributes that would make her an icon in the American culinary canon.

"It is important to understand that I was not raised as a girl," Martínez says.

"I was raised as a person who could do anything she chose to do, and I was expected to do that. It was not just a matter of being fearless, but feeling totally secure in what I was doing."

In the early 1970s, she was back in El Paso, working as a social worker, married, and pregnant with twins. Cooking continued to be a hobby, but it would soon turn into a career.

Finding Success: A Reputation Grows
Martínez eventually quit her job and went into the culinary business full time. In 1981, her life took an "abrupt Cinderella-Zarela turn," she writes in her 1992 cookbook and memoir, *Food from My Heart*, after a chance encounter with Chef Paul Prudhomme at K-Paul's in New Orleans. She and her mother had traveled there and found themselves seated in front of Prudhomme at his restaurant. Martínez struck up a conversation that ended up with him offering to teach her something about Cajun food if she would teach him something about Mexican food—which for most Americans at the time was fairly narrowly defined. "You know the combination plate? That's what they thought," Martínez says. "Brown gravy on everything, flavored only with

cumin." For the next three days, Martínez cooked in Prudhomme's kitchen, and everything, especially the *enchiladas de cangrejo*—crab enchiladas—were a hit.

The experience led to Prudhomme asking Martínez to prepare Mexican-inspired dishes for a dinner for the Maîtres Cuisiniers de France at Tavern on the Green in New York. "Needless to say," Martínez writes, "it was a watershed."

After the event at Tavern on the Green, the doors began opening in a domino effect. Craig Claiborne, food journalist and *New*

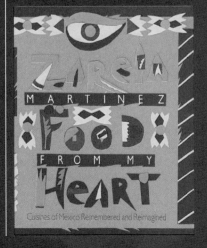

▼ While *Food from My Heart* contains recipes, much of it is a memoir detailing Zarela Martínez's life.

York Times restaurant critic, wrote an article about her, which led to her cooking at an event at the Reagan White House, and then for an international economic summit in Williamsburg, Virginia, in May 1983. Between these events, in April of that year, Martínez packed up her boys—she and her husband had long since separated—and moved to New York City.

Travels South: A Culinary Education
In 1984, she took a job as the head chef of Café Marimba. She wanted to know more about regional Mexican cuisine in order to represent it at the restaurant, and began taking trips the following year to all parts of Mexico, filling notebooks and taking photographs.

"I was flabbergasted when I started traveling in Oaxaca and Chiapas and to other places to discover the tremendous variety of Mexican food," she says.

Martínez brought her newfound knowledge to Café Marimba and then three years later to Zarela, the eponymously named restaurant she ran for 24 years, until it closed in 2011.

When she opened Zarela, she says, gone was the timid girl who initially told Paul Prudhomme she didn't know how to properly chop an onion.

"By now I had arrived at a cuisine representing, I felt, not just the mestizo character of Mexican food generally but my own personal process of *mestizaje*, synthesis," she writes in *Food from My Heart*. "I was making dishes true to their origins—whether simple, hearty ranch food, tropically flavored *recados*, or lavish *moles*—but I was experimenting by juxtaposing different elements. I might for example, take a thick blue corn tortilla

▲ Martínez—who grew up in both Mexico and the U.S.— traveled extensively in Mexico to learn about its regional foods.

from the state of Mexico, top it with a version of braised pork I'd known all my life from Sonora, and serve it with a Oaxacan sauce and Yucatecan *escabeche de cebolla*. In this way the layer of flavors that diners encountered in one of my meals reflected the depth of possibilities in Mexican cooking."

In 2001, Martínez was featured in a PBS series *Zarela! La Cocina Veracruzana* as a companion to her cookbook, *Zarela's Veracruz*. In 2013, the James Beard Foundation inducted her into the Who's Who of Food & Beverage in America, and the Schlesinger Library at Harvard acquired her papers—34 notebooks,

35,000 photographs, and a collection of personal effects— which reside alongside those of Julia Child, Elizabeth David, Avis DeVoto, and M.F.K. Fisher.

"When I came to New York, I was going to open a restaurant, write a book, have a television show and a product line, and the last thing I was going to do was leave a legacy," Martínez says. "Because Schlesinger acquired my papers, people can delve into the intimate lives [of people] and traditions from all over Mexico that live on there."

MANCHAMANTELES DE POLLO

Zarela Martínez grew up on a ranch in northern Mexico. This dish—Braised Chicken in Spicy Fruit Sauce—from the southernmost state of Chiapas, which borders Guatemala, was one of the first dishes she tasted that piqued her curiosity about foods from other parts of Mexico. She was introduced to it by family friends in high school. The name means "tablecloth stainer," and "the tablecloth really did get stained when we ate it!" she writes in *Food from My Heart*. "It was wonderful, rich and complicated, with a thick, succulent texture and different notes of sweet-tart fruit, fragrant spices, and chile. We would dip the chicken pieces in more of the sauce and suck blissfully. It has been one of my favorites ever since."

SERVES 6 TO 8

⅔ to ¾ cup vegetable oil

1 medium onion, sliced into thin half-moons (about 1 cup)

2 large garlic cloves, minced

1 can (28 ounces) whole tomatoes, with juice

2 bay leaves

½ to 1 teaspoon freshly ground black pepper or to taste, plus a little more for seasoning chicken

1 to 2 teaspoons salt

¼ to ⅓ teaspoon ground cloves

1½ teaspoons ground Ceylon cinnamon or ½ teaspoon ground U.S. cinnamon

1 teaspoon ground cumin

1 teaspoon dried Mexican oregano, crumbled

½ cup dried apricots, sliced

¾ cup pitted dried prunes, whole or sliced

½ cup golden raisins

1 can (20 ounces) unsweetened pineapple chunks, with juice

½ cup dry sherry or red wine

1 tablespoon cider vinegar

1 cup Adobo de Chile Colorado (recipe page 285)

2 chickens (about 3½ pounds each), cut into 6 to 8 pieces

1 to 2 medium tart apples, such as Granny Smith, cored and cut into eighths

Corn tortillas, for serving

1 to 2 tablespoons butter, optional

1 large ripe plantain, peeled and sliced, optional

Cinnamon sugar, made with 1 tablespoon sugar to 1 teaspoon ground cinnamon, optional

1. Heat 2 tablespoons of the oil in a heavy, medium-size saucepan over medium-high heat until hot but not quite smoking. Add the onion and garlic, and cook, stirring, until golden and translucent, 3 to 4 minutes. Add the tomatoes, breaking them up with your hand. Add the bay leaves, ½ teaspoon of the black pepper, 1 teaspoon of the salt, the cloves, cinnamon, cumin, and oregano. Bring to a boil, then reduce the heat to low and simmer, uncovered, 10 to 12 minutes. Working in batches if necessary, puree the mixture in a blender and transfer to a large Dutch oven.

2. Bring the pureed sauce to a boil over high heat, adding the dried fruits, pineapple with its juice, sherry or red wine, and vinegar while it heats. Let simmer a minute, then add the adobo. Taste for seasoning and add a bit more salt if desired. Reduce the heat to medium-low and simmer the sauce, uncovered, about 10 minutes. While it cooks, heat about ½ cup oil in a large heavy skillet over high heat until almost smoking. Sprinkle the chicken on all sides with salt and black pepper.

3. Working with 3 or 4 pieces at a time, brown the chicken on both sides (add a little more oil to the skillet if necessary). As they are browned, add them to the simmering sauce. Add the apple pieces to the sauce and chicken. Let the sauce return to a boil and simmer, covered, until the chicken is cooked through, 25 to 30 minutes. Serve with corn tortillas.

4. If you wish to garnish, melt the butter in a medium-size saucepan over medium heat. When the butter begins to bubble, add the plantain slices and cook, stirring, until golden on both sides. Sprinkle with cinnamon sugar and arrange over the *manchamanteles*.

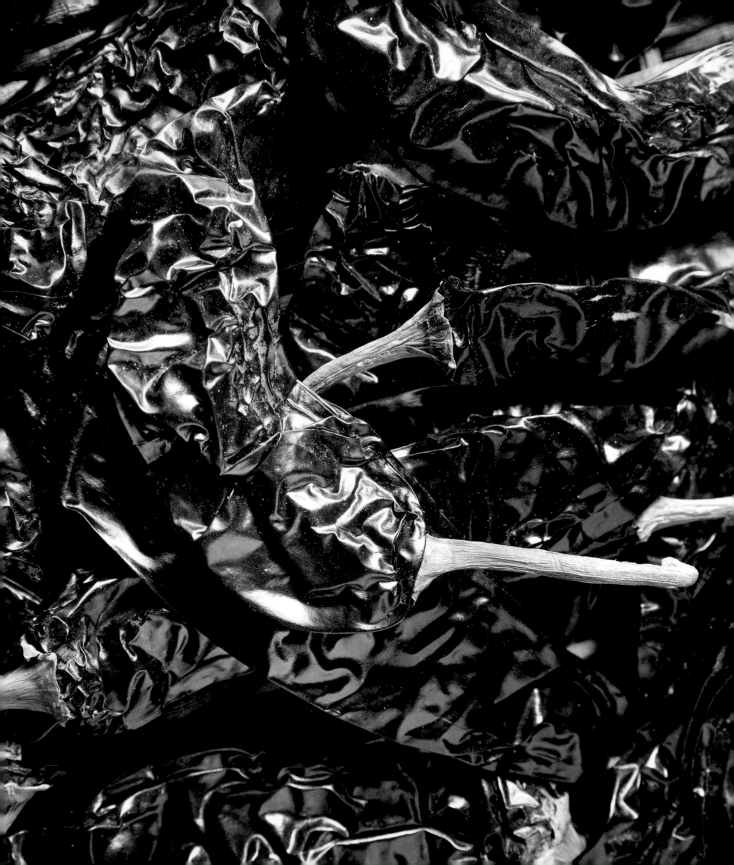

ADOBO DE CHILE COLORADO

"The flavor of this typical marinade/coating will depend on the hotness and the variety of the chiles used," writes Zarela Martínez in *Food from My Heart*. "The recipe illustrates one technique of preparing dried chiles so as to soften them and enrich the flavor, first by frying them in hot fat (being careful *never* to scorch—the dish will have a horrible bitter taste) and then soaking them in hot water. Usually they are roasted on a griddle, fried, or softened in hot water, or some combination of these steps. This adobo is good brushed on pork, grilled chicken, or fish. It also lends some real interest to Tex-Mex chili con carne."

MAKES ¾ TO 1 CUP

2 tablespoons lard or vegetable oil

4 medium-hot whole dried red chiles, either ancho, guajillo, or Anaheim, stems intact

1½ cups boiling water

1 large garlic clove, peeled and finely minced

1 teaspoon dried Mexican oregano

1. Heat the lard or oil in a small or medium-size heavy skillet over medium heat until rippling. Fry the whole chiles, one at a time, turning several times with tongs, until puffed and red or slightly orange in color, 30 to 60 seconds. Be careful not to let them burn!

2. As the chiles are done, add them to the boiling water in a bowl. Let soak until softened, about 10 minutes. Push them down if they float. Drain.

3. Pull or cut off the chile tops and scrape out the seeds. Discard the tops and seeds. Place the soaked chile pods in a blender with the garlic, oregano, and 1 cup water. Process to a smooth puree. Add a little more water if desired to facilitate blending, but the sauce should be thick.

4. Place a medium-mesh sieve over a bowl. Pour the paste into the sieve and force it through with a wooden spoon, scraping and rubbing to push through as much of the solids as possible. Discard any bits that won't go through.

5. Store, tightly covered, in the refrigerator up to a month, or indefinitely in the freezer.

NANCY SILVERTON

If you are of a certain age, you might remember taking slices of a familiar white bread and, because it was so soft and full of air, rolling bits of it into balls in your elementary school cafeteria or under the family dinner table. That pillowy, highly engineered bread was standard in America for decades since its introduction in 1921, until a baking revolution took hold in California in the 1980s pioneered by a few passionate practioners, one of whom became synonymous with an artisanal movement that opened the eyes of Americans to how much better bread could be when it was baked the way it had been done thousands of years ago.

From Poli-Sci to Pastry

Nancy Silverton was born in 1954 to a television writer and a lawyer and raised in Southern California's Encino Valley. When she enrolled in Sonoma State University, she signed up to study political science.

"I never ever intended to be a politician. Never," she told the *Montecito Journal*. "Isn't [poli-sci] the go-to major people who don't know what they want to study put down?"

While in college, she began cooking in the dormitory kitchen—in part to impress a boy—when she had an epiphany.

"I still remember that day," she told *Los Angeles Magazine* in 2018. "I was following the recipe for something as simple as lentil loaf or steamed vegetables and melted cheese, a chef's knife holding the pages of my cookbook open, and I thought, 'This is what I want to do.' From then on, my path never changed."

Silverton called her parents and told them she was dropping out of school—she was a senior—and that she wanted to cook professionally. Despite the fact

at the time (it was 1976), being a cook, or chef, or restaurant owner didn't carry the cachet it does now, her parents were very supportive. Her father told her that was fine, as long as she went to "the best" culinary school—Le Cordon Bleu in London. So she did.

Back to the Basics

When she returned to Southern California after graduation in 1979, Silverton worked as a pastry chef for two restaurants that were at the vanguard of what came to be called "California cuisine"—Michael's in Santa Monica, and Wolfgang Puck's Spago in West Hollywood.

While at Spago, she began to experiment with bread baking after reading an article about Steve Sullivan of Acme, an artisan bakery in San Francisco. She soaked grapes—which have naturally occurring yeast—in water and flour for days. She experimented with different flours, water and air temperatures, and rising times.

When she and her then-husband, Mark Peel, opened their iconic and influential

restaurant, Campanile, on South La Brea Avenue in Los Angeles in 1989, she knew that if she wanted the best bread possible, she would make it herself. Even before the restaurant opened, they opened La Brea Bakery in a space that adjoined the restaurant.

"In the process of what would eventually become La Brea Bakery, I talked to oven

▼ Nancy Silverton's 1996 book, *Breads from the La Brea Bakery*, walks home bakers through the steps of making artisan-style bread.

manufacturers, flour millers, bakery consultants, to any expert I could find," she writes in the introduction to her 1996 book, *Breads from the La Brea Bakery*. "I read crumbling nineteenth-century cookbooks and jargon-filled papers on the scientific properties of sourdough baking."

She refused to use commercial yeast and standard commercial bakery equipment, which flummoxed those she talked to in the bakery industry. She determined "the most frustrating and ultimately satisfying thing I discovered: Bread is alive."

La Brea Bakery was a breakout hit. On Thanksgiving Day 1990, the line to buy bread stretched around the block and down a side street.

The reason, it has to be surmised, is that Silverton's breads were so much more interesting than anything else that was available in most of the United States at the time. Silverton describes her ideal loaf as "neither squishy or pale." It is beautifully burnished—the color of "burnt sienna" on the outside, with a natural sheen on the crust, which should crackle. The interior should have a porous texture with an irregular cell structure, and should be elastic but not rubbery. It should feel cool to the touch, and have flavor that is complex—at once slightly sweet from the caramelization on the crust and tangy from the fermentation.

Continuing Impact
Silverton backed off from the bakery in 1993, and in 2001, she and her partners sold it to an Irish conglomerate that now

▶ Silverton prepares food at Cassia restaurant for the 2016 L.A. Chefs for Human Rights fundraiser.

sells La Brea breads to grocery stores across the country.

Though Silverton trained as a pastry chef, not a cook, she went on to be more active as a chef than a baker, opening up Pizzeria Mozza, Osteria Mozza, Mozza2Go, and chi SPACCA in and around Los Angeles—all of which focus on fresh, vegetable-centric Mediterranean-inspired dishes informed and benefited by Silverton's legendary palate.

"If someone asked me to fillet a whole fish, I wouldn't have a clue," she told *Food & Wine*. "But if I taste a dish, I'll know exactly what it needs." She'll add a drop of lemon juice or splash of balsamic vinegar, a sprinkle of sea salt or truffle salt, or a dusting of fennel pollen to "bring the flavor to another level." In 2014, she received the Outstanding Chef Award from the James Beard Foundation.

If she hadn't spearheaded the artisan bread movement in Los Angeles—and eventually across the country—she says, it would have been someone else a few years later. "People were saying, 'You're responsible for bringing bread to L.A.,'" she told *Los Angeles Magazine*. "Maybe I started a bakery, maybe I raised the bar for restaurant bread, but I certainly did not invent bread."

ROSEMARY-OLIVE SOURDOUGH BREAD

In Nancy Silverton's *Breads from the La Brea Bakery*, she writes, "Natural leavening, slow by nature, gives this more rustic loaf the time that it needs to develop texture and flavor." Her loaves start with a 14-day starter instead of packaged yeast. The starter creates its own yeast for rising and lactic-acid-producing bacteria for a tangy flavor. For this savory Silverton-inspired olive bread, use any sourdough starter that's developed and ready to use. Silverton recommends rustic breads be stored at room temperature, cut side down in a paper bag, because plastic bags tend to make the crust soft and encourage mold to develop more quickly.

MAKES 2 BOULES (ROUND LOAVES)

6½ cups white bread flour

2 cups unchlorinated water, room temperature

1½ cups sourdough starter (developed and ready to use)

½ cup raw wheat germ

½ cup whole wheat pastry flour

1 tablespoon kosher salt

1 cup pitted Kalmata olives or a mix of Kalamata and cured black olives (halved lengthwise)

1 to 2 tablespoons chopped fresh rosemary

1 tablespoon extra-virgin olive oil

1. In a large mixer bowl fitted with a dough hook, combine half the bread flour, the water, sourdough starter, and wheat germ. Mix with an electric mixer on low speed 1 minute; scrape down sides. Stir in the remaining bread flour and the pastry flour, and mix on low for 3 minutes more. Cover; let stand 25 minutes. Add the salt and mix on low 4 minutes more, scraping sides as needed. Add the olives and rosemary; mix on low 4 minutes more.

2. On a lightly floured surface, knead the dough about 3 minutes or until the dough is smooth and elastic. Lightly coat a clean bowl with olive oil. Add dough; cover and let rise until double in size, about 4 hours. Turn the dough onto a lightly floured surface. Cut the dough into two equal pieces. Knead dough a couple times to deflate. Form each piece into a boule (ball), tucking edges under. Cover with a clean towel; let rest about 15 minutes.

3. Transfer each boule, smooth side down, to a floured proofing basket or a bowl lined with a well-floured clean kitchen towel. Cover loosely with a clean towel. Let stand at room temperature 1½ hours. Uncover and wrap the dough in baskets or lined bowls with plastic wrap. Refrigerate 8 to 10 hours.

4. Remove the plastic wrap and cover the dough in baskets or bowls with the kitchen towel again. Let stand at room temperature for 2½ hours. Meanwhile, place a bread stone or baking tiles onto the middle oven rack. Preheat the oven to 500°F.

5. Remove cloth and lightly dust dough with flour. Gently invert each boule onto a pizza peel or bottom side of a sheet pan. With a clean single-edge razor or sharp knife, cut 3 parallel slashes in one boule, about ½ inch deep.

6. Fill a clean spray bottle with clean water. Open the oven door and spritz the water all over the oven. Shut the door. Immediately place the boule with the slashes onto the bread stone (leaving room for the second boule) and shut the oven door. Repeat with the second boule, spritzing the oven with additional water before adding it to the baking stone. Immediately reduce the oven temperature to 450°F. Open the oven door quickly and spritz oven (not boules) with water two more times in the next few minutes. Bake for 40 minutes more or until deep brown, rotating boules halfway through baking if needed. Transfer to a cooling rack. Cool completely before slicing.

JOSÉ ANDRÉS

In 1990, at the age of 21, José Andrés arrived in the United States from Spain with $50 in his pocket. By 2010, two of his Washington, D.C., restaurants, Oyamel Cocina Mexicana and minibar, were favorites of both local diners and visitors to the capital. In 2017, with 30-plus restaurants to his name, he helped provide nearly 4 million meals to the people of Puerto Rico in the wake of Hurricane Maria through World Central Kitchen, the philanthropic organization he founded in 2010. It has been a wild, rapid rise for a chef who is—by all accounts—brilliant and blunt, with a seemingly never-ending supply of energy and ideas, and a tendency to perfection. And he's not done yet.

A Boyhood Fascination with Food

Andrés was born and raised in northern Spain, the son of two nurses. His earliest and fondest memories revolve around cooking and visiting the markets to gather the freshest ingredients. "Going to these markets is what made me really appreciate the goodness of the earth and what first planted the seed of cooking," he told Andrew Zimmern in 2013. "As a young boy, I was always amazed by the possibilities of food, so these markets were always a big inspiration."

The metamorphosis of those ingredients in the kitchen only increased Andrés' fervor. "The touching, the transformation of things, the smells of it, the tastes of it, it brought people together," he told *Time* magazine in 2020. "I love clay. I love fire. Maybe I'm a distant relative of Prometheus." He frequently tells the story of how when he was a child, he would want to stir the paella—but his father wouldn't let him. First he had to learn how to control the fire.

Andrés entered culinary school in Barcelona at the age of 15. At 18, when the time came to complete his military service, he was assigned to cook for an admiral on the Spanish Navy's training ship, the *Juan Sebastián de Elcano*. The lessons he learned there would prove pivotal to both his work as a professional chef and first responder.

"Just watching 300 people working together, doesn't matter where the currents came from or the wind came from, the boat would always march forward," he told the *New York Times* in 2020. "Sacrifice, hard work, teamwork, belief in the person on your right and belief in the person on your left."

In Barcelona, he worked three years, 1988 to 1990, for Ferran Adrià—one of the most influential pioneers of molecular gastronomy—at El Bulli, considered to be the world's best restaurant in its day.

Small Plates Pioneer

Upon arrival in the United States, Andrés cooked at Eldorado Petit, a popular Spanish restaurant in midtown Manhattan. In 1993, Chef Ann Cashion hired him to head up the kitchen at Jaleo, a new tapas restaurant in Washington, D.C. It was the beginning of making his mark on the American restaurant world—Andrés is widely credited with popularizing small-plates dining in the United States.

In 2003, he opened his flagship restaurant, minibar, a six-seat restaurant at which diners sit at a bar and experience Andrés' creative imaginings. The restaurant received two Michelin stars in 2016.

The fare at Andrés' restaurants runs the gamut from the avant-garde to simple sandwiches. One iconic menu item at minibar is Fast & Slow—snail caviar, tapioca pearls, chanterelle mushrooms, and rabbit and snail broth with Jamon Iberico gelee. His Pepe food truck offers a grilled cheese sandwich featuring five Spanish cheeses.

A First Responder, with Food

Although Andrés continues to be highly influential in the food world, he has turned most of his attention to an entirely different way of feeding people. In 2010, he and his wife visited Haiti

after the devastating earthquake that killed 250,000 people and affected nearly 3 million others. Andrés returned home with the determination to do something.

The result was the founding of World Central Kitchen, an organization of chefs and volunteers that sets up field kitchens in the wake of natural disasters and provides fresh, hot, nourishing meals to people in need. Instead of relying on MREs flown in, World Central Kitchen turns to local supply chains. During the economic fallout of the Covid-19 pandemic, the organization played a huge role in addressing hunger, feeding 250,000 people a day in 34 states at the height of need.

The organization has been all over the world—to California and Australia during wildfires, to Albania after an earthquake, to Guatemala after a volcanic eruption, to Tennessee following tornadoes. As of 2020, it had been in 13 countries, served 15 million meals, and attracted 45,000 volunteers.

In addition to receiving both "Outstanding Chef" and "Humanitarian of the Year" from the James Beard Foundation, Andrés made *Time* magazine's list of the 100 most influential people in the world in both 2012 and 2018. In 2016, he was awarded a National Humanities Medal for 2015 at a White House Ceremony. In 2019, he received a nomination for the Nobel Peace Prize and was the recipient of the Julia Child Award.

Whether he's suited up in crisp chef's whites running the kitchen at one of the world's most exclusive restaurants or in his signature beige multipocketed vest and ball cap, sweating and getting covered in dirt and mud at the scene of disaster, he's always in the thick of things. "We need to make sure we are building walls that are shorter," he says, " and tables that are longer."

"He's a treasure," former president Bill Clinton, whose Clinton Global Initiative has supported World Central Kitchen, told *Time*. "He's a national treasure for us, and a world treasure now. He's really one of the most special people I've ever known."

▲ José Andrés at his minibar restaurant in Washington, D.C., in 2011. The food at the six-seat restaurant is wildly creative.

KWAME ONWUACHI

At the age of 27, Kwame Onwuachi published his 2019 memoir—*Notes from a Young Black Chef*—detailing his early life and evolution as a chef. He had, writes Priya Krishna in an April 2019 profile of Onwuachi in the *New York Times*, "already experienced the kind of head-spinning rise and fall that most chefs will never know in a lifetime."

His journey as a professional chef stems from a desire to tell his personal story through food, in addition to sharing the foods of his ancestors with the wider world.

"I come from a very diverse background—Jamaica, Trinidad, Nigeria, and Louisiana—and I come from a long line of cooks who couldn't go out to eat because of Jim Crow," he says. "Food can be just food. But it can be much more than that—it's history. It represents a group of people and what they stand for. It represents culture and tradition."

Onwuachi was born in the Bronx to a mother with New Orleans Creole roots and a Nigerian American father. His mother worked as an accountant, but her true passion was cooking. After his parents divorced when he was 3 years old, she quit her job and turned to catering full time as a means of supporting herself, her son, and Onwuachi's half sister from a previous marriage. The family struggled financially—often to the point of poverty.

By age 5 or 6, he was helping his mother in the kitchen, peeling shrimp or stirring roux. Bright and full of energy, he began attending a school for gifted and talented students from around New York City. By the age of 10, after many incidents of coming home smelling of cigarettes, or high, or having thrown a fellow student off the jungle gym, Onwuachi's mother announced one morning that he was going to live with his grandfather in Nigeria for the summer. His grandfather was born in Nigeria but spent much of his adult life in the United States as a leading academic voice on Black Liberation, teaching at both Howard and Fisk universities. When Onwuachi was sent to live with him, he had returned to his ancestral village of Ibusa and assumed the role of elder.

At summer's end on a phone call home during which Onwuachi asked his mother when he was coming home, she informed him that he would stay in Nigeria until he learned "respect." He was distraught at first, but over the next 18 months, as he absorbed the culture, ate the food, and learned about his heritage, "the concept of ancestors seeped into me, so much that after a while I stopped even thinking about them and they became a part of me," he writes. "I learned what it meant to have space, space at home, space to be who I really was without being penned in by what people *thought* I was."

In the years following his return home at age 12, he resumed the behavior that got him sent to Nigeria in the first place. He got involved with a gang, started selling drugs, got into physical altercations, bought a gun, witnessed a murder.

In college, he got deep into pills and pot himself. He decided to leave New York and stay with his mother, who had moved to Baton Rouge. He worked at a series of restaurants, first as a server.

A Turning Point: Ship to Shore
Then he got a summer job cooking on the *Maine Responder*, an oil spill response ship in the Gulf. He was technically assistant to the head cook, who made what Onwuachi

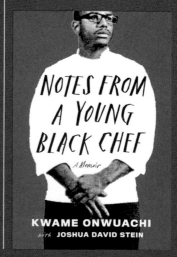

▼ Kwame Onwuachi's memoir details his growing up in New Orleans, his time with his grandfather in Nigeria, and the opening—and closing—of his first restaurant.

describes as "tasteless bland slop." One day he convinced the head cook to let him do the ordering and cooking. Without access to the internet or cookbooks, he cooked, as his mother had advised him to do, from his heart. He made his mother's shrimp étouffée, and the crew loved it. He continued to cook for them the rest of the summer.

"That time on the *Maine* made me a chef," he writes in his memoir.

At age 20, he began selling marked-up candy on the New York subway to finance a catering company start-up. He worked at Tom Coliccchio's Craft as a server, then cobbled the money together to put a down payment on his first year at the Culinary Institute of America. He secured an externship at the New York branch of Thomas Keller's Michelin-starred Per Se, and after graduating from the CIA, landed a job at another Michelin-starred restaurant—Eleven Madison Park, which topped the list of the World's 50 Best Restaurants in 2017.

Telling Stories: One Bite at a Time
As high in the echelon of the restaurant world as these were, Onwuachi wanted to cook his own food. He quit his job and signed on to cook a meal for a company that produced pop-up food events. At a venue in Brooklyn, he prepared a seven-course tasting menu for 130 people that traced his life's journey through food.

Out of that experience, he was offered multiple opportunities from investors to open a restaurant. In 2016, he opened the 32-seat Shaw Bijou in Washington, D.C. Shaw was the neighborhood—originally a freed slave encampment. Bijou is French for "jewel," partially an homage to his mother, whose name is Jewel.

Every dish on the menu was an extrapolation of an experience Onwuachi had in his life—from the jerk-marinated duck prosciutto with a "cigarette" of crackling pastry filled with La Tur cheese whipped with hazelnut oil to "steak and eggs" of Wagyu beef paired with an "egg" fashioned from a dollop of onion soubise topped with the pickled yolk of a quail egg.

The restaurant was plagued with financial problems from the start and closed after less than three months. In 2017, Onwuachi went on to head up the kitchen at Kith and Kin in the InterContinental Hotel in D.C.

"I could either do an elaborate tasting menu, or I could do something to honor my ancestors," he told the *Times*.

The Afro-Caribbean menu featured dishes that gave a nod to his ancestry, including the goat roti he ate at his Trinidadian grandparents' house on Long Island, jerk chicken, and jollof rice—a classic dish of Nigeria.

In 2019, Onwuachi was named the James Beard Rising Star Chef of the Year. In the summer of 2020, he left Kith and Kin to once again pursue cooking at a restaurant he himself owns. He wants to give opportunities to other people of color in the restaurant industry and to raise the visibility of the foods of Black cultures from around the world. As of this writing, he's not sure what that looks like exactly—especially in the middle of a global pandemic. What he does know is that it will involve him cooking—and doing so from his heart.

"You need to know where you came from," he told an audience at a TEDx talk published in October 2020, "in order to know where you're going."

▲ Onwuachi—whose roots lie in Jamaica, Trinidad, Nigeria, and Louisiana—believes in honoring his ancestors through his food.

CURRIED GOAT AND BLACK BEAN HUMMUS

Eating curried goat in his grandmother's kitchen is one of Chef Kwame Onwuachi's earliest food memories. "My grandfather is from Trinidad and my grandmother had it in the fridge," he told *The Splendid Table* host Francis Lam in an April 2019 interview. "I remember her opening the fridge, heating up some roti in a paper towel, raveling the paper towel and steam billowing out from it. She would wrap the curried goat in the roti and put it in my mouth, and it was one of those 'aha' moments at a very young age. At first, it's like, this is curry, and then things start to build and you get the heat from the back that comes from the Scotch bonnet chiles." This recipe from Onwuachi is reminiscent of that memory-making childhood dish.

SERVES 4

FOR THE GOAT CURRY

- 2 tablespoons grapeseed oil
- 1 pound goat shoulder, cut into large chunks
- 1 yellow onion, sliced
- 10 cloves garlic, peeled and chopped
- 2 tablespoons curry powder
- 2 cups recaito (cilantro cooking base)
- 8 cups chicken stock
- 1 Scotch bonnet chile, stemmed
- 4 sprigs fresh thyme
  Salt to taste

FOR THE HUMMUS

- 1 (15-ounce) can chickpeas, rinsed and drained
- 1 (15-ounce) can black beans, rinsed and drained
- 1 cup tahini
- 2 cloves garlic, peeled
  Juice of 1 lemon
  Salt to taste

FOR SERVING

- 1 small bunch fresh cilantro, chopped
  Naan minis, warmed

1. **FOR THE GOAT CURRY:** Heat the oil in a large pot over medium-high heat. Brown the meat in hot oil on all sides, about 10 minutes. Remove from the pot. Sauté the onion and garlic for 5 minutes. Add the curry powder and recaito, and sauté for another 2 minutes. Return the meat and any accumulated juices to the pot. Add the stock, chile pepper, and thyme. Bring to a boil. Reduce heat, and simmer, covered, until meat is tender, about 1 hour. Uncover and simmer until liquid has reduced and thickened, about 1 to 1½ hours. Remove the thyme stems and discard. Season to taste with salt.

2. **FOR THE HUMMUS:** In a high-powered blender, combine the chickpeas, black beans, 1 cup water, the tahini, and garlic. Puree until smooth. Season with the lemon juice and salt to taste.

3. **TO SERVE:** Transfer the hummus to a serving bowl. Top with the goat curry and cilantro. Serve with warm naan.

CREDITS

INDEX